Ira Mae: He is pursuing you with joy. Mt. 4:17

KINGDOM IN PURSUIT

JAMES A. WILSON

Copyright © 2015 by James A. Wilson

Kingdom in Pursuit
by James A. Wilson

Printed in the United States of America.

ISBN 9781498432092

All rights reserved solely by the author. The author guarantees all contents are original and do not infringe upon the legal rights of any other person or work. No part of this book may be reproduced in any form without the permission of the author. The views expressed in this book are not necessarily those of the publisher.

Scripture quotations taken from the New International Version (NIV). Copyright © 1973, 1978, 1984, 2011 by Biblica, Inc.™. Used by permission. All rights reserved.

www.xulonpress.com

PRAISE FOR KINGDOM IN PURSUIT

"James Wilson is an important and articulate voice in today's Body of Christ. He spans the various streams of the Church to offer a perspective at once broad and absolutely faithful to the Word of God. He sees Christians called to be active solution seekers in every dimension of life – from respecting life beginning to end to giving voice to God's cry for justice for all – and he knows God in Christ is the solution. He believes God has especially called the United States and Israel into a special and shared commitment to the purposes of God. He writes weekly to believing and not-yet believing readers to transform what we can scarcely imagine into something we can passionately seek at ground level. Kingdom in Pursuit combines some of the best if his offerings."

The Rev. Jim Garlow, Sr. Pastor Skyline Church, San Diego
Founder, Pulpit Freedom Sunday

"James Wilson's writing is a reflection of his entire life – devoted to healing cultures, nurturing the transformation of lives, and stirring revival in both hearts and nations through Christ's great redemption. His devotion and writing are quite admirable. His books are must reads for anyone seeking real change in today's world."

Bestselling Author and Novelist Cindy (Martinusen) Coloma

"Jim is a standard bearer. His ability to read and interpret the Word of God plus the signs of the times is insightful. He is a true 'son of Issachar,' one who knows the times and the seasons and acts accordingly. Not only is he a man of the Spirit, but he is extremely practical; this is a balance we can lack in the Church today. Hearing from God, then doing what it takes to get the word accomplished, is a gift that those who move in the prophetic should be working harder to achieve. Jim, you're there and you are leading the way for others to do so as well."

Weslie Leake, People Builder and Founder, Business Blessings
Principal Coordinator, Bible Breakthrough, Brisbane, Australia

"You're busy; I'm busy. But when I see anything written by Jim Wilson I stop what I'm doing and I read it. Often I re-read it, even chew on it later, because there are layers of Truth in whatever topic he's tackling. Because he's so often in prayer he hears from the Holy Spirit. When you combine that with a talent for words that God gave him, and his years of study and experience, Jim's words become a powerful vessel for the Holy Spirit, showering us with the Lord's Wisdom. Words of Truth coming out of Jim's writings are all the more important in these perilous times when good is called evil and evil good. Like the sons of Issachar he discerns the times. He sees the critical need for personal and national repentance to accelerate the next great move in the body of Christ. Take the time to read and re-read this book; you'll be more than just blessed. You'll go deeper in your walk with the Lord."

The Rev. Jeff Daly, Principal Director The National Day of Repentance
Attorney at Large, Pacific Justice Institute

"Jim Wilson's latest book, "Kingdom in Pursuit," provides Spirit-sharpened, keen insight into the most relevant issues of our day. Where other ministry leaders *fear to tread,* Jim steps boldly forward providing thoughtful and thorough analysis from a solidly Biblical perspective that takes away the fog and clearly frames the issues. You never put down his writing without having gained inspiration about the "*exceedingly above and beyond*" that God has in store for those who pursuit Him. Jim's leadership in the Kingdom pursuit will challenge you to "*subdue kingdoms*" and "*obtain promises*" you hadn't dared before."

Susan Johnsen, Pacific Regional Director,
The National Governor's Prayer Team

"Jim Wilson is an entertaining and enlightening Christian writer who knows how to "tell the rest of the story" while merging critical thinking and Christian world view."

Brad Dacus, Founder and President, Pacific Justice League

"Jim Wilson is a voice for our age, and his latest message is sure to bless all who hunger for hope and encouragement in these troubled times. Jim's ministry has touched countless lives, and his extensive travels across the nation and around the globe have helped lay the groundwork for the Great Awakening the Lord is preparing for His people. Jim is not only an eloquent writer and a compelling radio host, above all, he is a minister of the Lord and humbly acknowledges Jesus as the source of our strength. I pray this book will be a blessing to you. "

Dr. Katherine Albrecht
Host of the Katherine Albrecht Show and world renowned End Times expert
President of the Caspian Foundation
Best Selling Author of I Won't Take the Mark, Spychips, and The Spychips Threat

"For over a decade I have witnessed Jim Wilson flow in a variety of roles including Teacher, Preacher, Speaker, Evangelist, Ministry Leader, Priest, Prayer Bomber, Author, Counselor, and Shofar Blower. The LORD has also blessed Brother Jim with an anointed gift for clearly and succinctly writing what's on HIS Heart while gently, yet **passionately**, calling the Body of Christ to RISE UP, REPENT, and RETURN to Him and His Word! In his newest book titled "**Kingdom in Pursuit**", Jim continues to use his God-given talents through timely writings which are prophetically informative, strategically significant, and highly relevant today for ALL Kingdom Pursuers...are you one?"

Maryal Boumann, Executive Director, Pray California

"James Wilson is one of those rare leaders in the Church who combines God-given imagination, a strong prophetic gifting (they are not the same) and a thoroughly pragmatic grasp of living at ground level. His earlier books have inspired gatherings and reconciliations in multiple states and nations to bring the Word of God lovingly to bear in their communities. Kingdom in Pursuit, his latest effort, is a selection of his short writings on topics as varied as science versus scientism, addressing the culture, to acknowledging Christ before men in all our dimensions. He manages to keep his addresses to eight hundred or so words into the bargain. Pursuit is at once pleasure and exhortation for our time."

Dran Reese, Founder and President, The Salt and Light Council

ACKNOWLEDGEMENTS

As always I want to dedicate this book to my Lord Jesus Christ and my family; Diana, son Christopher, daughter Malorie, Chris Glavan (Malorie's awesome husband) and Baby Nicholas – our first grandson. But I want to make a special dedication as well to two men who have mentored me over the decades, had my back, and are today celebrating the abundant life my Lord Jesus gave on the Cross and from the Empty Tomb but which is only fully activated when we go to live with Him in His Father's House of many rooms – one prepared for each of us who love Him and are called according to His purposes.

I would like to acknowledge the publishers of the New International Version of the Holy Bible. All Bible quotations are taken from the NIV. I would also like to acknowledge Ugandan Evangelist Jackson Senyonga. I refer frequently in the text to his famous statement, "The condition of society is the report card of the Church." I first heard Jackson speak these words at a meeting at Neighborhood Church in Chico, California, sometime in 2004 or 2005. The statement is something of a signature utterance of his, and one we Christians need always to take to heart. God bless you Brother Jackson.

I specially dedicate this book in all humility to the Rev. Frank Maguire and the Rt. Rev. John-David Schofield. Frank, you will always be my father in Christ. John-David you will always be my father and bishop in Christ.

TABLE OF CONTENTS

KINGDOM IN PURSUIT

A few weeks before I received the Lord Jesus Christ as my Savior, my Best Friend, and my King, He came to me in a vision.

I was an undergrad at San Diego State University when the four young Christians knocked on my door wanting to talk about Jesus. My roommates were out and I invited them in–I had been looking for God most of my life but had long since written off Jesus because of the hypocrisy I saw in so many believers–but I was willing to let them say their piece on this evening in 1970. They were so interesting in their courtesy as well as their conviction that I let them say their piece four nights running. Still, I did not accept their invitation to invite their Lord into my life.

As I lay waiting for sleep to come following their last visit I saw a vision of clouds as dense as they were dark over my bed. A great and muscular hand cut through the cloud bank and was headed in my direction. I knew it instinctively to be the hand of my Father God; I knew just as surely that it wanted only to rest on my shoulder, giving it an affectionate squeeze, as I was welcomed into the family of my God and my Christ. But I also knew with equal certainty that if I permitted this hand to land, and it turned out to be nothing more than my fantasy, the disappointment would be more than I could bear.

I pointed my index finger at the descending hand and said, "No." The hand withdrew and the vision ended.

A few weeks later I was standing in a classroom at James Madison High School in the Claremont district of San Diego–I worked there as a teaching assistant–monitoring an exam. While I looked over the class, making sure no one was cheating on the exam, I carried on a dialogue-slash-monologue in my head. Being the Philosophy major I was, I wrestled with the question of what is truth and how would one know it if confronted by it. Without knowing why, or making a conscious decision to do it, I found myself demanding–in my silent conversation–that if there was a God and if He knew my name–and if that meant anything to Him–He should show Himself to me now. "Say something," was my belligerent way of seeking His face. Without hesitation He began to recite the words of His own Twenty-third Psalm.

I knew of the psalm well enough to recognize it, although I could not have recited it from memory if my life depended on it. That dual recognition was enough for my skeptical heart to authenticate the source of the revelation. I responded with a rather wimpy, "Then I guess you are my Lord now." There was nothing wimpy about the peace that flooded my heart. I was home at last and I knew it–was overwhelmed with the knowing of it. The peace stayed with me but–even so–I spent the rest of the day as I normally would, working and studying and hanging out with friends. I wondered on and off how my life would be changed now that I was a Christian–whatever that meant.

That night I decided to go out and sit on the lip of the canyon on which my apartment building was perched. It was a beautiful starlit night in San Diego; I prepared and relaxed for some stargazing and wake-dreaming.

The Cross appeared–broke out and into the night sky–as though it had always been there and yet had never been before. It seemed gigantic as it filled the portion of the sky right above me. I guessed, not knowing its altitude, it might be anywhere from twenty to two hundred feet in length. It was brightly lit and sun yellow in color. Certain it was an optical illusion, I tried looking at it from different angles, closing one eye, and squinting. It did not go away; it did not change in any way. At last I had to admit whatever I was seeing was as real as it gets. Gazing now in wonder, I asked out loud, "What do you want?" The answer was just as audible as my question. "All of you," said the Spirit of my Lord Jesus Christ.

I knew in this moment–more powerfully than I had that morning–it is all true. Everything the Law and the Prophets say about our God is true. And that includes the part about His coming in pursuit of us.

Matthew 4:17 records the earliest public saying of Jesus. Depending on the translation he says variously, "Repent, for the Kingdom of God is near," or "has come near to you," or even "has drawn near to you today." Repent, of course, comes from the Greek *metanoia*; it means to turn about or make an about face. Pragmatically speaking it is to focus or re-focus our attention on God in much the same way Peter re-focused on Jesus in Matthew 14 when his walk on the water went south. He was fine while his attention was on his master; the moment he looked down he began to sink. But in the instant he looked back at Jesus, calling,

"Save me, Master," his troubles are over. Jesus grasps his hand and walks him back to the boat.

The really operant term in this verse–for our sakes–is the Greek word *eggiken*. It does not mean anything like *is near*, or even *has drawn near*; it is nothing so passive. The word actually means *is in pursuit of you*. Jesus says He–and His Kingdom–are in pursuit of those for whom He came to die and to live, to strip off the crust of their shadows of human life and to usher them into the abundant life of His Father.

Imagine it. The Kingdom is in pursuit of us. All we need to do is stop running away, turn to face Him, receive Him as our life and lifegiver. "What do you want?"

Over the years He has revealed to me that He was pursuing me all my twenty-two years before I allowed him to catch me. That would include the time He sent me the dream when I was ten and gripped by an obsessive fear of death for as long as I could remember. Not instant death, not near death, just a terror that everybody dies and that includes me and then I am no more and nothing and it paralyzed me with fear whenever I thought about it. In the dream I was convicted of a crime I had not committed and executed by hanging. As the life left me I was conscious of being elevated–levitated, really–through bank upon bank of clouds and finally breaking out into heaven where the music and the peace were without end. My fear of death was permanently eliminated when I woke, but it never occurred to me that God had loved me enough to heal me. I was just glad to be free of it.

It would include the time when I was nineteen and flirting with psychedelic drugs. I was loaded on marijuana one evening while visiting a friend's apartment. The walls and ceiling were of knotty pine and I fantasized about becoming miniaturized and climbing into one of the knots of the ceiling so I could look down and observe the other people without being observed myself and so impacting their behavior. I had always rationalized my drugging by telling myself I was seeking a higher consciousness; when I heard an audible voice chiding me that evening, "Is that the best you can do?" I was jerked out of my hypocrisy–and there went the high as well–and I was permanently cured of doing drugs.

It even included the church summer camp when I was fourteen and every message drilled my brain with the idea God was calling me to serve Him when I knew I did not even believe He was real. The enemy showed up there too–in the form of the camp bully–and after I beat him senseless one day for having me stripped naked by his friends and thrown out of the cabins in front of a bunch of girls–I swore I would never enter a church again. And He was there the day I was stranded in a very dangerous–read gang infested and haters of white boys like me–part of Los Angeles. I had no choice but to hitch-hike out and hope I made it when a car carrying three angels–who looked like three young men having no more business in that neighborhood than I did–picked me up and drove me to safety. I have come to know over the years I have been with Jesus that He pursued me daily from the moment of my birth. It is what He does.

"Turn about for the Kingdom of God is pursuing you." He says so in Matthew 4.

This book is not like my earlier books. They told an extended story of one dimension of God's calling us in this time–the one of His passion for His people to represent Him as His ambassadors of reconciliation as that is depicted in 2 Corinthians 5:16-20–the other of His imperative to His people to prepare their cities and communities for His imminent return–whenever that may be–in keeping with Luke 1:17. In that passage we are instructed to go forth in the spirit and power of Elijah, to turn the hearts of the fathers to the children, to prepare a people for righteousness. But this book is not like those books.

Kingdom in Pursuit is an anthology–a selection–of my blog postings over the past four years. It is inspired by a vision God gave to one of my prayer teams–the one that visits our California state capitol each month and spends a couple of hours worshipping the Lord, celebrating His supper, and praying for the Great Awakening He has promised since 2008 to begin in California–or whenever else He has in mind–as the guest of one of the elected members of California's legislature. This Awakening is no longer just a promise. It is underway and–as He said to me in 1970–God says to all of us in this day, "All of you. I want all of you."

Reality is the Great Awakening has begun; it is underway. Just as crucially real is that it remains in its infancy, a spark waiting on God's people to nourish it into the Holy Spirit wildfire He has designed and inaugurated. When God wants our everything He means just what He says. A big part of what He wants from us is a will to partner with Him by tilling the land He has taken, provided, and impregnated–land which has laid fallow until the present moment.

The chapters that follow are stocked with brief essays on ten different topics; the essays themselves are diversified within their chapters. The trait they all share–besides having been previously published as postings for my blog–is that each calls on the reader to make an act of repentance–to sacrifice something belonging to the reader that our Lord, our Christ, our God wants as another portion of "All of you. I want all of you."

Chapter 1 is titled Waking to the Awakening. Each of the essays it offers speak to pragmatic ways and means for awakening ourselves and those we love to the majesty of what He is launching in our midst. Chapter 2 is A Culture of Repentance. It addresses many arenas in which we need to re-focus our attention on God from the sacred to the profane–from the heights of worship to stuff so Saturday-morning we are convinced He could not possibly care about it. Chapter

3 is Navigating the Season. It describes and commends practical stories and strategies for working and playing in the new things our God is releasing into our world.

The common thread in Chapter 4–Challenging the Culture–is affirmation of our culture and its leaders as they honor God and challenges to them as they dishonor God. The takeaway for readers is that each of us is called to speak truth in authentic and humbled love to the culture in which we live and move and have our being as the gift from God that it is. Chapter 5 is titled Challenging the Body Politic; it takes the same approach to political issues as does the preceding chapter on cultural issues. Chapter 6 is called Challenging the Faith of Scientism with Authentic Science. The thrust of this chapter is that real science makes real sense and has no fear of questions or alternative ideas. Scientism, on the other hand, cannot stand up to scrutiny and demands obeisance from all simply because its clergy have many abbreviations for advanced degrees after their surnames and publish in difficult to decipher journals. Chapter 7 is named Challenging the Church. Its focus is on a Body of Christ all too comfortable with programs and doctrines and rarely willing to journey from Jerusalem to Damascus and the rest of the world. The Church is historically the last segment of society to embrace Awakening. Movements to resurrect the Faith are typically as messy as the first Pentecost, when the crowds imagined the disciples in the upper room were intoxicated. In fact they were intoxicated–but with the Holy Spirit–and the Church needs to be lovingly challenged to abandon the safety of Traditionalism and embrace once again the riotous Father, Son, and Spirit as the foundation of Tradition.

G. K. Chesterton famously said, "Tradition is the living faith of the dead; Traditionalism is the dead faith of the living." God came in flesh that we might live.

The last three chapters are titled Witnessing in the Public Square, Israel, and Acknowledging Him Before Men–in that order. Jesus said we are to go into all the world, making disciples of all nations, and beginning with our own. The Israel of the first century was the most religious on earth–it still is–and the most secularized as well–it still is. Saying and even believing we are religious is not worth the price of a cup of coffee. Being in relationship with Him is everything, and the first and best proof we are in relationship is our hunger and thirst to share that relationship with those who too are hungry and thirsty. Chapter 8 is all about witnessing in many venues and contexts.

Jesus says in John 4–when he talks with and offers salvation to a Samaritan woman of poor character–Salvation is from the Jews. She receives His offer with joy and leads her whole village into new and abundant life. But salvation is still from the Jews. That means–of course–that our Messiah springs from His Jewish roots as to His human side. But it also means what Paul points out in Romans 9, 10, and 11.

We Gentile Christians are grafted onto the vine that is the Hebrew nation, the nation of Israel. Ultimately there is no salvation that does not include the Jews. Chapter 9 is all about a healthy relationship with Israel. It stresses that the Jews need their Messiah, but they do not need us. We need them. We need to be who we are in Christ, whether Catholic or other mainline denomination, Evangelical, or Charismatic, but we need to bless, uphold and support Israel (Genesis 12:3) if we would be blessed, upheld, and supported by Israel's God. We need to take hold of the hem of the garment of a Jew–as Zechariah prophecies–and beg him to guide us into the Holy of Holies.

Jesus says in Matthew 10:32 that when we acknowledge Him before men He will acknowledge us before His Father. When we fail to do that we can expect as much neglect from Him. Of course the context for the chapter from Matthew's Gospel is a time of persecution when we will be brought before hostile authorities and challenged to rehearse or renounce our faith. But Jesus is just as well known for saying when He learns He can trust us with a little He will be happy to trust us with much more. Chapter 10 is a series of postings about many times and places in which our acknowledgement of our Lord is the subject matter of the test to which we are put. The question is what will we do when the stakes are relatively low; our answer predicts what we will do when the chips are down and it is winner-take-all.

My blog is read by more than four hundred thousand readers. Anyone desiring to receive it–or to inquire about my previous books, Living as Ambassadors of Relationships and The Holy Spirit and the EndTimes–is welcome to contact me at praynorthstate@charter.net or by phone at (USA) 530-941-3470.

My prayer is that each reader will be blessed by every entry in Kingdom in Pursuit. Of course some entries will move some more and others less, and vice versa. But the most important blessing to be gained from this book is the sure and passionate recognition that God and His Kingdom are pursuing you in every dimension of your life from the magnificent and dramatic to the mundane and even the dull. That pursuit is unending and the news of it is the best news any of us will ever receive. It is one more way for God to say, "I love you. I love you just the way you are. I love you so much I have no intention of leaving you in the condition in which I find you."

It is also another way for God to say, "All of you. I want all of you."

CHAPTER 1:

WAKING TO THE AWAKENING

The Lord never does anything in a corner. He announces His plans and His accomplishments to many witnesses; this is one of the ways He gives for us to test the spirits. He has made a number of prophetic proclamations of the birth of this latest Great Awakening; they have come from multiple streams and nations in Church and world.

On July 3, 2014 the Lord gave a vision to a member of my capitol prayer team. The vision looked like this: There was a room with two large piles of bones on the floor. The bones rose to become animated and shaped – one looked exactly like a lion and the other exactly like a man. The two living skeletons were clearly friendly to one another as they moved about the room. The team member was unable to say anymore about what he had seen. But the interpretation of the vision came to another team member even as the story unfolded from the mouth of the one who first saw it.

The interp was this: The animated bones – in the spirit of the bones prophecy of Ezekiel 37 – represented the Son of God on the one hand and the Lion of Judah on the other. We could not have asked a clearer word that Israel and the Awakening are inseparable in the mind of the Lord. We could not have received a more direct statement that the Awakening is actually underway; the manger is once again full with the Baby. But there is more at stake than even this activation-with-blending of the Lord's plans for the worldwide Body of Christ and the firstborn people of Yahweh.

Our ministry is one of many calling for a prolonged season of repentance – a veritable culture of repentance – as the pathway to welcoming and supporting the Great Awakening when it comes. Others are the National Day of Repentance, the National Governor's Prayer Team, The National Day of Prayer, and many others in the United States and in those other nations in which faithful servants seek the Lord for all His promises rather than only those concerning individual salvation. He has made it clear that He brings salvation to the Jews and then to the world, just as Jesus sent the apostles first to His own people, later sending them on to the Gentile world. In our day that sending is simultaneous; His concern that none should perish remains paramount.

The Lord spoke clearly in that capitol hearing room. He said, "Do you see that these are not whole bodies? They are only the skeletons of the bodies to come. There are no muscles, organs, nerves, or other tissues–no skin and hair–these bodies are only just beginning to come alive. My call for repentance is more urgent than ever if the Awakening is to be fully embodied."

The articles in this chapter cover a range of topics–all related not to bringing the Awakening but to awakening to the Awakening God has already brought. Reality is God is not waiting for the Awakening–or for our readiness to participate. He has told His people over and over what we are to do–both to prepare and to participate. We are (Micah 6:8) to love and practice both kindness and justice–not to mention humble walking with Him. We are to make our lives and bodies (Mark 11:17) living houses of prayer as we walk out (2 Corinthians 5:16-20) being His ambassadors of His reconciliation. We are to acknowledge Him (Matthew 10:32) before men in all things great and small and seek first (Matthew 6:32) His Kingdom, expecting all we need will be placed at our disposal. Of course, that means all things we need in order to do what He calls us to do.

While we are at it we are called to know and recognize Him, distinguishing between revival–which is good–and Awakening–which is the best. We are charged with choosing the best over the merely good. Finally, we are called to remember and obey His word that He will teach us in the very hour we need to know it just what we are to say and do. We can pray–as I have for more than thirty years–"Lord, please fill my head with what I need to know and empty it of what I do not need to know."

This is the very essence of repentance practiced as a lifestyle.

GOD IS NOT WAITING FOR THE AWAKENING

The woman who asked for prayer for her cancer though neither she nor her church had any frame of reference for miraculous healing is one piece of evidence–her tumors shrunk before treatment could begin. The man whose immune system had shut down from the leukemia and whose anger at God so blossomed that he refused to come to church for prayer–his wife stood in for him, the leukemia is gone, and his immune system is fine–is another. California's three year drought–2008-2010–is broken by prayer, water pumps closed by a federal judge's order are opened by that same judge's order–after eighteen months of prayer–and Christians are gathering in stadiums and on capitol malls to repent and seek the face of the Lord all over the country. People are leading other people into life changing encounters with the Son of the Living God in bookstores, at high school reunions, and in the homes of friends after forty years' hiatus in the relationship. Can it be that God is calling for–and planning–a Great Awakening?

Whenever God's people come together to humbly seek His face and repent of the self-reliance and self-satisfaction they have practiced it is the result of God's prompting. But He is quick to respond to the desperation of His people. He is not driven by the sin of those who do not know Him, although He cares deeply for those harmed by it. But His attention is ever on His own people and whether they are giving glory to His Name. It is our righteousness that moves Him since the days when He would have shown mercy if even a small number of His own could have been found in Sodom. The outbreaks of miracles and decisions are His way of getting our attention.

The first Great Awakening swept the Eastern Seaboard in the seventeen thirties and forties–but it began in the fields of the Connecticut River Valley. When the churches rejected it the Holy Spirit found hungry hearts in those fields. When the fruit of empty jails and restored families became evident the churches embraced the awakening and the Lord treated them like the workers in the vineyard who came at the eleventh hour. Full pay and benefits were available to all. The Second Great Awakening erupted at the dawn of the nineteenth century–again the churches rejected it–but when the fruit of social ministries, temperance societies, the abolitionist movement, and an American people embracing prayer became evident the churches again embraced the movement and all was forgiven. The Third Great Awakening landed on the beaches of Southern California in the late sixties and seventies of the twentieth century. The church reaction was the same as it had always been until the fruit of dynamic missions, revitalized worship, lots of miracles and decisions, and a recovery movement that never drew breath before God manifested it was as it had always been as well. The churches were received and the Lord was given the glory He deserved. Shouldn't it be happening again? Is it not?

The Lord spoke prophetically about His intentions near the end of 2010. He said, "I have prepared a great harvest for you and you have gathered it into barns, and there it remains. I will tear down the barns and release the harvest." He said at another time in the same season, "I am coming soon, as I understand soon. You need to expect me tomorrow, as you understand tomorrow." And of the colliding seasons of unprecedented miracles and decisions for Him on the one hand, and unprecedented wars and rumors of wars, men calling evil good and good evil, and hatred of His people for His sake He has something to say as well. "It is as though there were two tsunamis about to collide on the ocean. I am at the crash site. That is where you will find me."

God is raising up a whole new generation of leaders. He is sick and tired of the idolatry of the rock star that we have created. His idea of repentance is to seek His face and voice in the still and in the seemingly small. He is waiting for His people to step through the walls of our churches to seek Him at that oceanic crash site. He is not angry or upset at His churches; he is simply unwilling to wait for the ship of the Church to turn itself about and head home to Him. He seems to think that if we would walk on water we must first step out of the boat. His idea of stepping from the boat is to continue to respect and love our leaders, but to decide not to wait for or follow them so much as to wait on and follow the Lord Himself. When the fruit of that decision reaches critical mass the leaders who failed to follow will come on board with all the respect and privileges due their ministry. But it is the children who will lead them.

In the meantime let us remember and walk in terms of the powerful words God released for this season when He launched it on the first day of 2008. He called us to release the Spirit of worship–to seek His transformation of us from people who worship to people of worship. He called us to choose not just this day but each day Whom we will serve–forsaking all others as we pledge marital fealty to the Bridegroom alone. He called us to rise, take up our palate and walk–understanding that our healing is not real until we begin to walk in its reality. And finally He said, "Relax; I've got more riding on this than you do."

IN THE BIRTHING ROOM – REPENTANCE JUST AS CRUCIAL

The 4th Great Awakening in American history is underway. There have been a number of words from recognized prophetic voices published in the past few weeks and there is a compelling co-incidence to their witness. We got the word ourselves when our prayer team made its monthly visit to the California State Capitol July 3. One of our members reported a vision in which the Lord showed him two piles of dry bones on the floor – reminiscent of the famous passage in Ezekiel 37 – and while he watched the bones rose to form two skeletal bodies, one of them a man and the other a lion. Putting aside the natural skepticism of many of our readers about revelations from God in capitol hearing rooms – or anywhere else – let's track with the internal logic of the vision. That too is supplied by God, but it is subject to rational critique.

The interpretation came to me instantaneously as the vision was described. The man represented Jesus Himself and the lion the Lion of Judah. Their rise to incarnation was clearly about the promised Awakening but the caveat is at least as important. Attention was drawn to the skeletal nature of these bodies; that is, to their lack of flesh, skin, hair, and organs. Clearly the Awakening is in its most fragile infancy. The present outpouring of signs and wonders has been with us for some time; it does not constitute an Awakening by itself. And there is much more at stake here than whether a bunch of charismatic Christians get to raise hands and shout glory to the Lord. The call to the people of God to practice ongoing repentance – re-focus of our attention on God – is even more urgent than it has been the past several years.

There is a dark side to this season which also grows exponentially. Jesus said the last days – whatever their duration – would feature worldwide wars and rumors of wars, and we have armed conflict on the five heavily populated continents. We would see men calling evil good and good evil; look no farther than the outpouring of sympathy for Hamas as it shoves women and children in front of its own missile batteries as human shielding. And we would see Christians hated by all for no other reason that that we bear the name of Christ; the legal assaults on American and European Christians in the name of political correctness pale next to the slaughter of the faithful in the Middle East but the source is the same and the escalation as certain.

Yet most of these so-called revelatory words are steeped in triumphalism. There is no acknowledgement of ongoing need for repentance. There is a childish obsession with the healings and the other goodies which are indeed part and parcel of any move of God in our midst, but which are anything but the whole package. Jesus was quite clear that as history winds down there is going to be hell to pay as much as heaven to gain; nobody gets a free pass. Any alleged prophet who claims it is all coming up roses for people of prayer is just as much a false prophet as the people who keep running up and down California claiming the drought is over despite the reality that reservoirs are less than half full and snowpack almost non-existent. So what is the reasonable and at the same time faithful approach? Just what it has always been.

John 8:1-11 is a story of authentic repentance. Pharisees who seemingly have nothing better to do on a weekday morning than look in someone's bedroom window drag a woman caught in adultery before the Lord and ask permission to stone her. Jesus uses the Law accurately when he says only the sinless may cast the first stone. Only the woman actually repents – she steps across the line Jesus draws in the dust and remains by His side – while her accusers refuse to focus on Him and slink away in shame. It doesn't matter who has done well or poorly; it matters only that His grace is sought and accepted by each and all.

Two apostles stand out for rejecting a portion of pre-resurrection revelation. Thomas is chronically convinced it will all end badly, despite what he has seen of Christ's power to bless and heal. Yet he is loyal and devoted to the end, saying, "Then let us all go and die with Him," when Jesus determines to go to Jerusalem despite being warned against it. One might say Thomas faces the darkness while doubting the glory. Peter, on the other hand, is the first to confess Jesus as Son of God; he gets into trouble with the boss when he refuses to believe the Cross is coming. Jesus rebukes Peter but lets Thomas slide. Why is that?

Thomas's rejection is wrong but not problematic for his faith. He will hang in there with Jesus in the hard times – he always does – and when it turns out exponentially better than he can imagine it is just that – exponentially better in the Kingdom. Peter's rejection negatively impacts his faith; he is in for the wild ride but the plummet of Good Friday can shock him right out of the Kingdom if he is totally unprepared. God wants us to enjoy the hurricane of signs, wonders and decisions for Jesus – not to mention the grace that will flow in many directions through the culture shared by the awakened Church. But if we imagine the glory is all there is we risk missing even that when the hurricane of hard times makes landfall.

REVIVALS AND AWAKENINGS IN AMERICA

The American colonies were the fruit of an English revival rejected by the English people and government. The Puritan vision was of a reformed and re-vitalized England brought about through enthusiastic embrace of the Living God. When the Puritans found themselves despised they came to America and set up a culture of that embrace, believing that when those they left behind saw what God did with them they would hunger for the same. The Pilgrims were more radicalized, but their sense of a city on a hill – observed and hungered for – was just as strong. Yet revivals do not form nations; awakenings do.

The first American Great Awakening rocked the Atlantic seaboard in the 1730s and 40s. It began in the pastures of the Connecticut River Valley as the Holy Spirit ignited preaching with signs and wonders. The Spirit drew hundreds of thousands and the emphasis was on receiving and growing a relationship with God in the Person of His Son. These relationships were as intimate as they were dynamic – and uncomfortable for observers. People coming under the Spirit would frequently cry out, weep, laugh, and convulse on the ground. Fruit was that jails tended to empty as people became less inclined to commit crime, families tended to come together as parents became parents and spouses re-committed to loving and faithful marriage. Colonists saw themselves as Americans rather than British ex-patriates. This social and spiritual cohesion enabled Americans to fight a revolutionary war and write a Declaration of Independence and Constitution.

Just as the first Great Awakening formed an American identity, the second formed an American character in which concerted efforts from barn raisings to spanning a continent to walkers on the moon were simply viewed as the American way. The kinds of signs and wonders associated with the first Awakening were just as commonplace in the second. But as it was in the earlier movement, these were not its fruit. Public schools and social welfare movements were its creations. It birthed a commitment to live in freedom for all – the commitment that abolished slavery and struggled for another century to make manifest what they had mandated.

Revivals often lead to Awakening – when they are not managed to death by the very people who triggered them – but revivals are confined to the Church while awakenings hit the streets and transform cities; they often begin outside institutional churches. The Charismatic Revival of the sixties featured thousands being healed, renewed in their faith and – in many cases – coming into a relationship with Jesus for the first time. But the cities at its heart – Los Angeles and Seattle – were no different after the revival than before it. The Toronto

Blessing that rocked churches all over the world is a formative influence on my own character and approach to God – but Toronto remains the city it was before 1994. Many want to hail the Azusa Street Revival of 1906 as an awakening, but that revival was destroyed by the failure of leaders to confront the racism that strangled it. Los Angeles remained as it had always been, only bigger and richer as the oil and entertainment industries came of age there.

It can be argued – and I would – that Azusa Street was resurrected in the charismatic renewal triggered by Dennis Bennett. This revival led into the Jesus People, which is the third Great Awakening in America.

The Jesus People began outside the Church – on the beaches of California and Oregon. It began with drugged out hippies who had radical encounter with Jesus and took Him along wherever they went. They birthed modern worship music, a renewed emphasis on families, and a normalized view of signs and wonders on city streets. The modern recovery movement and the Messianic movement among Jews are from the Jesus People, as is the worldwide missions paradigm that honors indigenous leaders and gets out of their way as soon as possible. The idea of vision preceding product in the business world is fruit of this movement, as is the movement for reconciliation with people groups and across all dividing lines. The Jesus People picked up where Azusa left off and got it right re racial integration.

I do not mean to imply the Awakenings are cool and revivals are not. Both have a place of honor in the Kingdom of God. But the one tends to be a fuller manifestation of the larger Kingdom while the other is more instrumental to it. Awakenings tend to be rejected by the larger Church until the fruit comes into the bin while revivals tend to dramatically stir the Church – or at least the streams in which they come. The kiss of death for either is the urge to manage and tame them by leadership. But the kiss of life from the Lord comes – always – in response to a season of repentance from that cross-section of the Body hearing the promise of the Lord without seeing its manifestation.

THE ROLE OF REPENTANCE IN AWAKENING

A pastor I know tells a story of his friend changing a tire on a dead flat road in Kansas. While he worked he saw an approaching car two miles away. He knew there was no chance it would hit him; he and his car were as visible to the driver of the other car as that car was to him. His reasoning sustained him until the moment he was hit.

He was drop-kicked fifty feet but sustained no injury beyond a few bruises from landing on pavement. The driver stopped and ran to him, amazed he was okay. When they both calmed enough to talk he asked her how she could have hit him when he was so visible. She said it was the strangest thing; the more she focused on avoiding him the more inevitable hitting him seemed to become. This true story forms a perfect illustration of our shared need to engage a lifestyle of progressive repentance.

The Bible calls us to renounce sin simply because it hurts when we abuse ourselves or others. But not bringing injury is not enough. The more we focus on avoiding the sin we renounce the more inevitable becomes its return to power. If we would be free we must re-focus on the God-in-Christ who comes into the world to set us free, just as that Kansas driver needed to focus on where she wanted to drive instead of where she wanted to not-drive. This re-focus is the essence of repentance and – because life is littered with people changing flat tires in our path – it must be a lifestyle if we are to live in freedom.

Every awakening is preceded by a necessary season of repentance in the Church. God is not waiting for the world to don sackcloth and ashes; we Christians are the model. But Christians must get a clue we are seriously off course and begin to act on that clue in order to clear obstructions from God's highway. Our own book says judgment begins with us; the abysmal track record of Christians choosing abortion, divorce, and a host of idolatries speaks for itself.

When John the Baptist proclaimed the near arrival of the Son of God he demanded more from people than renunciation of corruption. He called for fruit in terms of behavior imitative of the God in Whose image we are made, pragmatic fruit like feeding and clothing the poor. These behaviors are not repentance, but they are hard evidence we are re-focused on God instead of ourselves. Jesus said we must seek to become new wineskins in Matthew 9:17. The wine represents the Holy Spirit, but first century wine was still fermenting when it was placed in skins. If those skins are not new – and thus stretch-able – they burst from the expanding wine coming to full potency. The take-away is progressive re-focus of our attention and energy on the One Who pours out His Spirit in us.

One person repenting launches an expanding life. Many repenting make a culture opening for the Great Awakening God wants to lavish on His people.

It is what happened to Peter in Matthew 14 and Paul in Acts 9–in its discomfort and its amazing-grace promise. When Jesus calls Peter steps out of the boat and begins to walk toward his master on the water. The moment his mind drifts to his problem–a man cannot walk on water–he looks down and begins to sink. The moment he looks back to Jesus and takes His hand, he can and does walk on water. I like Paul on the Damascus Road even better. Paul has been serving God as he understands Him most of his life; yet he detours into vigilantism. The Spirit knocks him onto his backside and asks why he is kicking against the goads instead of serving the goatherd. The fruit of Paul's process of re-focus is the life of contentment and the confidence he can do all things in Christ who strengthens him described in Philippians 3 and 4. Nobody wants to be knocked on their backside, but if we repent instead of kick the rewards are incredible.

One thing we need to remember at all times, returning to that Kansas highway. The man was unhurt beyond a few bruises; that is a miracle by any conception. God has given us a season of miracles–of all kinds–beyond any season in history. There is going to be discomfort as we look up–rather dazed–from the pavement on which we have landed. But the deposit of grace is already in our pockets and more abundant life is the promise in our hearts.

THE PRAGMATIC FRUIT OF CONCERTED PRAYER

I encourage a lifestyle of prayer and repentance–understood as progressive re-focus of attention on God in Jesus Christ–as keys to the abundant life He came to bring. Skeptics wonder about the pragmatic benefits of seeking and praising an alleged all-seeing yet unseen King–and they are right to wonder. Tentative Christians say prayer does not change God; it changes us. They are right as far as they go, yet wimping out if they really think that is all there is to relationship with God. The pragmatic fruit of concerted prayer is all around us and easy for a repentant heart to discover.

We have prayed in concert with a coalition of thirty-five other prayer ministries called the Rain and Reign Coalition, for the past year. We have–of course–asked the Lord to end the drought begun in 2012, but our focus has been in the spirit of 2 Chronicles 7:13-14. In it the Lord promises to hear and forgive when His people humble themselves, seek His face, and repent of sin. Our prayers have focused on the historic sin patterns common to California (and virtually everywhere else) of idolatry, covenant breaking, shedding of innocent blood, and sexual sin. In the past two months rain and snow has averaged 150% of normal. The primary reservoir in my region has made up half of its deficit. Dry streams and rivers are flowing with waters bubbling from the ground in three counties following an earthquake. While the drought is far from over, this is a clear case of God's mercy in response to heartfelt prayer from a critical mass.

In this time of prayer we've seen a number of horrific bills fail in the California Legislature. One would have forced pre-schoolers into Kindergartens staffed by teachers uneducated in Early Childhood Education; another would have forced all children into Kindergarten regardless of their developmental readiness; still another threatened the tax exempt status of youth organizations not permitting homosexual leaders. A recreational marijuana initiative given a broad chance for success in last November's elections did not even muster enough signatures to qualify for the ballot. By the way, we do not pray failure for the bills; we pray that justice, wisdom, and the will of God be manifested. Just as important is that all these bills sailed through their committees, hailed as surefire by insiders, before crashing and burning.

Concerted prayer must be sustained for lasting impact to occur. PrayNorthState has conducted more than a decade of whole-Bible readings in public forums. Several projects of targeted prayer have accounted for large drops in crime rates, hospital cancer admissions, and plummeting rates of suicide and youth deaths. We pioneered Christian radio and television in secular venues beginning in 2001. Our programming expanded from one to five outlets and has enjoyed wide popularity from the get-go; it is no longer unusual for new offerings to do well on secular media. Secular periodicals that did not have them are now hosting Christian-themed features. Our blog has expanded from one thousand to four hundred thousand readers; the invitations to expansion have all been unsolicited. Prayer concerted across denominational and congregational lines and sustained over seasons has literally modified the cultural atmosphere on the ground; our region is not the only one in the state or nation to bear such fruit. Our ministry is just one leader of prayer plowing and preparing ground so others can plant and gather the fruit.

In my city of Redding a local church leased and took over the running of the city-owned–and bankrupt–convention center. There was the expected outcry over church-state-separation and so forth but the city council gave the church's separate holding corporation a chance and the center is flourishing under the new management as it has not in many years. Hard and creative work by management achieved this, but before the bedrock of concerted prayer over years this move was unthinkable.

Redding's convention center is only the latest God-intervention coming in the wake of concerted prayer. FAITHworks is a coalition of some seventy churches-in-support birthed from a half-day retreat where half a dozen pastors prayed, worshipped, and asked a vision of God's plans to address regional unemployment. The vision was grandiose–as authentic visions are. The pastors mobilized their congregations in prayer as others signed on. Eighteen months after a 1997 launch the coalition–in voluntary partnership with a softened county government–had reduced unemployment by half while sharing the Gospel and life-skills training with all who consented. The coalition built and operates two transitional living projects for marginalized families.

Another seventy-church coalition in our region followed concerted prayer with multiple community service and evangelistic concert events shortly after 2001. Hundreds came to the Lord and hundreds wounded by the Church came home as a result. The coalition engaging similar unity and fruit in Sacramento numbers almost five hundred churches at this time. When Jesus says, "My father's house shall be called a house of prayer," in Mark 11:17, He is not making a statement of obligation only, but of opportunity. And the verse offers a prescription for authenticity to churches.

This is not about designated intercessors gathering for prayer. It is about houses of worship–led by their pastors and those specially gifted in prayer–gathering in spatial separation and spiritual unity to plead for God's people as Moses pled for the Children of Israel and Jewish minions down the centuries pled for the restoration of Israel herself. All these prayers were answered – in their time – by God's sovereign choice to bless His people – but not before they were prayed. God's Word in 2 Chronicles 7:14, "If my people, who are called by my Name, will humble themselves and pray and seek my face, and turn from their wicked ways, then I will hear from Heaven and will forgive their sin and heal their land." He does not say, "If those people," but "If my people..."

TIME FOR A RESURRECTED ADVENT

About eighty per cent of the two billion+ Christians in our world observe the four weeks before Christmas as a season called Advent. The word itself means beginning–much like Genesis. It is a solemn season in which caring for the poor and lonely are stressed and readings from Scripture focus on John the Baptist. John breaks into history sometime before the Lord goes public. His story is presented–especially in Mark–as part of the seamless garment of the Gospel of abundant life in the Kingdom of God.

Mark begins with, "The beginning of the Gospel about Jesus Christ, the Son of God." The next two verses quote Isaiah saying God will send a messenger ahead of Messiah who will–in effect–prepare His way like paving a highway in the desert for the coming of the King. (Citizens in ancient times paved a new highway when their king approached.) The next verse depicts John preaching a baptism of repentance.

It cannot be plainer than it is. Repentance is turning about to face in a new direction. For those who already know the Lord it is about re-focus of our attention on the One we once adored; for others it is about gaining that focus for the first time. Other Gospels share the things John calls his listeners to do–as the necessary demonstration of that re-focus–forgiving each other; feeding the hungry and clothing the naked; carrying others' burdens an extra mile. But Jesus Himself makes it clear that repentance is itself the beginning of the Good News–the privilege of repentance–when He makes His first public statement. "Repent," He says, "for the Kingdom of God is near." The Greek we translate as "near" actually means "in pursuit." The Kingdom and its King are pursuing us; the privilege of repentance is the privilege of turning to be captured by Him.

As a Christian steeped in the recurring seasons of the Church year I used to correct my evangelical brethren when they celebrated the Christmas season throughout December and let it die on New Year's Day. "No," I would say. "Advent is December–the time of preparation–and Christmas-the-season begins on Christmas and runs through Epiphany on January 6." But in light of John's announcement of the privilege of repentance my friends seem onto something.

On the other hand, there is a lot to be said about the traditional view of Advent as a time of visible repentance-preparation–visible in the sense that we find ourselves doing good works perhaps neglected earlier in the year as–in this season–the Lord creates a heart of flesh in what has been a heart of stone. This is what the Baptist said. The idea is that throwing a few coins–or even bills–in the Salvation Army kettle is a good thing; calling friends, relatives, and even a needy family our church sponsors is as good or better. But these things can be done as add-ons, without a change of heart. When we take seriously the notion of a time or season for re-focus on God we begin to worship Him in times and places new to us. He sends our hearts in directions of caring we had not thought of on our own. We find ourselves caring more lavishly, and more as a result of His re-shaping our hearts. The horse retakes its rightful place in front of the cart and we are on more than a moment of generosity; we are on a journey of becoming the persons we are called to be and everyone we come across benefits as we do.

This is not some spiritual sleight of hand as opposed to a pragmatic seeking of peace and plenty for those who have little of either. It is a simple recognition that the One who creates, redeems, and resurrects our humanity wants and understands authentic peace and plenty better than we do. In the wilderness temptation episode Jesus is tempted to feed the hungry, secure His authority, and right the world's wrongs outside relationship to His Father. He knows such an approach never ends well. His idea is identical to the traditional sense of the Advent season – a time of seeking relationship with God and expecting the abundant-life-fruit-for-all-concerned to follow the seeking.

Even an Old Testament grouch like Jeremiah (29:12-14) knows that when we seek Him we cannot fail to find Him. What if readers of this blog dedicated the weeks preceding Christmas to that radical seeking? In this world, as it is today, what have we got to lose?

A SEASON OF UNUSUAL MIRACLES

Several years ago on a trip to New Zealand I was awakened from a sound sleep by the sound of my wife, Diana, saying, "Oh no!" It was not a dream, or telepathy, or even a prophetic revelation; I heard her cry out and it woke me up. When I reached her by phone and asked her what had made her cry out she said, "Let me tell you about that." It turned out that she had simply overslept–it was five hours later in California–and said, "Oh no!" when she saw the clock by her bedside. But the Lord's purpose in connecting us in that way was simply to reinforce the reality that He is our connection; distance does not matter. It was a miracle–albeit an unusual one–with a message.

When Diana and I were in Scotland we rented a car and returned it the next day. When I attempted to pay for the fuel we had used the agent said, "But Sir, there is more petrol in the tank now than when you took the car out." Agencies don't make mistakes like misreading gas gauges, but God has an agenda to remind us that–like the Twelve when Jesus first sent them on mission–we should expect to be provided for as we seek His Kingdom. And because we need constant reminding He showed me a bottle of anointing oil–the one I had used in Scotland–twice as full when I took it from my glove compartment in California as when I put it there on our return to the States. These are not the sort of miracles we usually expect, but we are in a season of unusual miracles and God is getting glory for Himself through them while we get a message.

Unusual miracles are most easily described in terms of what they are not.

They are, generally speaking, unsolicited. During our time in Scotland we had planned to gather a team and visit the battlefield at Culloden–the Scottish equivalent of the Little Bighorn. Our plan that year was to assemble a team of British and Scottish prayer people and fulfill the instruction of the Lord to make reconciliation by blessing the English who fought there. When the team unraveled and we found ourselves preparing to worship with only our assistant, Elizabeth, to accompany us we were at peace with it. Yet without our asking God orchestrated our lodging; we were hosted by a direct descendant of the English soldiers of Culloden. David went with us to the battlefield representing a family who–unlike those who merely pillaged after battle–remained in the Highlands to serve the people over two and a half centuries.

I did not ask the Lord to awaken me at 3:00 in the morning so that I could hear Diana's voice–had I thought of it I would have requested a daylight connection! But these miracles come as an unexpected token of God's overwhelming love for us–and His unspoken inquiry as to whether we are paying attention.

Unusual miracles are usually uncompelling–we can explain them away if we are so inclined. In Fiji one year I was called to a hospital because a member of our mission had suffered paralysis in a construction site accident. I also planned to pray for a woman recently blinded by diabetes. I believed that visiting hours began and ended an hour later than was actually the case. When I got to the hospital it seemed as though the Lord wanted me to visit the blind woman first, although the injured man was clearly the greater emergency and I thought I had plenty of time for both of them. I followed the nudge and went to see the woman. It turned out that visiting hours were nearly over and I would not have been permitted on her ward later.

After praying with her I went to find the young paralytic. When I arrived they were about to take him to x-ray; half a minute later and I would not have been permitted to see him either. The timing of both visits was as precise as it was perfect; my role was to obey the Lord's prompting even–and all the more–when it was counter-intuitive to the max. I could have explained away nudging as coincidental, or I could choose to act on the unusual.

(The woman's sight was restored that afternoon and the paralyzed man was so thoroughly healed within ten minutes that the x-rays showed no indication he had been injured at all. But the unusual miracle was God's ordering of both visits without which there would have been neither praying nor healing on that day.)

Just as undemanding–unless we are predisposed to see God's hand at work–is the sign of an inch-and-a-quarter rainfall in my home city of Redding in the middle of July–where everybody knows we are in severe drought and rain never falls in the summertime even when we are not. Anyone could rationalize the fact that our mission team in Fiji sounded like a professional choir each morning as we sang the Doxology at worship even though we had never met or sung together before. Message received: God really wants us at this time to be seeking first His hand in all of our adventures.

A third feature of unusual miracles is that they are frequently unspectacular. We all love to shout from the rooftops when God heals blind eyes and deaf ears; it is wonderful to watch a leg grow out or a tumor disappear. Not so dramatic are signs like the level in a speaker's water glass that does not lower after fifteen or twenty big gulps–that happened in a Northern California conference I attended some while back–or the fact that some pastors in Scotland thought it important that we meet their leadership even though we were not scheduled to be in the country at the same time–and suddenly we found that we and they were arriving at Glasgow Airport at precisely the same time on different flights. Message #1: Are we seeking God's face only in the speaker's teaching or in every dimension of the time and place appointed? Message #2: Are we leaning on God or on our own understanding of what can be orchestrated for His Kingdom?

More than three hundred people prayed daily this summer for a reduction in traffic fatalities and–while fatal bike crashes are skyrocketing around the state–there were at least three NorCal collisions during this period in which the bike was totaled and the riders walked away with minor injuries. Supernatural prevention of the crashes would have been spectacular; handling them as He did was simply God telling us softly that He is calling each of us by name. The message is the same as that given to Elijah three millennia ago–listen for the still small voice and recognize in it the Word of God.

All of this asks us to reason against the logic we have invented in our fallen state. It requires us to do the math as the Bible does the math. Jesus paints the picture for us in Mark 8:14-21 when He finds the disciples arguing over whether they have brought enough bread along on a boat ride. He reminds them of how they gathered twelve baskets of fragments after feeding the five thousand on five loaves of bread; he moves on to the seven baskets recovered after feeding four thousand on seven loaves; he concludes with the question, "Do you still not understand?" What they–and we–don't always understand is that–by conventional worldly math there should be more left over from seven loaves than five. Jesus did it again in His own way and He is calling on us to look for Him instead of what we already recognize as the signs of His passing.

On another ministry trip to Scotland in 2007 Diana and I saw an unusual miracle played out on a strategic Scottish moor. As we prayed for the revival of our ancestral homeland we saw two male deer grazing and hanging out together. The older looked for all the world as though he were mentoring the younger. It was unsought, uncompelling and unspectacular–and it is a phenomenon that does not occur in nature. (Bucks come together only to fight over the females.) Our hearts were drawn to Malachi 4, in which God connects calling the hearts of the fathers to the children as a precursor to revival and transformation. On our return to the States, one of our intercessors related that she had seen the same miracle on the road from Redding to Weaverville, a town in the next county. I have long believed that God is linking the calling forth of His Kingdom in regions like Scotland and Northern California. His promise is real; it is clear; and it requires us to pay special attention at this time to miracles so unusual that they occur outside of even the miracle box.

PROPHETIC ACTS TRUMP DECLARATIONS IN THE PROPHETIC COMMUNITY

In 1984 Roger Ralston had a dream in which God called him to found a ministry of care for women caught in unintentional pregnancy–and for the men in their lives. God said that if he would be faithful the ministry would one day span three counties and occupy the building of an abortion referring agency. The Lord instructed him to cooperate with the prophetic word by prayer walking the property that was already leased to the other agency. Ralston and his wife, Joann, walked and prayed, and went on to found the Crisis Pregnancy Center on another piece of property.

By 2005 the center had known several executive directors and scores of dedicated volunteers. The staff had cared for thousands of clients and gone from one day of operation each week to four. They had a mobile unit in Trinity County and an ultrasound machine for which they had no funds but a mighty God. The director, Sharre Littrell, heard God say that now was the time to move into Red Bluff in Tehama–the third county. She continued to the evening worship service led by a prophet named Joe Cicchino. When Cicchino spoke that night he stopped in the middle of his message to speak the same word to Littrell that she had heard in her car earlier.

The next morning a girlfriend gave her the identical word she had received twice on the previous evening. She called the Salvation Army in Red Bluff and they offered space in their already overcrowded building; within weeks the ministry–now Carenet Pregnancy Center of the Tri Counties–moved into two rooms in the Salvation Army building, hired a Tehama County director, and opened for service. (Eighteen churches came together in support.) In 2006 the facility expanded to a three bedroom house and three days a week of operation; in early 2007 the Redding branch of the ministry began operations in the former family planning clinic building. Family Planning offered them the facility when they lost government funding. The change was friendly and full of mutual blessing.

It is exciting and impressive to watch a prophetic word first delivered in 1984 come to fulfillment in 2007. But that word could not have come to pass without the faithful obedience of two generations of servants of the Living God–most of whom never heard the word uttered. The staff–past, present, and yet to be anointed–of this ministry acted prophetically to pave a straight highway in the desert for our God. That is to say they acted in accordance with God's Word for more than two decades while He established fulfillment of a specific word–given to successive leaders and confirmed by others–on the shoulders of their faithfulness. Their service has resulted in a full-service medical clinic and a full blown men's ministry in addition to the prophesied developments. God gets all of the glory and the rest of us have the privilege of partnering with Him to establish another outpost of His Kingdom.

In the Old Testament God created a community in which prophets sometimes resided. These prophets spoke whatever words God laid on their hearts and often acted in accordance with what they uttered while the people watched in awe–when they weren't stoning the prophets. In the New Testament God has created a prophetic community in which the Spirit of the Living God is progressively poured out on all flesh. Many prophesy and many more act on the prophetic word. It is the unfolding activity of the prophecies–sometimes over many years and through multiple groups within the community–that is truly prophetic in the New Testament Body.

The difference between the two covenantal communities is the difference between a spiritual economy in which the prophets are the members responsible for announcing the coming Messiah and one in which all of the members are responsible for establishing the Kingdom won by the Messiah on the Cross. Although prophets still function in the New Testament community–and we should thank God that they do–their primary role is now to mentor and manage the prophetic release into the whole community so that all of the members can become the prophetic people God has called forth. The books of the New Testament contain as many prophetic utterances as do the pages of the Old, but they are usually spoken by Christians who do not hold the office of prophet–from Peter and Paul to the Ananias who breaks the scales from Paul's eyes. And it is the Church acting on the prophetic words–as when Paul and Silas are sent to Antioch and Philip is sent to a lonely road in the desert to minister to an Ethiopian eunuch–that provides the excitement and action.

In Redding PrayNorthState will organize a prayer project called Paah-hoammi in the first week of May. 2007 will be the third incarnation of this project in which teams of Christians pray for issues of Kingdom significance–like violent crime, traffic fatalities, and unemployment levels–for approximately ninety day periods. Statistics for the issues prayed over are then compared to the same period a year earlier and the resulting changes are proclaimed in a very public manner. In 2006 more than two hundred Christians committed to daily prayer for their assigned topics. Crime was reduced in the county areas by twenty-two per cent according to the sheriff's office. Traffic deaths went down by forty per cent according to Highway Patrol figures, and county officials logged about a one per cent decrease in unemployment. The shape of the project was given to a pastor in Nevada County–first conducted in 2003–and the name was given to me by prophetic revelation. But the action was performed by dedicated people who went before the throne of God every day–and that action is what gives God glory and His people cause for celebration.

PrayNorthState was called to organize a reading of the entire Word of God over the city of Redding in conjunction with National Day of Prayer ceremonies. More than three hundred people from some forty churches have come out each year since 2003 to read the Bible in fifteen minutes increments. We obtain a permit from the city and set up shop at City Hall. The project is called The Bible: Up Close and Personal and it goes on round the clock for three and a half days. (We begin this year at 6:00 AM on Monday, April 30.) We believe that many of the cooperative activities in which churches are partnering with government and business in our city are facilitated by the atmospheric changes brought about by simply seeding the city in this way; we know that a zone of the peace that passes all understanding is palpable at City Hall during the reading and this is confirmed by believers and non-believers alike from city workers to the film crews that cover the event. As it is with Paah-ho-ammi, the prophetic word to launch the reading was uttered by several; the action that shapes and empowers it is undertaken by the Body itself.

Last year in California a several communities outside of Redding held their own Bible reading marathon. More are planning for this year, and we look forward to seeing Paah-ho-ammi spread throughout the state as well. The word is wonderful but the action that springs from it trumps mere declaration every time.

The Walt Disney classic *Twenty Thousand Leagues Under the Sea* remains one of my all-time favorites. Within the story of three castaways attempting to escape from the tortured genius, Captain Nemo, and his nuclear powered submarine seeking vengeance in the South Pacific, there is presented a stark contrast between a prophetic community and the best that technology and human genius can achieve. Captain Nemo is more articulate and more organized than any of the castaways will ever be. Everything aboard the Nautilus is ship-shape and designed for maximum efficiency. Nothing ever happens that he cannot ultimately bring to heel. The castaways, on the other hand, bicker and bump into one another. They cannot seem even to agree on a simple plan. But in Nemo's world only he is even permitted to speak–it is all about him and his crew has abandoned the freedom for which Christ has set us free in favor of allegiance to the one who makes all of their decisions for them. The castaways ultimately live for one another–as God both commands and demonstrates in the Son and in the Spirit. At the end of the day the submarine is a suicide and the castaways enter into a larger life.

The Kingdom community that Christ founds on the Cross and the Spirit launches on Pentecost is not efficient by human standards – or even by Old Testament norms. There are too many moving parts and they all too often march to many drummers. But when God decided to pour out His Spirit on all flesh He also determined to accept no substitutes and no shortcuts. His word – delivered in Scripture and through the mouths of men and women just as in Bible times – gives birth. But it is the action in response to His word – in which the whole Body is called to participate – that trumps the mere declaration of His word every time. And for that we can praise Him in the highest.

CHRISTIAN LOVE CROWDS OUT TOLERANCE

The writer said, "I am not a reader of the Bible, nor am I a practicing member of a church...However, I am a Christian who believes in the message that God gave us when He sent His Son into the world on Christmas Day. We are to care for the poor, the needy, the less fortunate than we are..." She then attacked a local church she judged deficient in carrying out this message. The trouble is, she has no idea what the Gospel is about. She would have to read and believe the Bible to know that.

Jesus does set a high priority on caring for the poor. But the Gospel itself is much more personal. The message is we cannot make it without entering a radically dependent relationship with Him. Once we engage that relationship one of the signs will be caring for the poor. God's Word is just as clear, however, that we can care for the poor apart from Him and achieve only evil; read the temptation narratives in Matthew 4 and Luke 4. Of course, this was a letter to the editor. The attack e-mails I receive are personal.

Some would instruct me about prophecy, but I often get correction regarding the "Christian principles of love and tolerance." The writers–who are rarely believers–want to remind me of my responsibilities to these principles. The trouble is, while love is paramount in the Christian faith, there is no such thing as Christian tolerance. There are four ways to say "love" in the New Testament alone, but each of them means to embrace the other with compassion and committed relationship–treating the other as though he is more important than me. The same principle applies to the radical act of love we call forgiveness. Jesus requires that we approach our brethren seeking reconciliation (Matthew 5) before we approach Jesus Himself in worship. He expects us to extend ourselves to the one who holds something against us before we offer gifts to Him–even if the other has no legitimate grievance. Love–by the way–is action leading to warm feelings–if practiced consistently; it is not feelings that lead to action.

Tolerance–toleration–is simply putting up with something or someone we detest and reject out of hand, hoping it does not show too much. We tolerate bad weather, long lines, and dead-end jobs. Christian love crowds out tolerance every time. The crowding occurs because love is real and substantive while tolerance–applied to human relationships–is nothing but hypocrisy masquerading as apathy.

The folks chanting tolerance as though it were a mantra understand this as well as I do. If I own a business–from a bakery to photography–that caters to weddings in Oregon or Colorado–where, incidentally, gay marriage remains illegal–the government will run me out of business if I refuse to serve a gay wedding. It is not enough that I make no fuss, that I am tolerant; I am required to embrace the people and the concept if I am to do business without serious penalty. If I own Hobby Lobby it is not enough that I tolerate the legality of elective abortion in the land; the government expects me to supply abortion services to my employees because it expects me to embrace something that spits in the face of my faith convictions. Tolerance is not enough; only loving embrace will do. But those who insist I love have no clue what love is.

As it is depicted in traditional wedding services, love hangs in there through thick and thin with people who may disappoint or even disgust the lover. But like the famous expression of patriotic love spoken by Stephen Decatur, "Our country…may she always be in the right; but our country, right or wrong," love is anything but a blanket endorsement of self-destructive behavior. Jesus loved lepers; He hated leprosy. I love my addicted friends and relatives; I hate their addiction. I will speak against it whenever I can and tolerate it whenever I must.

Some things are simply not tolerable. Governors, attorneys general, and even presidents who won't enforce–or will unilaterally re-write–the laws entrusted to them are not tolerable; they are to be opposed. People who bully and terrorize those who do not conform to their ideas are not tolerable; they are to be stopped. Non or marginal Christians who think they know my faith better than I do are to be ignored. Yet Christians are called to love even these–and even as we ignore, oppose or stop them. We're called to love, not tolerate.

THE ANDREW ANOINTING

Diana and I did not plant the sandalwood grove on the back slopes of the Haleakala volcano; Native Hawaiians re-introducing native vegetation did. We did not plant the nearby settlement at Kahiki Nui; Hawaiians entitled to land under the ethnic homestead law built their homes. But we did help.

When wildfire erupted in 2003 – threatening to burn out the settlement and trees that had not grown on Maui in more than a century we were there. We called people of prayer back in California and soon had about fifty praying round the clock – while firefighters fought their hearts out in the almost inaccessible terrain and braved the rifle fire of marijuana growers in the same neighborhood. Our team prayed nothing but blessing on all concerned. In a few days the fire was out and – though flames came within a few feet of settlement and sandalwood – no harm was done to homes or trees. The marijuana growers were burnt out and – yes – they too were blessed because the evil they represented was short-circuited. Settlement and sandalwood continue to flourish today.

We did one thing while others did many things. Others remained to build after we went home. But the one thing we did helped a lot. We exercised the Andrew Anointing.

Andrew is one of the obscure apostles. In John 1:40-42 Andrew hears what John the Baptist says about Jesus being the Son of God and believes it. He immediately goes to find his brother, Peter, telling him the Messiah has been found. Peter becomes the most famous of the apostles; he does many things that are recorded in scripture. So far as the Biblical record can show, Andrew only did one thing. But exercising the anointing that carries his name helped to advance the Kingdom of God a lot.

There is no way to know which thing we do will leave the world a better place but we can know what things are worth doing. We know it every time we act to serve the least of these – as Jesus instructs in Matthew 25:31-40. We know it each time we have each other's backs – as Jesus declares in John 10 and 15 – defending the weaker brother from the bully. We know it each time we confess Jesus as Lord, as He promises in Luke 21 and Matthew 10. And we know it each time we make sacrifice – for Him or for one of His little ones – because that is why He came into the world – to make sacrifice for each of us. Each time we do a thing just because it is worth doing we exercise the Andrew Anointing… at the very least.

There are typically many "one things" we have the opportunity to do in a lifetime. Taken alone they seem small – because they are – but the Lord knits these little things into a tapestry for His glory. I had forgotten the little thing I did more than a decade ago until the Wintu leader spoke of it during the recent dedication of his tribal cultural center. This leader needed to pick up another leader and his car was not functioning. I loaned him my car for the afternoon and he was able to pick up his colleague – no big deal. But as he tells the story the seemingly insignificant assist I provided led to introductions with the leaders of Bethel Church in Redding and the church soon began monthly donations to the tribe. They called it "rent" because their buildings sit on land that once belonged to the Wintu and for which they had never been compensated. The relationship deepened and the leaders honored the church that day for facilitating the building of the cultural center in ways large and small. It began with the loan of a car. Who could know?

In the famous story Loren Eiseley walks a beach after a storm. Thousands of storm-tossed starfish on the beach are dying; a young boy walking along is throwing the starfish back into the water one at a time. Eiseley approaches the boy and asks why; with thousands of starfish stranded, he says, the effort cannot make a real difference. The boy responds, "It makes a difference to this one," as he throws another one back. What Eiseley does not express is the reality that it makes as much difference to the boy as to the starfish.

Our Lord says if we are faithful in small things He will begin to trust us with much more. He wants us to use all of our anointing and gifting. But the Andrew Anointing is a real good place to start.

CHAPTER 2:

A CULTURE OF REPENTANCE

The Lord and I were walking a trail in the Appalachian Mountains of western Virginia one day; the scenery–the very air–was unspeakably lovely. The closeness with my Lord was best of all. He pointed out a turning point in the trail about fifty yards ahead and told me that was as far as we were to go this day. I agreed to turn back at that point, but when I got there I saw so much beauty down the trail after it took its sharp left turn that I decided to go to the next bend and turn back there. After all, I would still be enjoying Him in the midst of all that He has made for the enjoyment of His creatures–and especially me on this day–I knew He would be fine with it. I took the left turn and tripped over an exposed tree root about ten feet past where I was to stop and gave my ankle a very painful twist.

I cried out to the Lord, demanding to know why He would let me hurt myself when we were having such a wonderful time together. He answered, "I didn't let you; you insisted on it."

I don't know many–if any–activities we would call sin that are not fully rationalized before commission. We can always think of really good reasons for going our own way. On my walk in the forest I "knew" God would not mind if I just enjoyed a little more of His beautiful creations before I obeyed. The time I arranged abortions for two of my friends who were panic stricken over their pregnancies I "knew" the only standard for my behavior should be loyalty to friends in trouble. Trouble is, my knowing fell short of knowing Jesus in both cases–the only One worth knowing.

The consequences were far more serious in the one case than in the other, but the issue is identical in both. The good news is the forgiveness which follows repentance is just as thoroughgoing in both cases as well.

The word itself–whether rooted in Greek or Hebrew–means literally to miss the mark aimed at. In other words it is not necessarily that sin has independent existence as a phenomenon; it is actually a lesser–albeit inexcusable–falling short of goodness. And since Christians who know the Word of God recognize that goodness is only realized in obedience to God, sin is pragmatically understood as anything we do or fail to do in disobedience–less-than-obedience–to God. Romans 1 makes it clear that even if we do not know God's will, nature itself makes clear what is expected of us.

This chapter examines repentance in for-instance-types. The National Day of Repentance is a grassroots ministry observed twice yearly in forty-two (and counting) of the United States. It has caught fire in thirty other nations as well. The Rain and Reign Coalition is an independent yet affiliated ministry of repentance coordinating thirty-six similar ministries within California. The common element is a dedication to accepting the responsibility assigned each of us in Romans 3:23 that all of us have fallen short of God's glory. That responsibility means a culture in the Church of a 2 Chronicles 7:14 lifestyle–If my people, who are called by my Name, will humble themselves and pray and seek my face and turn from their wicked ways I will hear from Heaven and forgive their sin and heal their land. Any time we recognize that our land is not as it was in Galilee in Matthew 11:2-6–the dead raised, the sick and injured healed, the poor encouraged, and blessing abounding for those not offended by the Christ–repentance is the antidote.

The good news is repentance is not a punishment, but rather an earth shaking privilege. Mark 1:1-4 depicts this privilege not as preparation for Messiah but the first step in receiving Him. The privilege of repentance is the Gospel.

The chapter addresses the four classic categories of sin–the shedding of innocent blood, sexual sin, covenant breaking, and idolatry. It reminds us that the real essence of repentance occurs after we abandon the sins we have rationalized so ineffectively; the trainwreck we make of our lives proclaims the truth whatever we may say about it. That real essence is the opportunity to re-focus our attention on God. We have that opportunity every time He calls us to obey Him–whether or not we have disobeyed.

One day I entered a supermarket looking for a soda on a hot day. I saw a woman obviously conducting a survey; I hate surveys without exception and was already changing course to avoid her when the Lord said, "You are to stand with this woman." I obeyed this time and let her ask me her survey questions.

When she was finished I was again prompted by the Lord–this time to ask her about faith. She acknowledged that she was a believer, but she did not have a team of intercessors praying daily for her and for her family. She also said she did not share her faith with others, not being very good at it.

A friendship has developed between us over the years and one of the ways I have spoken into her life is to encourage the re-focus of her attention on God in those areas about which I questioned her that day in the supermarket. She is today an internationally known figure in a growing edge ministry who needs and appreciates her prayer team every time she dodges a dart from the enemy. She shares her faith on her nationwide talk radio over secular airwaves. My contribution? One day I did something I did not want to do–a small thing–but a choice to re-focus that is the essence of authentic repentance.

My small choice to re-focus–in the doing of what I did not wish to do–led my friend to a choice to re-focus–in the doing of what she did not wish to do. Our choices have become catalysts for others to re-focus–in the doing of what they (perhaps) do not want to do. This is the seedbed for a culture of authentic repentance.

A NATIONAL DAY OF REPENTANCE

(Author Note: This piece was written in 2012, the inaugural year of National Day of Repentance. The day is presently observed in more than forty states and more than thirty nations. American observations occur in the Fall–on Yom Kippur–and in the Spring on April 30. The Spring Day celebrates Washington's first inaugural address and the Day of Fasting, Prayer, and Humiliation proclaimed by Abraham Lincoln in 1863.)

In the verses leading to 2 Chronicles 7:14 God calls His people to repentance not when they perceive a moral need for it, but whenever disaster is seen in the land. Then He says, "If my people who are called by my Name," not "If those people I believe have sinned…" He promises healing when we have turned back to Him. In the chapters preceding Joel 2:28 and the wonderful promise to pour out His Spirit on all flesh God first calls on His people–and His people alone–to fast and pray and hold solemn assemblies–inspired not by consciousness of wrongdoing, but by awareness of needing God in the land. Jesus calls on His own people to "Repent, for the Kingdom of Heaven pursues you," in Matthew 4:17. Mark's Gospel (1:1-4) begins with a call to repentance in the ministry of John the Baptist–as though that privilege were itself the Good News of Jesus Christ. And so the disasters in our land provide us with the greatest opportunity of all time–if we will choose to see God's call in it.

The National Day of Repentance follows in the footsteps of Scripture, and in those of events–such as the recent Luis Palau Festival in Sacramento–gathering hundreds of thousands of Christians over the past twenty months. I am privileged to serve as one of the national directors that responds to a persistent call in these events to prepare our hearts for the next great move of God in our land. Our purpose is to educate the Body of Christ to the need for and the value of repentance at this time of our life together. We envision an annual event filling the twenty-four hours of the Jewish Yom Kippur with ongoing acts of repentance locally conceived and conducted around the nation. The Day of Repentance begins at Sundown, September 25, and continues to Sundown, September 26.

This is an everyone-can-play opportunity whether as individuals, church congregations, or simply as groups of friends if a couple of things are remembered. The first is that we are not called to beat our breasts about how bad we are. (If we are conscious of fouling pitches into the seats we need to confess and let it go, as always.) The second is this call is for people who name the Name of Christ as their Lord to turn themselves–not to wish others would turn–back to a focus on God instead of on self. (Of course, any who don't identify themselves as believers and yet feel called are welcome to jump in.) But the most important thing is to focus on Whom we are turning toward and what He may want us to do about that. I know a man who was hit by a car because – as the driver said – he was so intent on missing the man that he drove right into him. We tend to steer into what we focus upon, even if that is the very thing we mean to avoid. Let all who participate in this day be intent on what they want to start and enjoy rather than on what they want to stop and regret.

For more information go to www.dayofrepentance.org. All participants are invited to post their events on the web site (if they wish) so that others may be inspired and challenged. All are welcome to take what they find on the site and do it as is or adapt it as needed. No national, state, or regional format will be imposed. We ask only that the day itself be devoted to repentance activities, that we be permitted to help spread the word about what you are doing, and that we understand ourselves as contributing to a culture of repentance in the Church itself rather than issuing a call to a nation that does not know Christ. We are confident that as the Church begins to live the victorious life that is the fruit of repentance the nation will beat a path to our door – and not before. Let us begin and let us rejoice.

Culture is not something you think about so much as something you think through. In our American culture, for example, we don't think about why we use a fork; we simply use the fork and think about the food we place on it. A culture of repentance beginning with a national day of repentance just begins the building of an opportunity to refer our lives more and more back to their source, living though that reference point. Only good can come of it.

THAT HIGH PRESSURE RIDGE–A SPIRITUAL AND SPATIAL REALITY

Meteorologists say the worst drought in California history is caused by a high pressure ridge of air in the upper atmosphere that has hovered over the state for more than a year. The ridge deflects storms. Such ridges are natural phenomena when they coalesce for days or even weeks; to hover over the state for sixteen months–and counting–is simply not natural. It can only be called supernatural. And if it can only be called supernatural it must be addressed in supernatural terms.

The Bible provides that address. In 2 Chronicles 7:13-14 God tells the Jewish People whenever He shuts down the heavens so that no rains fall they ought to "humble themselves and pray and seek my face and turn from your wicked ways." His promise is to hear from heaven, forgive their sin, and heal their land.

There are a couple of caveats before we proceed. One is that God is not vindictive, but He is a God who stops at nothing to get our attention–even to shutting down the heavens. The other is that the Hebrew word *ra*, or wicked, means literally inadequate or dysfunctional. God is not judging us for inadequacy; as human beings we are naturally inadequate. But the state of inadequacy becomes the sin of choosing dysfunctionality when we worship it, placing human efforts and understanding ahead of God. California leads the nation in elective abortions–at a rate exceeding our share of national population; biblically that is shedding innocent blood. California is a national leader in breaking all kinds of covenants, from the marriage covenant to holding Native American slaves in our early years to statewide officers refusing to enforce our laws and constitution; we are in denial of these things as a state. California hosts the pornography and sex trafficking industries as just two examples of the sexual sin that is rampant here. And California pays tribute to pagan deities by placing their statues in public buildings and worshipping them in some of our religious buildings; that is idolatry in Biblical parlance. In each case we believe we are doing what must be done to cope with an inadequate world. We place our understanding above what God says in Scripture. That especially is idolatry–at its most subtle and most damaging.

These four categories of sin–if we believe the Bible–are adequate to literally pollute land and atmosphere. Most people believe human moral choices cannot impact the environment unless they literally target it, but we have already demonstrated our drought is not of natural causation. I recommend believing the Bible–not just for explaining the problem, but for solving it as well.

The Rain and Reign Coalition is a gathering of approximately thirty-five extra-parochial (not limited to one denomination or congregation) ministries committed to praying for an end to California's drought. We are committed to prayer for more than just relief. We pray repentance – first and foremost for ourselves – and then in identification with our fellow Californians. We repent of the sins cited above and beg our God to release His blessing over our state – first in the restoration of relationship with Him that we Californians have stretched to the breaking point, and second by releasing the rain and snow we so desperately need in such a way that everyone will know it comes as a gift from Him. Those who think our prayers and repentance silly need not join in. For those who see wisdom – if not logic – in prayer of this type, please add your voices to ours. We ask nothing more than that prayer be daily and heartfelt.

On my recent ministry trip to Malaysia I went out one evening with a small group of young adult leaders to do some stargazing. Heavy cloud cover hid all but a handful of stars. As we sang praise songs and enjoyed each other one of us suggested we point our index fingers at the sky, count to three, and blow. When we did this the clouds visibly moved. After the third repetition the sky was cleared and we watched with wonder the stars as we praised the Lord. And no – none of us is so foolish as to imagine our counting and blowing actually moved the clouds. But we do serve a God who loves to play with His children if we will just let Him draw near enough to take hold of us. He waits for California to get that message.

RAIN AND REIGN–AND A SUNDAY FOR REPENTANCE

I wrote in my last posting that the high pressure ridge keeping precipitation from the state hovered over us sixteen months and counting. As the good rains of March and April came about that ridge began to disperse; it reappears, but for more natural spans, since a large cross-section of the Body of Christ has begun a particular process of sustained prayer and repentance over the state.

The Rain and Reign Coalition is a gathering of some thirty-five California ministries agreeing with each other to pray repentance–understood as re-focus of attention on God and His Kingdom–on behalf of ourselves and the state we love. That re-focus includes renunciation of California's historic sins. We renounce shedding of innocent blood–from the unborn to Native peoples to victims of gang violence–and the idolatry of human ingenuity without reference to God's vision and provision, the sexual sin of a state hosting the pornography industry and closing its eyes to human trafficking, and the many broken covenants past and present–from treaties with tribes to abandonment of families by their heads. We do not dwell on sin, but we do commit ourselves to seeking opportunities to eliminate its presence and legacy.

The coalition is committed to daily prayer asking God to break the drought cycle, thanking and praising Him for the rain He has sent. Some reservoirs are full and the hillsides are green already. But we recognize that rainfall is hovering around half normal levels for this time of year even as the natural rainy season draws to a close. The snowpack on which we depend for sustained water is less than a third normal depth. We serve a God Who answers prayer quickly, and this is a deposit on His promise to bless the state. Our resistance to accountability for past and present behavior is still in His Face, effectively blocking the fullness of His blessing. Ongoing drought–and make no mistake the drought is indeed ongoing–comes not from divine rage but from God's love which says He is absolutely determined to see us become all that we can be. And so the coalition continues to pray and to call for prayer.

Why do the heathen rage? That is the question in Psalms 2. The heathen are those who do not accept God as authoritative; it is an archaic term with no judgment in it. But those who reject the notion that God's Son died for them and so bought their abundant life often rage at any hint of accountability to a higher power. Throw in the notion of responsibility for their ancestors' acts and the rage becomes monumental. (Never mind that we cheerfully accept the passed-down benefits of ancestral achievement.) Frankly, I am not writing to or about the folks who reject God and His claim on our lives. It is the Body of Christ God calls to repentance. When the fruit of our repentance comes into the bin is time enough to look to a clueless world and ask if they want to share the bounty through joining us in repentance.

National Day of Repentance is calling on churches across the nation to name May 4 Repentance Sunday. Those who accept the call will engage some form of corporate repentance or re-focus on God and His Kingdom–as depicted in the Scriptures and not as we imagine it to be. The willing are exhorted to renounce participation in the categories of sin cited above. This is no call for sackcloth and ashes, much less self-flagellation, but for a humble acknowledgement that we have messed up and it is time to fess up. Then and only then can we credibly ask God to lead us in the transformation of our communities and states into provinces of His Kingdom in the power of His Holy Spirit. Then and only then can we say we are preparing for the Fourth Great Awakening in our land that He promises.

In the meantime, many claim there is nothing you can do about death, taxes, and weather. They are wrong; we can pray and then walk through the doors we see opened only after concerted prayer. Others travel the state claiming the drought is over. They are wrong; we pray they–and we–become filled with God's humility. (Coalition members have committed to repenting until even secular authorities affirm the drought's end.) What is right on is the certainty God loves His people more than life itself. There actually is a pony under all this...drought.

The next four postings deal separately and respectively with the patterns of historical sin in California.

SHED BLOOD AND A CULTURE OF SACRIFICE

I met Jesus in April 1970 in an encounter both dramatic and intimate while proctoring an exam in a public high school in San Diego, California. Two years prior I helped two friends abort their pregnancies; I found a doctor willing to perform (then) illegal abortions and borrowed the money from a relative. I had nothing to do with creating these pregnancies but in my mind there was no higher value than having your friends' backs; I did what I believed needed to be done. When I met Jesus He did not condemn me for what I had done in 1968. It did not come up at all for a few weeks.

In a Holy Spirit show of irony this hippy (me) was led into one of the most traditional and structured denominations; they even practiced "going to confession." When I asked the pastor what I should do next–as a new member with no previous experience of church–he told me to show up for confession the coming Saturday. When I asked how I should prepare–seeing as how I lacked even a grasp of what might be called sin–he told me to write down everything I could think of in my past that might stand between me and God. He said I should include even the apparently trivial and then he said something I thought odd but encouraging. He said if some sinful incident came to mind after my confession I was not to worry about it; if the Lord had wanted me to deal with it then He would have brought it up in time for the confession.

I was surprised at how much I remembered of clearly out of bounds behavior even to someone as clueless as myself; I had a laundry list by the time I got into that little booth I had only seen in movies before. Midway through the exercise I heard a voice as clear as my own saying, "Don't forget the abortions." There was no condemnation of me as a murderer of the unborn; neither were excuses offered on account of my ignorance. There was only the instruction. I walked out of that confessional convinced of two things. Abortion is murder–the unjustified killing of a human being–and I dare not condemn those who have done what I did; I must speak the truth about this heinous act in love and humility.

California leads the nation in elective abortions; our lead is far in excess of our share of the national population. Our legislature recently adopted a law permitting even non-physicians to abort pregnancies despite the fact I could not abort my dog unless I have a doctor of veterinary medicine perform the procedure. In each case we are doing–as I did–what seems the only realistic option in the face of emergency. But we are so committed to aborting all unwanted pregnancies we forget Ludwig Von Beethoven was an unwanted pregnancy; we forget God knows more about what is both best and most realistic than we do. And we forget substitution of our best for His is key to many sins.

Shedding innocent blood is sin that–when it becomes a social pattern–pollutes the land and atmosphere under and over wherever it is welcomed. California taxpayers fund thirty thousand abortions yearly–on top of the multiple thousands paid for by the panicky parents seeking them. It always seems like the only way out of a bad situation until we consider the overwhelming medical odds against any one pregnancy resulting in a live birth. Truth is there is simply no way a pregnancy comes to term without the intervention of a loving God; if one were truly unplanned it would self-abort. With the large numbers of couples desperately seeking to adopt there is no way a woman must be saddled with raising a child she does not want. When we choose to bail out on a baby we are shedding innocent blood and spitting in God's eye at the same time. But what should we do?

The first thing is to adopt the Forty Days for Life approach. Bless and do not curse those with whom we disagree. The second is to repent of our role in creating a culture where dealing death is so easily rationalized. The silence of pastors, leaders, and everyone else is the reason it flourishes. And last is to commit to a lifestyle in which we sacrifice ourselves for others–as Jesus did and does–instead of expecting others–whether unborn children or the driver one lane over–to sacrifice for us.

THAT IDOLATRY THING – ENOUGH IS ENOUGH

By secular standards Herod the Great is one of the greatest kings Judea ever had. He produced public works from aqueducts to arenas, kept most people working, and had enough foreign policy savvy to keep Roman occupiers at arms' length. Of course the prophets reject Herod as an enemy of God because he kills any who cross him and puts himself in the place of God for all practical purposes. Jesus tells his disciples to reject the influence of both Herod and the Pharisees in Mark 8:14-21. He rejects these influences because they are idolatry, which is nothing but the elevation of our creations onto a throne reserved for the real Creator.

The Pharisees – dominant religious authorities – were no better. Their idolatry was to elevate their law, inspired by Ten Commandments but bloated to nearly seven hundred commandments of their own invention, to obsessively cross every T and dot every I they could imagine. When Jesus heals on the Sabbath – in fulfillment of God's Old Testament admonition to show mercy at all times – the Pharisees demand an accounting. He violates their law – which they worship – mistaking it for the God they reject.

In the Garden of Eden the first people disobey God by eating forbidden fruit despite His admonition to leave it alone. But their sin is to place their will to know and understand on the throne of the One who already does. Idolatry goes back a long way and it keeps on returning to the prominence it demands for itself in California.

During California's Gold Rush we placed our will to strike it rich ahead of God's commands to love one another, treat one another honestly, and steward the environment of the most wonderful place on the planet. We slaughtered Native inhabitants – and any Euros we considered to be rivals – while we stole claims and goods from one another and raped the environment to get at the gold. We enslaved Natives, Blacks and Asians even after California was admitted to the Union as a free state because we decided our legal rights (the 13th Amendment had not yet become law in 1850) trumped God's word that His Son sets all free. Today the state government – through taxpayers – funds thirty thousand annual abortions; we place our love of self-determination in all things above the overwhelming witness of science that every pregnancy is against all odds. California leads the nation in abortion and suicide disproportionately to our share of the population; this is the fruit of militant self-determination. That's right – abortion AND suicide.

Today we adopt laws denying young people seeking to escape same sex attractions the right to counseling and – in the same spirit – adults the right to work if advocates of small fish or opponents of fossil fuels are offended. We mandate the end of privacy for school-aged young people in misguided efforts to help the gender dysphoric feel better about themselves despite the fact these measures help none. And we preside over an economy so dysfunctional through over-regulation that five of the ten most difficult US cities for young people seeking work are in California. This is the fruit of idolizing the human will to make things and people better. This is sin of which we in the Rain and Reign Coalition repent on behalf of ourselves and the state we love. But what do we need to do; what is the practical outflow of repentance after prayer?

That outflow should re-focus our attention on God Himself and His vision for our state–any state–as a place that maximizes opportunity for all and places a premium on permitting each of its citizens to "work out your own salvation in fear and trembling," as Paul writes in Philippians. The outflow of that is to stop honoring the expressions of our idolatries from the Gold Rush to politically correct thought and from the slaughter of the unborn to the excesses of the environmentalist movement. Our laws should reflect stewardship of the human and physical environment without the manipulation of it. Thus ends the influence of Herod.

Those churches and leaders who absent themselves from public affairs because their concern is otherworldly need to get a clue: this is the influence of the Pharisees–don't look and don't touch because you might make a mistake. Jesus calls us to walk on water; Peter is repenting when he begins to sink and calls on His Lord to save him.

What is required of us is both difficult and risky. But it is not complex and it is our participation in the Kingdom of God in California if we choose to believe.

SEX AND SIN – NO NECESSARY CONNECTION

God has given no more beautiful gift than the sexual union He makes possible between a husband and wife. It is the fullest expression of "having one's back" – understood as total commitment. There is good and credible evidence the Jews invented romantic love as expressed in their practice of kissing and making love in the frontal position, making possible the intimate engagement – looking one another in the eye – we associate with "knowing" in the Biblical sense. Sexual union is also the way we give birth to children whose purpose is to provide an opportunity for sacrificial love as much as to reproduce our species. This approach to union is unique to humankind.

God clearly intended this as His gift from the beginning. A proper translation of Genesis 2:18 reads literally, "one who can look him in the face," as egalitarian a term as anyone could ask for the status of a wife; "helpmate" is simply not it. Meanwhile, Genesis 2:24 depicts God declaring a man leaves his parents and becomes one flesh with his wife. Jesus calls this foundational in Mark 10. Only then is sex the gift He intends.

Tragically, we have not been content to walk out God's plan, and California leads the nation in walking out the tragedy. Many studies – conducted by major secular universities over the past four decades – show marriages sturdier and stabler when the couple marries prior to co-habitation. Others show children far less at risk for poverty, crime, or addiction when raised in traditional families. Studies touting the benefits of raising children in alternative households have been debunked as junk science by studies actually employing the scientific method and painting a picture much more grim. Although there are times when a marriage cannot endure the strains placed on it, and the one entrusted with the children does the best and often most successful job possible against odds, there is no alternative model in which adults and children consistently thrive than the Biblical one. Yet we keep trying to do the same dysfunctional stuff while expecting a different result for ourselves and our children.

California plays host to the worldwide pornography industry. Between eighty and ninety per cent of pornography produced worldwide comes out of the greater Los Angeles area – ironically a place named for the angels of God – and its use is as common in the Church as outside it. Pornography is by definition an appeal to the absence of covenant relationship in which only the pleasure associated with sexual union is entertained. The people on both sides of the screen are treated as objects – pieces of meat in essence – and even Christians tend to deny the destruction this wreaks on authentic relationships, although numerous studies document the reality. Add that to the social tendency for engaged couples to focus more on the wedding than the marriage in their preparation times and it is small wonder our state leads the nation in divorce and marital dysfunction. What can we do as people of repentance?

For openers we could check out Ephesians 5:21-25 in God's Book. The world was grounded in sacrifice from the beginning. (I have made my case for this in previous blogs and will doubtless do it again hereafter.) Verse 21 calls on husbands and wives to submit to (read sacrifice for) one another out of reverence for Christ. The rest speaks to how wives and husbands can accomplish this mutual submission within their respective spheres–and nothing more nor less. There is no subordination in marriage; only mutual submission leading to mutual joy, if we accept the counter-intuitive precept God gives.

We are indeed called to repent in this season of spiritual drought leading to physical drought. Repentance is not about beating ourselves up over our own behavior, much less that of others. It is about re-focus on God and on the life He offers to us. The people of God who observe the lifestyle of repentance as the privilege it is will look first at how they can be better spouses and parents according to the Biblical model. They will re-discover the joy of covenant engagement with one spouse viewed as a person and not as an object. And we will beg God on an ongoing basis to lead the rest of us Californians back to Him and to His ways. Repentance is about seeking abundant life from its Giver through practical acts. And we can start by celebrating that–while there are sexual sins and they are rampant in our state–there is no necessary connection between the one and the other. Authentic sex is anything but sin.

ANOTHER SHOT AT KEEPING THE COVENANT

Human beings are designed for covenant. Unique among the creatures of God we are capable of voluntary, reciprocal, and developmental relationships. Dogs are either pack or solitary–they don't choose social or solitary each morning. If your dog bites my dog, mine will likely bite back, but if your dog bites me I will likely call a lawyer. And when a dog reaches maturity he is all the dog he can be. When I reach adulthood I will continue to change and–hopefully–grow the rest of my life. This maturity occurs in relationships in which I live and move.

Covenant–as opposed to a contract with fixed terms, conditions and boundaries–is a shaped relationship remaining open at the front end. When God tells people (Micah 6:8) they know what He requires–to act justly, love mercy and walk humbly with Him–He shapes the relationship without limiting its growth. Ditto when Jesus calls the heart of covenant with God that we love God with all our might and neighbor as ourselves. We are not just designed for covenant living; we attain the fullness of humanity only within that context, whether in the most intimate setting of the marriage covenant or in the social covenants of friendship and constitutional community.

In California we've done a poor job–at best–of keeping covenant with God and with one another.

We lead the nation in divorce and co-habitation without marriage, and these are covenant breaking and refusal to covenant at all, respectively. Yet most of us remain blissfully unaware of–and in denial of–the degree to which covenant breaking is a lifestyle in our culture and history. When our ancestors arrived in California they discovered more varieties of Native American tribes than in any other state. They entered into covenants–treaties–with more frequency than in any other state–and we have broken virtually all of them. That breaking has often been accompanied by violence of a unique ferocity.

The Natural Bridges Massacre is one of the worst examples. The gold miners of Weaverville lived in peace with the Nor-el Muk band of the Wintu nation until a famine came and six Indians begged food from a hate-filled Weaverville grocer. He suggested they eat grass instead. When his body was found with grass stuffed in his mouth a posse formed and reacted. They never found the suspects, but they murdered more than one hundred fifty women, children and elderly Wintu at Natural Bridges for revenge. To this day tourists and locals alike think the area a playground instead of the shrine it ought to be; graffiti covers the rocks where the dead are still not permitted to rest in peace.

Even worse was the Etna area massacre of Shasta people. Whites entered into a peace treaty with the tribe and–to celebrate–invited the tribe to a barbecue. They laced the beef with strychnine and three thousand Shastans died. Those who did not succumb to the poison were gunned down as they fled. To this day the federal government denies the event took place, but I have seen xeroxed copies of contemporary newspaper accounts of the slaughter. It happened; denial only worsens the atrocity.

Covenant breaking is unique among the master sins of California in that it does not stop with polluting the physical environment as much as the hearts of we who live in it. It degrades our very nature as beings designed for one way of living and one only. What does repentance resemble?

The first thing is simple enough–fess up where we have messed up. The second is just as simple–choose to recognize the God Who makes us as the God Who understands our best interests far better than we; re-focus our attention on Him and His ways and forget our excuses that too much time has passed or we are not our ancestors. We accept the Gold Rush benefits they bequeath cheerfully enough; we can accept responsibility for righting their Gold Rush wrongs with the same cheerfulness.

Of course such recognition would change our decision-making–one decision at a time–from whatever seems necessary to me to whatever seems important to my Maker. It would embody Jesus' words that when we sacrifice life claims for others we come into His abundant life, but when we hang on to self-serving survival we only postpone death for awhile.

Prayer is the most important third dimension. When we pray before and after doing we are reminded–should we forget–that the Good Samaritan remains the model of ultimate covenant keeping and Micah 6:8 still defines the covenant lifestyle.

AMERICAN EXCEPTIONALISM AND THE GNADDENHUTTEN MASSACRE

One of my favorite books as a teenager was Zane Grey's *The Spirit of the Border*. I was thrilled by this tale of quiet courage in Moravian Christian missionaries to the Native Americans of the Ohio River Valley set against the earthquake valor of the famous Indian fighter, Lewis Wetzel, at the close of the American Revolution. Nearly all the characters are historical realities excepting the twin brothers, Jim and Joe Downs, the sisters they love, and some of the Indian leaders. A key element is the destruction of the missionaries' Village of Peace–they called it Gnaddenhutten–by Indian warriors incited by American renegades while an equally real band of American militia looks on because they are not large enough to interfere without bringing certain destruction on themselves.

As an adult with leadership responsibilities in the Christian community–the American Christian community–I recently re-discovered this book and did a little research into its historicity. I discovered the truth that the Christian Indians were massacred by that very body of American militia led by David Williamson whom Grey depicts as helpless to intervene. The band–actually twice the size reported by Grey–gave the Indians a night to pray and prepare themselves for death before bludgeoning and scalping them into eternity. The missionary leaders, David Zeisberger and John Heckewelder, were not present. They were later captured by the British and tried and acquitted of treason against Great Britain.

The historical incident should be as shameful to our people as it was thrilling to the heart of the fourteen-year-old boy reading the fictionalized account. It becomes more horrific by the very attempt to sanitize it. Yet in either version it seems to spotlight the struggle for us Americans–since the beginning–between the God-breathed opportunity to build a shining city on a hill and the human demand to build a city in the image of our warrior and entrepreneurial tradition. Reality is both sides of the American character are exceptional and have been used by God to temper and activate each other. Reality is that the city on a hill metaphor–whether spoken by Isaiah or Ronald Reagan–reflects our God-given nature and needs to be in command when we strike out into the wilderness on the shoulders of the other side, the Wetzel side.

Our God is a God of quiet courage in the middle of sacrifice, forgiveness, and mercy. He revealed His plan for every social and political institution we hold dear in words uttered in His Name from New England pulpits that gave rise to our Declaration of Independence and our Constitution. He shaped our character and identity as a nation in the first three Great Awakenings. He also gave us the spirit of aggressive courage that invents the plow that breaks the Great Plains and feeds the world–but also breaks people and fights tooth and nail to preserve an institution as foul as slavery until other people–fueled by that same spirit of courageous aggression–put an end to it. Both spirits are of God, but the latter must be the servant of the former if we would be the people we have always been called to be, just as we Christians say the flesh must become the servant of soul and spirit. And we need to remember that God's unimaginable power is released only in submission to His known will, however counter-intuitive it may seem. At that point we become people of redemption, restoration, and resurrection. We become the only nation in history to re-build nations like Germany and Japan after having defeated them in war. We become uniquely transparent in acknowledging the areas in which we fall short–such as our treatment of Black and Native peoples–and in seeking to fully right those wrongs. And we become the first to come to the rescue of even those nations that despise us when they are in distress.

The American track record in caring and generosity–not to mention mercy and forgiveness–is unmatched among the nations. We are not perfect. But we do not need to paper over events like the Gnaddenhutten Massacre. We need to address them in repentance and humility. And we need to remember the words of the only King we will ever need. "Remain in me and I will remain in you. No branch can bear fruit by itself; it must remain in the vine. Neither can you bear fruit unless you remain in me." This is not a call to the nation first; it is first a call to the people of faith on whom the nation rests.

RECONCILIATION IS A TWO-WAY STREET

It was my privilege to make apology for some things my countrymen have done over the years when I gave a plenary address to the World Christian Gathering on Indigenous People, meeting in Kiruna, Sweden, in August 2005. My statement was not the politically correct apology favored by purveyors of shame. I acted as an authentic ambassador of reconciliation. Authentic reconciliation is a two-way street and anyone who has been reconciled to God in Christ is obliged to walk it.

I prophesied – spoke what God had spoken first – that God's plan was to launch a worldwide Great Awakening beginning with the indigenous peoples of the world. Most of these peoples are scattered, poor, and pressured to assimilate into the larger cultures in which they live. Absorption conformity threatens to effectively eliminate them in terms of their identity. Standing at the podium I apologized for what people who look like me have so often done – in both malice and uninformed goodwill – to people who looked like them. But I added a note that is all important if we are to operate in truth. I said my apology did good for me, clearing my own soul of spiritual barnacles that impede a smooth passage through the waters of God's lifegiving seas. I said the Word of God is clear – check Romans 3:10-18 – that all have sinned and fallen short of God's glory. The Gospel according to Mark actually begins with the bald statement that the privilege of repentance is a gift from God and the beginning of His good news in Christ. I challenged my listeners to go beyond forgiving those who had injured them to seeking the forgiveness of those they had injured. I added that only their own apologies to those they had oppressed would trigger their own liberation. It is repentance that opens a clear channel in each of us for God's will.

When I finished speaking the coordinator of the gathering declared we had just heard a word of God. He called on us to spend the rest of the afternoon seeking first forgiveness from others. More than eighty tribes and nations were represented at this gathering. We spent the next four hours seeking each other out for authentic reconciliation. I approached the delegation from the Philippines to apologize for the way we treated them in the days following the Spanish American War; our armed forces suppressed their insurrection with a brutality that matched the Spanish from whom we were supposed to be setting them free. Had Cuban people been present I would have asked their forgiveness for supporting the dictator Batista instead of the Cuban people and so paving the way for the Communist dictatorship of Fidel Castro.

I did not just apologize; I did not grovel and bleat how bad we Americans are. I declared that we are the only people on the planet who have always rebuilt whatever we have torn down. We are–and the Philippines is a case in point–the only nation to voluntarily release a nation from our control as soon as we believe it feasible. But we are also capable of being as ham-handed, foolish, and even nasty as the next nation. I am proud to be an American. I am proud to be a citizen of the greatest nation in the history of the world in terms of our national commitment to doing good wherever we go and to being the very blessing we seek. That is the very essence of the American Exeptionalism we speak and we live. I am not afraid of confessing areas in which we–and I–have fallen short of that tremendous vision and destiny so long as we speak and celebrate the whole truth. That whole truth includes claiming and celebrating the closest approximation in history to that freedom with liberty and justice for all for which Christ came into the world to set us free.

I read in the news recently of the death of Captain Matt Manoukian, USMC. The captain was gunned down by an Afghan police officer assigned to work with him in Afghanistan. His is one of more than more than fifty deaths this year of American servicemen and women murdered by representatives of the very people they have committed their lives to serve. The captain himself was a local legend because of the devotion he had shown over multiple tours of duty to caring for the people and families he encountered in Afghanistan far beyond the needs of his military duty. I would like to know when the Karzai regime is planning to apologize–to seek reconciliation–over these American deaths that are the fruit of treachery. I would like to know when the Afghans are planning to apologize for harboring the 9-11 terrorists that attacked our nation simply because we decline to live according to Sharia law. Reconciliation is a two-way street and if it is good that one party attempts to walk it without reference to another it is better when all are honest enough and humble enough to do the right thing. I am especially interested to know when Libya and Egypt are going to beg our forgiveness for the brutal death of an ambassador and the desecration of our flag and property at the hands of a mob that included their own security personnel.

I ask this question of Libya and Egypt while remaining mindful of the fact that Libyan authorities did warn our government of the danger of an attack. I understand that our own president and state department continue to pretend they did not receive embassy requests for more security. They continue to lie about what they knew and when they knew it. It is still a question worth asking.

I won't live forever in that mode, because I am also proud to be descended from Scottish Highlanders–indigenous people as abused as any on the planet. I want justice for my people–and for all peoples–but I want the grace, the mercy, and the destiny God has planned for us even more. I will forgive and I will repent, and call others to the same.

Some think repentance a sign of weakness, and so it is when reduced to politically correct behavior. Honesty is a sign of that strength God perfects in our weakness. It is fruit of that repentance which is the process of turning progressively from focus on self to focus on God. That repentance is the shape of real life. Like reconciliation it is a two way street, and an honor to walk wherever God may lead along it.

WHAT WILL WE DO?

I will never forget the day in Mindanao when the mini-van transporting us to Davao City broke down in a cane field. Al Qaida agents were identified at the gathering when Diana and I spoke and we knew for the two insurgent groups in the interior killing Americans was a hobby. But we also knew we were in God's will and were not afraid–until the breakdown.

As our drivers attempted repairs I kept visualizing insurgents carrying AK 47s crossing the field and trying to figure some way to protect Diana. Suddenly I heard the voice of God as clear as day. He said, "That's right, Jim, what are *you* going to do about this?" Now I got it long ago that when God asks a question He is not seeking information. That afternoon I got it that His burden is light (Matt. 8:28) only when He carries it. I responded, "Okay Lord; it's all about You." Our drivers got the vehicle started.

God does expect us to participate in the unfolding of His purposes, but as very junior partners. He gave us gifts of skill and imagination so we might offer them to Him; He loves it when we solve problems and give Him the glory. But it should always begin with submitting the problem to Him in the first place and–sometimes–that is how it ends too...if you are an unarmed civilian stranded in a cane field.

California is mired in the worst drought in eighty years. Meteorologists say the cause is a high pressure air ridge anchored high off the California coast the past thirteen months; such ridges normally locate no more than a few days or weeks. The ridge deflects storms seeking a California landfall and thus our desperate water situation. Experts say the phenomenon is unnatural, but it clearly resides within the parameters of nature and beyond any human ability to alter those parameters. Many churches and ministries are calling on their members for prayer; I have been asking my own network to pray for more than a year. Some would say, "Really? Then why hasn't it worked?" The answer is simple enough–prayer is not something that "works" but rather something that is submitted. Praying people depend not on the power of prayer but on the power of God. That power is under His control, not ours, but we can depend on the reality that He loves us more than life itself. He always exercises His power for our benefit and no other.

Possibly He wants to teach us something fundamental that we have forgotten–like that day with me in the cane field. Perhaps He waits on enough of us being consistent enough in prayer that we are less likely to forget we are His anytime soon. I do know prayer is one thing–like love–of which more is always better. I know that nothing can possibly be lost–except a bit of human arrogance – by engaging in concerted prayer to the God Who sends His Son to now rescue some forty million of the people for whom that Son gave His life. And I know focusing on God in prayer is a specific act of that repentance for which He has been calling the past five years. He says a season of repentance – in His Church – is the necessary precursor on our part to a Great Awakening that will rock the world in the best sense. Some say it is to begin in California. I know there is but one way to find out.

Following Him is lots easier than figuring Him out.

Northern California was threatened with devastating floods in 1997 because of abundant rain and unseasonable warmth. Local Christians begged His intervention and the snows came the very day meteorologists predicted the next rainstorm. Southern California was ravaged by wildfires in 2003 and hundreds went on our faces before the Lord; a storm front changed course off-shore and provided enough precipitation to enable fire fighters to douse the flames. The whole state lay under drought more than two years with prophetic voices predicting a three years' duration – if people prayed – and the Lord lifted it just when He said He would.

It doesn't matter how long or articulate our prayers; it's not about ritual or technique. It does matter that we pray daily, and that we remember prayer is not something that works or fails; it is something submitted. But it's a drought, not a car running rough. We can pray or we can think and strategize until we hear, "That's right, what *are* you going to do?"

CHAPTER 3:

NAVIGATING THE SEASON

This generation of the Church was born for such a time as this. We are privileged to see the wonders of God's promised love in forms and dimensions never before–and never after–to be seen on the earth. From the resurrection of the nation of Israel to the unprecedented outpouring of signs and wonders to the doubling of the numbers of us who know Jesus as Lord in the past half century there is no comparable season in history–not even the season immediately following the days of Resurrection and Pentecost.

The rise of worldwide darkness–featuring wars and rumors of wars, men calling evil good and good evil, and the persecution of Christians and Jews for the crime of naming the Name of Jesus is equally without precedent. In their day the Nazi effort to snuff out the firstborn people of God set new standards for brutality and efficiency, but the offspring mentored by the Nazis are already operating in a territorial scope Hitler could not have imagined; the numbers will just as surely dwarf his evil.

How do we navigate this season of glory and terror?

The first thing we do is thank Him for privileging us to live for an in such a time as this. He tells us in the Gospels when we see these things coming to pass–the good, the bad and the ugly–to lift up our heads for His return cannot be far behind. But our thanks is more than obedience; it gives us a new perspective through which we can see His activity and our privileged part to play in it with a clarity that is impossible when our attention is focused on what we do not have. Thanksgiving is an act of repentance that sets us free and heals our blind eyes at the same time.

This chapter identifies that perspective and leads us into the good news it holds. It identifies some myths we tend to believe about ourselves and our God for no other reason than that they too can be repented. At the same time the three powerful words God released over His whole Body in 2008 – the year of new beginnings – are addressed in practical terms. This chapter can be seen as a journey not unlike the journey Isaiah leads as he travels from his own chapter 5 – in which God warns those who call evil good and good evil of the destruction that will be the fruit of their perversion of truth – through chapter 55 – in which God promises the fruit of repentance will be that His people Israel will "summon nations you know not, and nations that do not know you will hasten to you because of the Lord your God, the Holy One of Israel, who has endowed you with splendor."

These splendid ones are the same people who courted ultimate doom with their wicked ways in that first Isaiah chapter numbered five. Each decision made for the Lord is a decision for life; many such decisions are habit forming in the best sense. Many people becoming habituated to life-launching decision making become a culture of repentance as we saw in the last chapter. Our God is so in love with us the path of repentance is always open, no matter how far we have gone in the other direction. The challenge to us is His equal commitment to judging us as we are rather than as we like to see ourselves. Isaiah 55 also speaks of aligning our thoughts with His thoughts, not the other way around.

We close this one with the good news of what God means to draw from the evil days in which we live as surely as we live in the time of His glory – by remembering the Alamo – of all things, and remembering we are called to war ourselves, but only with His weapons in our hands. Those weapons are blessing, forgiveness, and the Supper through which His disciples recognized their Risen Lord in a little village (Luke 24:13-35) called Emmaus.

A NEW GREAT AWAKENING

When the crews of the 1942 Doolittle Raid – better known as *Thirty Seconds Over Tokyo* – were forced to launch their planes four hundred miles further from Japan than they had planned they knew they were on a suicide mission. Not only were they planning to bomb a day early and in daylight, but there was no way they could carry enough gasoline to make the relative safety of the Chinese coast – not with the easterly winds that have blown off the China Coast every day for all the centuries in which records have been kept. But the miracles began when the planes reached Japan.

The whole Japanese Air Force, manned by veteran pilots, failed to shoot down a single bomber even though the Americans were forced to fly in virtual single file with defensive arms and armament largely inoperable. Once over the China Sea the winds suddenly about-faced; each aircraft was given an added range of about two hundred fifty miles when headwinds changed to tailwinds. All reached China safely – although the planes were ultimately lost – except the one that landed in Siberia. At least one miracle of healing was recorded for an injured airman and another – whose hatred of the Japanese was almost biological – met Jesus while in Japanese captivity and became one of the two most famous evangelists to Japan of all time. The other was Mitsuo Fuchida, leader of the attack on Pearl Harbor and led to the Lord by that same airman turned ambassador of Christ's reconciliation.

There was something the aircrews had to do – not to create or cause miracles, but to place themselves in the path of the Creator of miracles. They had to gun their engines and race down the deck of their aircraft carrier toward the water.

It was the counter-intuitive but necessary thing to do. To get their heavy bombers to take-off speed they needed that assistance of gravity which could only be had traveling *down* the deck; they had to be full-throttle when the deck was in a trough and pointed toward the sea floor. Only then would they reach the end of the deck when it was rising into the wind that would lift them into the sky. The very same truth applies in the very same way if we would answer the call of God for a new Great Awakening in our time.

The eastern seaboard was dotted with churches of every denomination in the first half of the eighteenth century; they were filled with uncommitted Christians who did not want to be confronted with their lack of commitment. George Whitefield and the Tennent Brothers, among others, took to the open fields with a message of total commitment; the Holy Spirit did the rest and people began to fall out and sob their love of Jesus by the thousands. Marriages were transformed in the towns and the jails emptied. The established churches rejected the awakening until the fruit was so visible they could no longer deny it was of God and the result was an American nation that loved God and had the cohesion to win a revolution and write a constitution. But the decision to preach to birds and squirrels if no one else would listen made about as much sense as barreling down the deck of an aircraft carrier pointing into the water. Yet God provided the wind beneath their wings.

As the nineteenth century dawned the nation had again settled into a combination of spiritual complacency and a focus on the urgent political crises of the day; the Kingdom of God would just have to wait. Circuit riding preachers with no more support than the Bible and the extra shirt carried in their saddle bags went to the frontier cabins of Kentucky and Tennessee – and the frontier caught fire for God. Once again the established churches rejected the awakening until the fruit was so evident that they could not but embrace it as a sovereign act of God. The Second Great Awakening shaped and strengthened American culture to the point that we abolished slavery and made the spreading of the freedom for which we are set free – to paraphrase Galatians 5:1 – our national creed. Our reputation as the place of welcome and opportunity for the huddled masses was established in this crucible and we got used to the ecstatic manifestations of the Spirit that came with it. But repeated decisions to seek the Kingdom in the wilderness instead of the cities were as counter-intuitive then as now.

The nineteen fifties and sixties were times of high church attendance and low interest in the Kingdom. Then a Third Great Awakening broke out on the beaches of Southern California among surfers and hippies. Leaders like Chuck Smith and John Wimber saw the hand of God and reached for it; others did the same. The onrush of God's Holy Spirit shaped an American generation that spread God's message around the world, birthed the short-term missions movement, resurrected the gifts we associate with the First Century at street level, introduced the modern recovery and inner healing movements, re-shaped music and the arts, and soldiered to victory in the Cold War. We still feel its effects in every ministry from pregnancy care outreaches to inner city missions to localized healing rooms to efforts to reclaim the entertainment industry. Again the churches rejected the movement until God's favor became obvious. (Some of the churches birthed in the sixties and seventies reject the newer permutations of the Jesus People Awakening we see today.) Certainly decisions to seek God and His People on the beach, in the business community, or in the tenderloin district of San Francisco, are spiritual kin to a bomber pilot gunning his engine when the bow points down – just because the air boss signals, "Do it now!"

There are a few things leaders of all of the Great Awakenings have in common. They make a repeated decision to come into and remain in the presence of the

Lord–wherever He may be found. They drop their agendas–especially the praiseworthy projects they have undertaken in His Name–believing He is a better guardian of their plans than they are. They assert the authority He gives in John 14:12-14 to do what they have seen Jesus do, and greater things than these. He calls for a new generation of leaders for a new Great Awakening today.

These leaders are not often recognized superstars; they are ordinary men and women who place their faith not in their ability to hear, but in God's ability to speak. They are the called who say, "Yes," not the qualified who say, "Let me understand you better before I act.," or, "We don't do it that way here." God has a recurring habit of qualifying the called who answer rather than calling the qualified who do not. And oh yeah–when the Boss says, "Gun it!" they gun it toward the water, relying on Him to raise that deck by the time they get there.

A MINISTRY OF GATHERING

(Author Note: This article was first published in 2012 and I have updated it for this book. I include it here in order to stress the point that we have done nothing in PrayNorthState that cannot be done by any Christian who is willing to trust in the Lord and lean not on his own understanding, as He says in Proverbs 3:5-6. This is how we navigate this season of God's promised Great Awakening. This is authentic repentance.)

PrayNorthstate is a ministry of gathering and reconciling the Body of Christ. Founded in 2001, based and focused in Northern California, our vision has roots in the worldwide Transformation movement. Our full-time staff consists of my wife, Diana, and me; we are entirely donation supported. We partner with any group of Christians who are ministering beyond denominational boxes, seeking reconciliation and healing in their communities, and accepting no substitutes for God's Kingdom on earth. We draw from the charismatic, evangelical, and liturgical streams of the Kingdom without prejudice and we love to see miracles that don't look like traditional signs and wonders but which display God's overwhelming love all the more for that. When the vision is given to someone else we offer help; when the vision is given to us we ask for help. We understand that God is calling for a fourth Great Awakening in America and we live to respond to His calling in Great Commission terms.

We have come alongside ministries and their projects as disparate as creating a festival to honor single parents, making a night to honor Israel, and holding multiple prayer summits for regional pastors. With the help of many congregations we led our eleventh annual speaking of the entire Word of God over our city from the breezeway of our local city hall in 2012. We accepted leadership of our city's National Day of Prayer observance and have seen the support of the community and the variety of activities included undergo a major league expansion. Many communities in which we have taught now include Bible reading marathons in their own cycle of events, including Malaysia and Australia; we offer ongoing training and support as we are invited.

We've led multiple annual editions of Paah-ho-ammi, a project of targeted prayer in which teams pray daily for assigned topics of community–and Kingdom–concern. We document baseline statistics for issues such as violent crime, unemployment, traffic fatalities, and cancer admissions to our local hospital. We then proclaim the difference between the time of prayer and the same period a year earlier. Our first foray into this arena recruited one hundred and thirty-five Christians from many churches; we saw God reduce crime in the county sheriff patrolled areas by more than 20% and He gave similar fruit in the areas of traffic deaths and cancer admissions. Next time out more than two hundred Christians joined us for daily prayer. Traffic fatalities were cut by 40% while cancer admissions went down by a whopping 58%. A dozen churches spent time in Sunday services each week praying all seven of the Paah-ho-ammi prayer topics.

The needed gifts for a ministry such as ours are Kingdom vision, persistence, and a willingness to look foolish in the Name of Jesus. A talk show on secular radio was in the background of the original vision God gave for PrayNorthState; the intention was to interview a couple of Christians who were ministering outside of the box and share their relationship to Jesus and how it led into a particular manifestation of servanthood for them. I was advised by some Christian leaders that I would run out of guests to interview in three months; to date we have been on the air in Redding for fifteen years and we are booked three months in advance with servants to showcase. We had a television program on Fox of Northern California 2005 to 2011; we let it go when the Lord opened up four more radio stations to double and then quadruple the already doubled coverage area at the same time He was greatly expanding the scope of our writing, teaching, and traveling. He called for a shift of focus and we simply obeyed the new calling once we heard it.

In 2010 we launched a new effort focused entirely on celebrating the leadership and initiative God has birthed in the younger generation. We called it Genesis Generation Radio. We have invitations to expand the radio program to the Sacramento and San Francisco areas as soon as sponsors can be found.

The willingness to be foolish may be the most essential gift of all. When the Lord blessed us with permission to begin a prayer project in 2004 that was first conducted under another name and in another region he stipulated that we call it Paah-ho-ammi. He did not tell us what the words meant–or even in what language they were found–but He did tell us to solicit support from the churches and go for it. Many leaders questioned my sanity when I brought them the vision. Eventually He led me to check the Hebrew dictionary in the back of my concordance and I discovered perfectly good biblical Hebrew meaning "Cry alas, My People."

The project eventually boasted some three hundred fifty people committed to team membership and daily prayer; between fifteen and eighteen churches committed to corporately support the project through a one-to-two minute focus time in their services. Diana and I have taught the principles of Paah-ho-ammi–or any of the other prophetic acts with impact in which the Lord has demonstrated His delight to us–in more than thirty states and twenty nations. We are willing to share in any community that hungers for God the way we hunger for Him.

PRAYING FROM A EUCHARISTIC HEART

God performed a massive miracle of healing on the land in 2005. It became a gift that keeps on giving in terms of the transformation of human hearts. He called a half dozen of us to make a prayer journey to the headwaters of Butte Creek in the hills above Chico. Our assignment was to pray blessing, forgiveness, and to share the Supper of the Lord on the banks of that creek with a special intention to seek healing of the waterway after years of spiritual pollution that had morphed into a very physical pollution of the waters themselves. These things happen when there is a legacy of practiced witchcraft, the shedding or enabling of the shedding of innocent blood, idolatry, or sexual sin on the land or waterway in question. The first two criteria were historically met along Butte Creek, and the presence of pollution coupled with that knowledge would explain God's call to us on that September Saturday.

After several hours of worshipping and calling on His name–and sharing the bread and the cup together–we cast the remainder of the communion feast into the water. (We call this addressing the bloodguilt with the Blood.) We then tasted the formerly polluted water and found that we suffered no ill effects. But we were only able to objectively document the healing of the stream in the past few weeks.

Government studies of Butte Creek showed a major league resurgence of the salmon in Butte Creek in the year 2005. This seemed ample documentation of the clean-up the Lord had orchestrated supernaturally–and in which our prayer group was privileged to participate. But further checking led to further perplexity for us; the salmon counts documenting the resurgence were actually taken up to two months prior to our visit to the stream! What were we to conclude or believe from this?

Reality is that God prophetically called us to undertake that prayer journey. We did as He had called us to do in His Name. Reality is likewise that He did as He had promised and He healed the stream, albeit outside the boundaries of what we understand as the flow of time. But wait a moment; time is a human construct and God is not bound by it. He demonstrates his lack of concern for time each time He flips back and forth on whether repentance must precede or follow forgiveness of sin, as just one example. In the case of the stream He simply gave the blessing before we came along and offered the obedience. And the beauty of the whole thing is that only God can get the glory in such a scenario; there is no way we can claim the power of our prayers achieved anything but His own exaltation. But to come to this conclusion requires that prayer proceeds from what I know as a Eucharistic heart.

In my branch of the Body we refer to the Lord's Supper as the Holy Eucharist. The term is Greek for Great Thanksgiving, but to have a Eucharistic heart is much more than a mere heart of thanksgiving for the Lord's gift of Himself. We understand the stuff of Eucharist in terms of people being permeated by His Word; practiced and commissioned in the exercise of His gifts; fed, forgiven, healed and prepared for apostolic journey; and sent on our way as His Great Commissioners, the ambassadors of His reconciliation. When we pray from a Eucharistic heart mysteries like the healing of a stream – before or after the prayers He calls out of us – get somehow presented and correlated through His unfolding revelation. His thoughts and His ways may not be ours – Isaiah 55:8-12 – but He has provided a process of personal transformation through which we can join Him across the divide – Jeremiah 29:11-14 – and His Word is good. We have only to say "Yes" and "Thank You" to Him in advance of our understanding.

Diana and I have made strategic visits to our ancestral home – Scotland – over several years. Each time we visit we have been called to pray at the battlefield of Culloden – a place of massacre and the unraveling of the Scots' dreams of independence. The slaughter was so intense on the battlefield and throughout the region that popular wisdom holds there can never again be heather – symbol of the highlands – growing from the graves of the fallen. Yet God had called us to seek a specific sign of His healing intention for the nation in the growth of the heather where those wise in the flesh claimed it could not grow.

We prayed blessings, forgiveness, and shared the Supper on our 2007 visit just as we had on previous occasions. Other prayer teams had been doing the same for more years than we had. But God privileged us to see the first sprig of heather growing atop one of the graves. We reported this clear sign of God's healing hand upon the land to our hosts back in Glasgow. We prayed and proclaimed that God had signed His intention to heal the Scots through this token of His healing the blood soaked land of Culloden. When these same hosts visited us in Redding last Fall we asked them if prayer was still offered regularly for the promised revival in Scotland and they answered, "Didn't you know? The revival has begun, and it is rolling down from the Highlands, just as it was prophesied by you and others over the years."

As it was with Butte Creek, we are enabled to see God's unfolding plans through the lens of the Eucharistic heart He gladly gives to those who keep asking for it. In the Holy Eucharist we are expected to give back – to go into the world to love and serve our Lord as His faithful witnesses – but we can only steward what we have been given. We can only give what we have received. We become dramatically aware, through that lens, that we are no more causative of the heather growing and the revival beginning in Scotland than we were the instigators of the healing of Butte Creek. But we become just as dramatically aware of the fact that He chose us to go, to pray, to worship, and to see what He has done before anyone else gets to see it. We learn the difference between privilege and prerogative.

Healing the land is a precursor to transformative revival in God's heart and mind. It is a simple miracle for Him to perform because the land must obey His healing word. The revival that His healing announces is something that can only occur with human cooperation–a critical mass of us must be seeking God's face for revival. A Eucharistic heart–as essential as that seems to be if we would be enabled to appreciate His subtler interventions–is even more dependent on request. Each of us must ask in turn. But the rewards are like a blind man receiving His sight–a gift that grows farther and broader as we ask and ask repeatedly for more of Him. In Jeremiah 29:11-14 we are assured of the Lord's intention to do good for us–to give us a hope and a future, but we are promised even more that when we seek His face we cannot fail to find Him.

THE CALIFORNIA GOVERNOR'S PRAYER TEAM AND THE DAMASCUS ROAD

The Paul who wrote more of the New Testament than anybody else began his ministry–the one he received from God–in an encounter with the Living God on the road from Jerusalem to Damascus. On a mission to arrest followers of Jesus he is struck to the ground by a vision of the Risen Jesus who asks why he is persecuting the Son of God. Jesus then remarks that it hurts Paul to kick against the goads–the revelations of Christ that are transforming the world and directing travelers like himself to their destination in Christ. Paul–known as Saul prior to the Damascus Road–is transformed and re-booted as a man created in the image of God and he never looks back over the rest of his earthly life. In the California Governor's Prayer Team we always begin our times of worshipping God and praying for His blessings on California with a plea to provide every leader in the state with a Damascus Road experience–beginning with ourselves as we pray.

The Governor's Prayer Team is an interdenominational ministry with chapters in every state. Its founder and national director is a pastor named Tom Walker who is based in Indianapolis, Indiana; I am the state coordinator for California. Although the state governor is aware of us–and we do pray for him–the governor referenced in the name is the Governor of the world referenced in Psalms 8 and in other scriptures as well.

Our goal is to have coordinators in each of California's fifty-eight counties; we are presently represented in more than thirty. Coordinators receive an e-mail from me at least once monthly in which I share whatever I know about what is going on in our state that could use concerted prayer. We host weekly conference calls and we take a team into the state capitol once each month to pray inside the building–with the blessing of hosting legislators. (Actually, PrayNorthState has been doing this since 2005; I became the state's CGPT coordinator in 2012.) We teach our people to pray only for blessing and transformation in our state; we exercise Our Lord's mandate to forgive if we would be forgiven, and we worship and celebrate His Supper at every bend of the road. County coordinators are required only to meet regularly with their own team of praying people and to fold the points in my e-mail in with whatever else they are praying. Each has a history of his or her county provided by Reformation Prayer Network to guide the long term intercession over the county in terms of what God is up to locally. We are, of course, on the look-out for seasoned and trustworthy people to become coordinators in unrepresented counties.

What do we pray for?

We pray God to shape each of our leaders – beginning with ourselves – into the people He intended when He knew us in the womb; that is the meaning of the Damascus Road for us. We pray for the culture and season of repentance that has preceded each of the previous three Great Awakenings of the Body of Christ in America. We include prayer for wise stewardship of our state's resources and a commitment to justice for all – not just those we deem excluded from it – as legislators allocate those resources in the state budget. We pray that God would cause leaders to fall in love with the limitations placed on their power in our state and federal constitutions. We ask God to shine the light of day on the many scandals plaguing our state and nation. We acknowledge that the condition of society is nothing less than a report card on the state of the Church. When the one is healthy so is the other – and the Church is called to lead in the process.

We do pray over specific pieces of policy and legislation, especially when it concerns the most basic rights to life, freedom of conscience and expression, and the unrestricted pursuit of prosperity for the benefit of our families and communities. These are rights given by God and guaranteed in those constitutions we love. But we do not curse anyone or anything; we simply ask God to transform hearts in whatever terms seem good to Him.

God never asked His people to transform the Roman Empire. He commanded us to become so transformed ourselves that we effectively infiltrate the empires in which we live with the life, the love, and the peace of God. We get it that when we Christians are living God's life others are attracted. This works fine for us.

THE MYTH OF THE UNFORGIVABLE

Among my favorite memories of recent trips to Penang, Malaysia; Philadelphia, Pennsylvania; and the Eastern Sierra of California are the people who approached me after I taught to say they believed they had done things that permanently separated them from God. They believed this lie until they heard my stories about the permanence of God's love–and I praise God that they listened.

Truth is we do possess the awful power to separate ourselves from God. But the larger truth is nothing can separate us indefinitely beyond a stubborn refusal to accept His forgiveness and be reconciled in Christ.

There are passages in Hebrews 4 and 10 in which the author says sin after baptism leaves no going back, and persisting in sin places one outside the Kingdom for which Christ once redeemed him. Jesus Himself says in Matthew 5 that if salt (us) loses its saltiness it is nothing. But the Hebrews passages use sin in its Greek noun form; it is a no-brainer to see that there can be no contact between a state of sin and a state of grace. It should be just as much a no-brainer to see that repentance–turning back to face and re-focus on Jesus Christ–is all He has ever required to cross over from the state of sin into the state of grace. The over-riding word against the Matthew passage is always Jesus' other word that what is impossible for men is possible for God; he who abides in Christ will never be forsaken or overthrown.

One of the stories I told that so moved these estranged children of God was of the bridesmaid who approached me at a wedding rehearsal years ago. She said she could not bear to be in church. I asked her why and she explained that she had been so strung out on heroin at one time that she prostituted herself to get money for the drug. At this point, although she had been clean and sober for some time, she was convinced that God could not stand the sight of her. When I asked her if she wanted to come home she burst into tears of YES. When I said, "In the Name of Jesus welcome home," she fell into my arms–really the arms of her Lord Jesus as represented by this priest–just like the prostitute who washes His feet with her tears in Luke 7:36-50.

Another concerns the elderly woman with such serious arthritis in her hands that her fingers could not be uncurled from the twisted claws they had become. She confessed that she had been in a state of unforgiveness with members of her church for more than twenty years. It was not that she wanted or accepted that condition; she found herself helpless to leave it after stating she had forgiven her friends over and over. When I, speaking as a representational leader of the Body of Christ, released her from her unforgiveness, she too burst into tears of joy. Before I could reach down to touch her hands in prayer her fingers were already uncurling as God's healing spread through her body. God's love trumps all our inadequacies. All He expects of us is that we stay in the game until He catches and releases us.

Let no one reading these words misunderstand that one must be a priest or pastor to assure a lost sheep of the Lord's love and forgiveness. I may be designated and set aside – professionally and sacramentally – to perform this work on a regular basis, but the Body of Christ is also known as the Priesthood of all Believers. The sharing of God's mercy is no more dependent on the presence of the professional – thanks be to God – than was caring for the man left for dead when the priest walked on and there was only a Samaritan left to minister. I am called to do this every day; every one of us is called to do this when the occasion arises in our presence.

The most helpful illustration in the scriptures addressing that crossing over from the state of sin to the state of grace occurs in John 8 with the story of the woman taken in adultery and dragged before Jesus in the Temple courts. As Jesus listens to the Pharisees' incompetence – they mis-read and mis-apply the Law in Deuteronomy 22 – and being unable to certify themselves as the sinless witnesses the Law requires – He says (in multiple albeit later places) they remain in their sin even though they retreat after being unmasked as hypocrites. What He waits for is those of us who are so hungry to hang with Him that we will step across the line He has drawn in the dust of the Temple floor – sometimes known as the Line in the Sand. He waits on people so hungry for His company that they don't care who else they stand beside as long as they can stand beside Jesus.

The only unforgivable sin – the sin against the Holy Spirit – is the refusal to accept His forgiveness and step across that line. Even that sin is forgiven once we stop committing it. He is always ready to do the heavy lifting in forgiveness; all He asks of us is that we stay in the game.

THREE WORDS: A SPIRIT OF WORSHIP

This is the first of three articles about three Words the Lord released over the Body in late 2007

Israel reaches the Jordan early in the Book of Joshua; God has promised Jericho as their first conquest in the Promised Land–but they must cross the river first. God will halt the stream to enable a dry crossing–with one catch. They must enter the raging waters first. In fact, they must enter in procession; the priests carrying the Ark of the Covenant in the lead. Then God will act.

This would be a truly frightful test of faith–even for people who have witnessed the many miracles in the desert; yet they march as He commands. (They must have looked very much like a modern processional with robed clergy and the symbols of faith elevated so that all can see.) This crossing is a worship event. They are releasing the Spirit of Worship and surfing the wake. On the other side they think they are ready for Jericho, but God has other plans.

In successive revelations He calls on them to escalate the release of worship in His Spirit–first in the ceremonial circumcision of their men of military age, later in the observance of Passover, and finally in the week-long march around Jericho that culminates in walls coming tumbling down. These are all worship events of escalating duration in which the people honor and celebrate God at the cost of extreme vulnerability. (The *bris* or circumcision ceremony for Jews is an act of worship itself, and not a mere adjunct to worship as we Christians often make our dedications of newborns.) As the Hebrews assembled to worship in their camp they were well aware that the people of Jericho would be curious as to why the river stopped; they are completely dependent on God to defend them in case of attack. Their vulnerability can only increase as they give themselves over to escalating worship in the Passover and then in the unarmed march around the walls.

God released three words over His Body in December 2006. The first was, "Release the Spirit of Worship;" for by so doing we remove all obstacles to His activity in our midst.

When we release the Spirit of Worship we morph from people who worship to people of worship–people for whom worship is defining activity, the very shape of our personality. It is a process, an escalating process, and the Lord is the driver. But He expects our courageous participation in the same way that the Hebrews kicked things off by stepping into that raging river with the ark high on their shoulders. The next step was to remain in camp unarmed while conducting the massive *bris*, and it was followed by the ecstatic worship associated with

Passover, and the resolute worship of the march around the city. In every case the people gave glory to God in pragmatic ways that were yet counter-intuitive to what they thought they had come to accomplish. And God did so much more.

Tom ministers in North Carolina. His vision for a local trailer park is that each of the druggies, prostitutes and ex-convicts in the park come to know Jesus. He and members of his church pray daily–and praise God as though it were already accomplished–but that is only the beginning. They have begun presenting people he knows in the park with MP3 players loaded only with praise music–and he has non-stop praise music playing in his home–the place where he invites people to a Bible study each Wednesday. Worship leaders from all over his city have been coming in to lead worship and to bathe the park in it. He is doing all of the things you do when your heart is for evangelism–making relationships, sharing and blessing, witnessing when it is appropriate and acceptable–but the Spirit of Worship he has released in the park is helping decisions for Jesus come fast and furious.

I have written before about the powerful prophecies over Redding's Downtown Mall that it will become a center of service and ministry in the Name of Jesus. A small band of Christians walks and prays the mall–we pray for people we meet as they share their needs–each month. Public worship is being lifted in the public areas of the mall on a regular basis. Business owners in the mall are meeting to pray for the mall and its destiny as they also seek His face and His strategies to prosper their business enterprises. The mall was about sixty per cent dedicated to service and ministry in 2005, at the time the prophecy was released, although some of the services were not Christian and a couple of cults had their offices there. Today the mall is about ninety per cent service and ministry and the cults are gone.

People in the trailer park are coming to the Lord left and right–and Tom's church is enjoying a renaissance as their house of worship becomes a focal point for transformational activity in their region. The downtown mall has gone from about 60% service orientation to about 90%–with more and more of it dedicated to the Lord Himself. When we progressively release the Spirit of Worship we progressively become the images of God's personality that we are created to become–and the walls come tumbling down.

THREE WORDS: CHOOSE THIS DAY

This is the second of three articles about three Words the Lord released over the Body in late 2007

Our God is a God of faithfulness–make that duration. In Joshua 3-7 He takes the Children of Israel from helplessness to power as they worship. But the process occupies several of their first weeks in the Promised Land, and the Father continues to up the ante for centuries as He prepares a people to receive the Righteous One–the Messiah. Our God is faithful, and He expects us to become faithful–as we image Him.

Jesus promised that His Kingdom would come in power almost immediately in Mark 9:1, and His Word is kept on the day of Pentecost when disciples become apostles ministering a Gospel of power and not of mere words. But the Book of Acts spans some thirty years of faithful apostolic activity from Peter to Philip and from Barnabas to Paul. Dramatic miracles are just punctuation in a text filled with more unsung characters than we can count thrown in for good measure. Paul makes his boast on the fact that he has run his race and counted all other things as rubbish, not on all of the healings he has seen. Jesus says, "He who endures to the end will be saved." The Christian life is about faithfulness–but it all begins with a choice. Each of us must choose each day whom we will serve.

The second word released over the Body in December 2007 was, "Choose this day whom you will serve." This is a word of duration. We can choose to serve the Lord on this day, but tomorrow soon becomes today and the day after follows quickly enough. Choosing this day Whom we will serve is a choice that must be made repeatedly over a lifetime because our lives are an unfolding process with new challenges and opportunities. The choice of whom we will serve is always before us and the Word of God is full of its permutations.

It is as fresh when God calls upon the people through Elijah to stop limping back and forth between Baal and Yahweh as it is when He exhorts Solomon to lead the people in seeking His face in 2 Chronicles 7:14–in which the very word chosen to connote prayer implies sustained prayer. It is the same when God speaks in Isaiah 62 that we should give Him and ourselves no rest, and it is the most pragmatic approach of Jesus when the disciples wonder (Mark 9:29–the same chapter in which He promises the Kingdom in power before his audience passes away) why they cannot cast out a demon; He replies that this kind comes out only through sustained prayer.

My friend, Ken, has made more than thirty trips to Fiji in the past six years. I have accompanied him on four of them. We have participated in more than a thousand power encounters resulting in healings, weather miracles, housing built for the poverty-stricken and polluted land turned productive as ancient curses were cast out of it through prayer and worship. We have seen more than a thousand people let go of their pagan idols and come to know Christ, and Ken has been a person of influence in the government of the nation. He has been used of the Lord in these ways through his patient cultivation of relationships as he has demonstrated to the powerful and the powerless that he can be trusted. He has – in short – chosen each day whom he will serve and he has encouraged others to make that same repeated choice. Each of us are called to choose and to choose daily.

I have recounted tales of limbs growing out and paralyzed men being made instantly whole, not to mention the heart conditions healed, sight and hearing restored; rains stopping on command and hardpacked soil opening to receive pilings for housing after frustrating the efforts of the construction crew. This just in Fiji; God is doing these things on a wholesale basis in every nation I have visited and right around the corner from where any of us live. These are the fun and exciting witnesses we love to share. But the foundation of it all is the repeated choice to seek and serve Him by the people on the ground and the prayer warriors at home who hold the mission teams before the throne with patience and persistence.

In our own region we have seen ministries such as the Carenet Pregnancy Center taken from a dream given to a man and his wife in 1983 to its fulfillment as a medical clinic operating in three counties and taking over the family planning property at their invitation. God supplied the vision and the wherewithal while hundreds of volunteers supplied the faithfulness. The same principle applies across the board in our communities as we seek their transformation – on earth as it is in heaven – through the hand of a judge much more in love with us than the one confronted by the widow in Luke 18. Our God is a God who practices and rewards faithfulness.

THREE WORDS: RISE AND WALK

This is the third of three articles about three Words the Lord released over the Body in late 2007

Paul says, on multiple occasions, that we preach a Gospel of power, and not of mere words. Jesus says – in Mark 9:1 – that the Kingdom will come in power before death takes those who are listening to Him. The writer of Acts chides the apostles for their foolishness – gazing into the sky after Jesus' ascension – when He has told them to go into the city and wait for the promised Holy Spirit to bring the Kingdom in power.

The apostolic Church dealt in signs and wonders on a wholesale basis. It's not that each one had to perform a miracle before breakfast to maintain status – the Book of Acts is a story of witness and service punctuated with the miracles that facilitate both witness and service – but the bottom line is that the Lord went before the *sent ones* (apostles) just as He promised at the end of each of the Gospel accounts. It is equally clear that in each time zone of explosive growth for the Church – whether when the apostles went to Antioch and beyond or when contemporary *sent ones* go to Africa or South and Central America or to the Pacific Rim – or to the streets of American cities over the past half century – they walk in all of the Holy Spirit power they need – and in whatever form. So why are we told to rise and walk – as though we were paralyzed?

One of the first miracles accounted to Jesus is recounted in Mark 2:1-12. Jesus is healing and a paralyzed man is unable to get past the crowds at the door. His friends remove a section of roof and lower him into the presence of the Lord. Jesus takes one look at him and forgives his sins – restoring the relationship that is our heritage in the Lord. As the crowd is astonished, Jesus completes the healing by ordering him to rise and walk. The scripture quotes Jesus saying that the one miracle is as easy as the other, but it is all about restored relation to the Author of health and wholeness. And when we are restored we expect to reflect the Author in our lives – His powerful Gospel.

The Reformation stands as one of God's great gifts to us. Through it He demystified faithful relation to Himself and restored the intimacy of relation that needs no intermediaries. But the Reformation also threw out the baby with the bath water when it declared that miracles were for the first century and had become a matter of superstition in later times. The Church has been paralyzed – with many noteworthy exceptions – in her reliance on the written Word alone, stripped of its demonstrative power. In the past fifty years we have seen more miracles – and more decisions for Jesus – than in all of previous history combined. The Lord says, "This party is just getting started," for the coming season. The third word He released in December 2006 was, "Rise, take up your pallet and walk, for the time of paralysis is past."

The good news is that we need not place our faith in miracles, or in our ability to perform them–even in His Name. We do not have spiritual gifts so much as the gifts have us, because we have the Spirit living inside us. Jesus is teaching us in the very hour in which we live just what we are to do and say, as He promised in Matthew 10 and Luke 21, to name a couple of places. If we believe Him our doubts about dimensions of His love manifested in us will be dealt with–like the time I was called to pray for a paralyzed man and I knew that God was not going to heal him. I prayed anyway, and with authority, and was shocked out of my shoes when the man stood and walked ten minutes later. (I still remember hearing the Lord laugh at me as He said that He didn't care what I thought or felt as long as I would obey Him.) There was the time I prayed for a woman blinded by diabetes and her sight was instantly restored. I led her to the Lord and expected–after such a great beginning–that the next time I saw her she would be healed of the diabetes. (When she died I questioned the Lord; He said, "I gave back her sight; she gave me her heart, and now she is home. What is your point?") This walking stuff is a re-education in the Kingdom perspective; it requires an earthly lifetime to learn.

But God is good and–with Him–all things work together for good. We just need to get on with it–not our leaders, and not our superstars; we are the ones called.

REMEMBERING THE ALAMO

An obscure occasion has passed into history once again. Most Americans remember the Alamo–especially if they are old enough to remember Fess Parker clubbing the soldiers of Santa Anna in the old Walt Disney portrait of Davy Crockett. Not so many recall the date of the fall of that old Texas fortress–March 6–and even fewer have any idea of what God was up to in unfolding the story the way He did. I was lucky enough to be let in on His intentions when I visited the Alamo in 2009.

As I entered the land the Lord spoke clearly that I was not there as a tourist, but rather to pray that His original intentions for the Alamo would be fulfilled and manifested across our land. (Readers who think the Lord cannot or does not speak to folks like you and me should remember Who invented speech.) When I admitted I did not know those intentions He said He would share over time, but that I knew enough to obey. I found a place in the plaza and prayed the fulfillment for which He called. Over the next three weeks or so He shared the shape of those intentions with me–one at a time.

He showed me that the Alamo garrison was as multi-ethnic a group as ever was. All parts of Eastern and Western Europe were represented as well as people of Hispanic, African, and even Native American heritage. They were as suspicious of one another as any such group might be in our time, and each was convinced that he was right and the others wrong. Over thirteen days of bombardment, assault, and death they were welded into one tribe and nation. They became what God intended for humanity from the beginning, but it took the pressure of the crucible of the Alamo to make them so.

Later He showed me that the defenders were of many denominations of the Body of Christ. He pointed out, for example, that the co-commanders were a Catholic and a Baptist. Like their ethnic tensions, they wore their religious superiority on their sleeves. Yet under the unrelenting pressure of the thirteen days' of siege and blood and thunder from which there would be no relief except in the Kingdom of God they became one faith in the sharing of one baptism. They became the answer to Jesus' prayer in John 17 that we all may be one in Him.

Finally He showed me the thirty-two men from the town of Gonzales who rode into the fort on the ninth day of the siege. These men were not in the least suicidal, but they had to know–this late in the game–that other men were not coming to help. They had to know that in riding to the defense of their friends and neighbors they were riding into the valley of death. And yet they came–and they be-came part of that movement of God to forge them into one tribe and one faith in Him. God's purposes can indeed only be fulfilled when we are willing to ride toward the place of danger, knowing that when we are with His Christ the closer we are to danger the further we are from harm.

So what is God attempting in our nation during this time of increasing division between our peoples–after all the gains of the past half century–and higher taxes and more punitive rhetoric about who should pay more and why they should? What is He planning as our families disintegrate and our very central government seems determined to expand the destruction of the unborn and those least able to care for themselves? What does He want in this culture in which we abandon our foreign service workers to death at the hands of terrorists and our military to death at the hands of neglect? And how about the general lack of commitment to law and order in our highest governmental officials–whether by following the rules they set for the rest of us or by refusing to limit their activities to constitutional norms–and the abrogation of duty on the part of so many leaders in the Church?

He wants the same things for us as He always has. He wants us to seek each other's joy in Him, to have each others' backs, and to be unalterably committed to our own children as primary. He wants us–by so doing–to become one tribe, one faith, and to recognize that riding into danger to seek Him is a privilege, not a punishment.

THE LORD'S SUPPER: A WEAPON OF SPIRITUAL WARFARE

Nearly twenty years ago the woman entered my office to say that she needed serious inner healing. She claimed that Jesus told her, "There is healing in the Eucharist," and that my church offered Holy Communion every Sunday. The woman remained to worship with us for several Sundays, seeking healing prayer during the week. When the Lord had completely healed her heart He also healed her knee – which had been scheduled for arthroscopic surgery – and she returned to the church from which she had come.

More recently a friend called to say that satanic ritualists were performing their revolting rites less than one hundred yards from her home – on a weekly basis. She and her husband own property in common with other families in their neighborhood and this stuff was taking place on the commonly owned land. In addition to the crawly feeling of knowing what was happening just beyond their windows was the knowledge that traffic accidents just outside of their neighborhood had increased exponentially as the spiritual atmosphere darkened over the roadway. We agreed to meet on-site with a small group of intercessors and wage spiritual warfare as Paul commends in 2 Corinthians 10.

On the agreed-upon afternoon we went to war. We walked the land, praying for those who lived on it and for those who were defiling it. We repented – of any sin that might give legalistic legitimacy for the enemy's activities – and we exercised the authority of the Body of Christ to forgive. We completed our time by celebrating the supper of the Lord on the very stone slab that the satanists had used for their altar; we poured out onto the land the remaining bread and wine after we had eaten and drunk the sacred meal. The fruit was as pragmatic as it was spiritual. In the past ten years the satanists have not returned to the land and the traffic accidents have disappeared from the road that passes the community.

The weapons of our warfare are not named in 2 Corinthians – they are simply accorded the unlimited authority and power of argumentation for the destruction of demonic strongholds – but Jesus gives three weapons of such potency. Blessing is the first – Romans 12:14 commands us to bless and curse not while Matthew 5 calls us to bless those who persecute us: blessing is the perennial remedy to persecution. In Luke 10:1-9 Jesus calls on the apostles to bless the people in the towns they visit as the first order of a business that ends in witnessing to the faith that is in them. The authority and commission to bless is without limitation.

The second of our weapons is forgiveness and this too is simply and clearly found as unlimited authority and binding commission in John 21 and Matthew 16 and 18. In John Jesus simply says that those sins the apostles forgive stand forgiven and those they retain are likewise set into stone – around the necks of those who retain them. In Matthew He declares that what we set free in His Name on earth is likewise loosed in Heaven and that forgiveness is a way of life for the Christian. Recognizing these first two weapons is not a stretch–although it may come as a surprise. But Holy Communion is more difficult to recognize as a weapon, even though Scripture is shot through with illustrations of this reality.

In the Old Testament the Israelites are commanded by God to eat the Passover before going out to invest Jericho. Gideon worships outside the camp of his enemies before he goes to report the Lord's promise to the waiting army. The famous verses of Psalm 23 declare that God prepares a table for us in the presence of our enemies. Elijah prepares a burnt offering in the very heart of his critical confrontation with the forces of Baal on Mt. Carmel. Are these worship-through-holy-feasting activities preliminary to the real business of war or are they among the most potent weapons in the arsenal of the people of God? We know that God does nothing as a mere decorative item.

We also know that the principal effect of spiritual warfare is to modify the atmosphere over the place of battle in such a way that God has readier access to it–this is clearly the impact of Daniel's twenty-one day prayer effort prior to the arrival of the Archangel Michael. Moving to the New Testament, we recognize that Communion comes as fulfillment of the Passover meal and sacrifice–an activity initiated to coordinate the militant travel plans of the people with the militant liberation plans of the angel of the Lord. But God presents it in a specifically militant frame of reference more than once.

In the triumvirate of events recounted in Matthew 16 and Luke 9 we find the feeding of the five thousand–long considered by scholars to be a type of the Lord's Supper–directly preceding the journey to Caesarea Philippi. At Caesarea Jesus takes the Twelve to a wall that is the very heart of paganism in Palestine and there asks the famous question, "Who do men say that I am…(and) who do you say that I am?" Peter's famous confession, "You are the Christ, the Son of the Living God,"–the most militant words ever spoken up to that moment–is set up by the sacred meal as the confession itself paves the road for the Transfiguration that immediately follows it.

Jesus prepares the atmosphere around His people for the greatest battle ever fought on earth–His own crucifixion and subsequent resurrection–with the sharing of His Body and Blood in Matthew 26:17-35, Mark 14:12-31, and Luke 22: 7-22. But the most explicit expression of the communion as an act of spiritual warfare comes in 1 Corinthians 10 when Paul asks, "Is not the cup of thanksgiving for which we give thanks a participation in the blood of Christ? And is not the bread we break a participation in the body of Christ? Because there is one loaf, we, who are many, are one body for we all partake of the one loaf."

It is a Christian truism that we gain victory over sin and death through the blood of the Lamb and the strength of our testimony. In the Supper of the Lord His blood and our testimony are mingled as we declare His death, resurrection, and return in glory as we confront a defeated demonic enemy of life. And by the fruit of reduced traffic accidents and satanic absence we come to know what our Lord is about in our midst as we "do this in remembrance" of Him. The power to demolish strongholds that is unleashed in this simple act is unimaginable; yet the apostles understood it well enough to exercise this event every chance they got.

It would be a horrific perversion of all that we know and believe in Christ Jesus to imagine that the communion event is nothing more than a means to an end–something of God that we utilize for reasons and purposes that seem good to us. Every act of worship is an end in itself. All that we dedicate to the glory of God is for that purpose alone. Yet we recognize that worship is itself warfare–that is why Jericho fell to the sound of the trumpet and kings sent the choir out ahead of their armies when Jerusalem was threatened. If God is enthroned on our praises then the enemy is unseated when we offer our sacrifice of praise and thanksgiving as Jesus commanded us to do.

It would be just as wrong to imagine that one denomination or stream had some sort of monopoly on the offering of Communion to the Body. Scripture offers no prescription for the correct way of observing this feast of feasts, and no analysis of how He becomes present so long as we commit to His recognition (1 Corinthian 11:29) in it. I do believe that whatever we do must be more on the side of fine dining than that of fast food, but the Lord clearly gives great latitude in how we set the table. I know that He gets glory each time we eat and drink in His Name–and the demons tremble–as the people of God march to a war that is already won.

Some weeks back we were asked to come and pray with a man who had suffered a stroke. The Lord had promised to heal him over time and his caregivers believed that the next healing stage involved the adjustment of his blood circulation–which was so poor that he required constant heat in his bedroom. He was also afflicted with epileptic seizures that seemed to be triggered by the invocation of the Blood of Jesus in words. We laid hands on the man and prayed–binding the spirit of infirmity as we declared the Blood over him ourselves and asked God to heal him completely. Then we celebrated communion with the man and his caregivers. Since that day there have been no seizures and the man's blood circulation is so good that he now requires a fan going all of the time to cool him.

Do we worship the communion–or any other rite or ceremony or procedure? Certainly not! We worship the Lord our God and Him alone. But that means we strive to obey Him–especially when He says, "Do this for the remembrance of me."

CHAPTER 4:

CHALLENGING THE CULTURE

Culture is not something we think about; it is something we think through. It is the wallpaper of our hearts and every tribe and nation has a culture that is the gift of God. Yet it is just as true that every tribe and nation – because all have sinned and fallen short of the glory of God – has managed to twist and pervert aspects of the culture into which they were born out of God's generosity and provision.

Culture dictates how we interpret experience without our ever asking a question about the dictate unless God gets hold of us and calls into a new or renewed revelation. Such a dictate can be as innocuous as the fact that some Asian cultures eat only with their hand while most western cultures use a fork to spear food from the plate. We tend to look at them and say, "I prefer a fork for serving as well as for eating because I don't know where your hands have been or how well you might clean them." They look back at us and say, "I prefer my hand for serving and eating because I don't know where your fork has been or how well you might clean it."

They can be as significant as the Hawaiian practice of greeting people with the Honi. In their culture the foundational word, Aloha, is a combination of three phonemes that represent Father, Son, and Holy Spirit – and have carried that representation since many centuries before the missionaries came. The original meaning of the word is, "May the Spirit of the Living God be all over you." When Hawaiians greet one another they say, "Aloha," and breathe (their spirit) into the face of the one they are greeting. But when they offered this honor to the first Europeans to land in their islands the Euros – our culture dictates we do not exchange breath because of the airborne diseases we can carry – drew back in alarm. The Hawaiians called us haoles and we thought it meant foreigners. Actually it means "breathless ones," and the seeds were sown for two and a half centuries of mutual suspicion and rejection.

It only got worse when both sides sought to exploit the other and the Euros proved more adept at the exploitation – we nearly wiped out the Hawaiians and we did destroy much of their culture – but there was sin in both camps.

The Hawaiians perverted the culture God gave them by worshipping idols instead of 'Io, the Father; His Son whose name they did not know but of whose existence and sacrifice for them they were quite sure, and the Spirit symbolized in aloha's meaning. But we have surely perverted our culture – at our own expense and that of everybody else we encountered as conquerors instead of brothers and sisters in Christ.

In our culture today we claim our Bible says God helps those who help themselves and cleanliness is next to Godliness. Such perversion of the Gospel message leaves no room for the vulnerability displayed by Paul when he says God's strength is perfected in his weakness – or in the helplessness of a Christ who accepts crucifixion when He could have called legions of angels to His rescue.

We descend further into impotency – thinking it strength and sophistication – when we relegate the God of wonders to a back room in our hearts. Being afraid to receive Him in His radical potency – the kind that creates a world based on an economy of sacrifice rather than survival – we believe in randomized evolution of our society as well as of our planet – and relieve ourselves of responsibility for its horrors. We think it okay to torture, massacre and displace the first inhabitants of our land because they were not – in our view – making proper use of it. We use the same logic to justify the torture of prisoners we take because – after all – they would do the same or worse should we fall into their hands. The end never did justify the means and it does not now.

As the Body of Christ we have no mandate to pull down the culture we were given by God. But we do have an obligation to honor what still holds itself accountable to Him and challenge that which does not. We offer a plan of restoration to our culture because we serve a Lord who came that we might have abundant life in all of life.

This chapter contains essays as fundamental as choosing life over death when that is not a no-brainer choice, and challenging our mindless rebellion against authority on the one hand and our slavish and equally mindless obedience to usurped authority on the other. Some pieces offer a critique of artistic endeavors that seek to re-invent what God has spoken into a more acceptable – read watered down – witness. Others call us to remember we need to forgive – in the secular world – if we would be forgiven, and to celebrate and support art that honors the Great Artist at any level. Still others challenge the notion that boys will be boys with a vision of – not perpetual boyhood but – authentic manhood. We are – in this great season – called to turn our father hearts to the children. We cannot be fathers if we insist on remaining children ourselves.

Each section of the chapter hopes to function as a parable, introducing a common enough dilemma that our culture has chosen to wink its way through and says, "Hey, not only is our God not winking; He has a life giving alternative and there is no reasonable alternative to that."

CHOOSE THIS DAY LIFE OR DEATH

I will never forget the inner healing session I conducted with the distraught widow of a member of my congregation in Virginia a quarter of a century ago. Her husband had hanged himself in the entryway of their home and she found his body when she returned from grocery shopping; their six-year-old found it with her. During the inner healing session she had a vision in which The Father allowed to see her dead husband–alive with Him. When He asked her if she had a message for her husband she replied, "I want to beat the stuffing out of him." The Father answered, "Well, he owes you at least that," and she proceeded–in the vision–to punch him until she was out of breath. She opened her eyes and said to me, "Now I can forgive him."

That may not seem like a very Christian way to forgiveness–it doesn't to me at least–but reality is the husband brutally injured the wife and young son. He left himself in the front hallway deliberately and with calculation. We do not belong solely to ourselves; we belong as well to the God Who created us and the loved ones we invite into covenant with us. G. K. Chesterton calls suicide an ultimate expression of a will to destroy. That young widow was entitled to express her own rage. When it was done–in the vision and not to the husband's physical self–she was truly able to forgive and begin to heal and move on.

Equally burned into my memory was the time I had to forcibly restrain my own mother from swallowing a whole bottle of pills in our front hallway. I literally held her by the throat until she spit them onto the carpet. Another time I restrained her as she screamed she would drive her car off a cliff; I had my brother disable the car.

Please don't misunderstand me. The despair that can drive a person to want to end his own life is real and compelling. It runs in my family and I neither question it nor mock its gravity. On top of this, there are mind altering drugs that can produce suicidal thoughts and motivations; some of these may have played a role in the death of Robin Williams. But if we learn anything from the Word of God and our own pre-disposition to admire sacrifice and sacrificial heroism it is that only a life lived for others has meaning. Our original fall from grace was all about human beings deciding to live for their individual selves instead of for God and each other. Jesus Christ came into the world to restore the natural created economy of sacrifice with His own sacrificial death and resurrection.

Suicide is an ultimate choice to seek one's own good at the expense of others. The greatest irony is that it turns out to be the enemy of all life doing a number on one more victim every time. Attempted suicides for whom intervention was successful are virtually without exception the first to admit how grateful they are. It may sound like old fashioned guilt-tripping but it is appropriate to point out that every person has forged interdependent and covenantal relationships that carry mutual obligation. The so-called right to die is a non sequitur; rights are for the living.

When my mother entered the last stage of her battle with an atypical form of tuberculosis she asked me to do something that was unthinkable for me as a Christian. She wanted me to connect her with a Dr. Kevorkian type who would usher her out of this life. I told her I would gladly prevent doctors from taking heroic measures to extend her life, but under no circumstances would I play God by facilitating the termination of her life. Once she knew I was serious–over the next few days–she became interested in asking Jesus Christ into her life for the first time in her life. When she actually popped the question she said it was because she had never known the peace she saw in me even when the world was crashing down around me. We prayed and that peace entered her even as the Spirit of God entered. Four days later she lapsed into a coma and went home.

Had I cooperated with her expressed desire for suicide assistance she would not have gone anywhere. Our choices are seldom easy, but they really are that simple. Jesus says, "I came that they might have life, and that abundantly." This is true, and it is good.

A KOBAYASHI MARU FOR A GENERATION

Every Boomer remembers the Kobayashi Maru in *Star Trek II–the Wrath of Khan.* A young officer encounters the no-win scenario and fails–as everybody does–except James Tiberius Kirk. When Kirk is asked repeatedly how he beat Kobayashi Maru he finally 'fesses up to re-programming the computers. Some would say he cheated; he says he created opportunity by re-creating the rules. We Boomers love our Captain Kirk because he does what we did–creating opportunity by re-creating rules.

When they told us living in space beyond the life of batteries was science fiction we perfected fuel cells and taught ourselves to make atmosphere aboard space stations. When they told us computers required entire rooms and massive cooling systems we invented micro-chips and the rest of the hardware needed for miniaturization. When they told us only star trekkers had wireless communicators we invented cell phones and placed our miniaturized computers inside them. And when they told us there were limits to communication and information storage we invented the internet. We needed the scientists and engineers of an older generation as much as we needed our own, but it was the heart of the Boomer Generation that said, "Go for it!" and we did.

It took Ronald Reagan to call for and conceive of the Reagan Revolution and Morning in America, but it took a generation to make it happen. It took a generation that refused to believe we were finished as a nation in the wake of defeat in Vietnam and the social and economic wreckage of Lyndon Johnson's Great Society. It took Werner Von Braun to design the rockets and Buzz Aldrin to invent the math that understood orbital mechanics well enough to enable space rendezvous, but it took that same younger generation to implement their designs and concepts. It took a generation willing to re-create the rules for the doable to become comfortable living in space–and invent the hardware and the software to move beyond the vision of just getting to the moon and back before somebody else did.

When they told us we would never change the racial climate in the South–and pretended it didn't need changing in the North–we marched and sang and voted and paid no attention to what could not be done. Mostly we hung out with people who were different than the people from our neighborhood and proclaimed that men are men and women are women whatever they look like and whatever they eat and however they speak–and God intended it that way. When they told us the age of miracles was ancient history we began healing people in the power of God's Spirit on California beaches and when they told us God expected us to wear the right tie and the right dress to church we discovered a God who loved us right where we are and just as we were. (I speak of the Jesus People and their Great Awakening.) And when we began to take the Gospel of God out to the nations we listened to Him–not to the purveyors of that old time religion–and respected and empowered the local leaders we met on the mission field. After sharing the Gospel we left them to figure out how best to serve it up to their people. We gloried in the fact that we are not the Savior; just His close personal friends.

The book says there is no hope for substance abusing addicts beyond a lifetime of meetings, once a person comes out as homosexual there is no going back, and young people will just become more and more promiscuous and inclined to abort the babies that result. Our parents and the experts they listened to wrote that book. We Boomers re-wrote the book and the faith-based recovery movement that emerged from our generation boasts up to 70% of participants in recovery. I personally know some two dozen healed homosexuals and the experts in the field of their healing report similar stats to those we see in the addictions arena. Our teen children–largely due to revitalized and re-visioned abstinence education–have cut the numbers of the sexually active in their generation in half and their abortion rate by 40%. We are a John-the-Baptist generation going forth in the spirit of Elijah, turning fathers' hearts to the children, preparing a people for their coming King.

All that is needed is a heart to seek the Lord of Life and a will to re-program the experiment in His image. This heart, this Lord, and this will is enough for any generation. Right on, Captain Kirk!

NOAH–TEARING THE HEART FROM THE STORY

The filmed version of *Noah* is a produced version of the Biblical story of the Great Flood, well acted and well written. And it tears the very heart from the reality portrayed in the Word of God. Daniel Patrick Moynihan famously declared everyone is entitled to his own opinion but nobody is entitled to his own facts. If a film producer wants to tell a story–any story–he is welcome to any way that seems good to him. But he is not welcome to tell his story and claim it is really some other story on which the copyright was established millennia ago. Such a producer is a cinematic fraud.

The Genesis account of the Flood depicts a God who tells Noah in great detail how to build the ark; the cinematic Noah tries to contact God repeatedly and receives only silence. Noah's three sons are all married and planning future generations in Genesis; God actually commands them to multiply in Genesis 9. But the movie Noah believes God intends humanity to end with the deaths of his own family; he lets one fiancé die and threatens to kill the offspring of the only married son. The most serious about-face in the film is having Noah and his family worship the serpent. In the Genesis account the serpent in the garden is the enemy of all life and the usurper who would steal God's throne out from under Him if he could. In other words the film presents nothing original in itself. It is merely a darkside rendering of the antithesis of the Biblical story. And I will say again the producer is welcome to tell his own original story if he will, but to simply counterfeit the Bible is nothing less than fraud and nothing more than lying under cover of the art form.

My purpose here is not to make a case for the truth of the Bible; that case has been made. But I would make a case for letting the Bible–or any literary work–speak for itself without people who do not believe it presuming to re-write it to suit themselves or their need for self-justification. This is a matter of integrity–artistic or otherwise.

"But"–some would argue–"how much difference does it make, these details of the story you cite in your second paragraph." It makes the difference between a God who loves and a God who hates, between a God who makes provision for the continuation of humanity despite the trainwreck they have made of His creation and a God who apparently wants all human life destroyed. (God never does tell Noah to show mercy to his grandchild; Noah is simply unable to complete the killing.) It is the difference between a God who longs to communicate and have intimacy with His people–and has provided a means to that end–and a God who broods in silence over the men and women scurrying about trying to avoid His wrath like some gigantic spider contemplating the next meal of its helpless prey below.

Do we want a God who loves and reaches out to us despite our persistence in provoking Him by our treatment of each other? Or would we prefer a God who obviously hates the very people He has made, giving us first the silent treatment and then a cosmic waterboarding? More to the point–for this piece–will we let the competing versions of God's story stand against one another that the better prevail in the marketplace of ideas, or do we honor the one that masquerades as the other?

Of course the ultimately guilty parties are not the film producers but credulous people who–for the most part–claim to be Christian, but are so Biblically illiterate they have no idea whether they see truth or fiction when God is depicted on-screen. The solution is simple enough: Read your Bible before watching a movie that claims to tell you what it says.

The Apostle Peter tells us to be always ready to account for our faith. That is for the sake of those who have none, but equally for those who believe we do. Jesus says–Matthew 10–those who acknowledge Him on this planet will be acknowledged by Him in the presence of His Father; those who don't, not so much. This can be construed as a threat to the unfaithful, but it is really a promise of never ending devotion. The Son says again–Matthew 28–He will never ever leave us behind or alone. But it all kinda begins with a commitment to truth.

EXODUS: GODS AND KINGS – SOMEWHAT

I have nothing but the highest respect for storytellers. I am one myself. The film, *Exodus: Gods and Kings*, develops an interesting premise. It depicts Moses as a dedicated atheist who is unmasked as a closet Jew and himself shocked to discover his real origins. He is exiled after attempts made on his life by Pharoah; upon his return from the burning bush and a boy representing God he leads an insurgency. Failure moves him to let God free his people. God wins in the end and Moses comes to faith. He exhorts his people to live on faith alone hereafter. My problem is it is only a story, and a stolen one at that.

Storytellers should let imagination soar anywhere it wants to go. But to take an existing story, recast it to suit ones' prejudices, and palm it off as the authentic version is both fraudulent and arrogant. The result is usually sub-par on multiple levels.

Exodus defies logic when it depicts the Hebrew people as having the faith Moses lacks; their collective witness leads their leader to recognize God and to follow Him. Liberation movements have never worked that way and–of course–the authentic story in Scripture has it the other way around–the way it would have to be to work. Pharoah's repeated attempts to kill Moses while negotiating with this man he believes invincible make no sense and–of course–the real story expresses Pharoah's impotent rage, fueled by fear of a man clearly backed by a mighty God. The film defies common sense when the unbelieving Moses offers unquestioning acceptance and grudging obedience to a vindictive little boy who claims to be an incarnation of the very God in whom Moses does not believe.

Ridley Scott justifies his abuse of scripture in an interview prior to release. He says only an atheist can storybook God objectively; atheists alone insist on a story that works. Why someone ignorant of God is less biased than a person who knows Him personally is beyond me. But Scott's ignorance explains the cruel hatred of this God toward the Egyptians who displease Him. The Bible account–rooted in personal relationship with God–declares God's desire to save even the Egyptians if they but humble themselves.

His objectivity falls flat again as we see the whole conflict beginning. Pharoah–who with Moses believes they are brothers at the outset–unquestioningly believes the corrupt official that Moses is Hebrew. His hostility is rooted in a prophecy by an Egyptian priestess he scorns that the one saving his life in battle will one day usurp his throne. When Moses saves his life in battle it is all over but the shouting. Really? This "objective" story does not work.

Truth to tell, the Bible's rendition of the story works quite well on every level. We find a man raised as Egyptian royalty due to the intervention of a daughter to the older Pharoah – everybody knows where he comes from but he is treated as an exception so long as he lives as an exception. Schooled in the arrogance of ancient aristocracy he expects to be welcomed as a liberator after killing an Egyptian he sees mistreating a Hebrew. When the people do not bow to him and he fears exposure into the bargain he flees into the desert. Arriving in Midian he takes a wife and settles down to raising his family and his flock of sheep. Shocked by an encounter with God in a burning bush that will not consume itself, he finds every excuse he can to avoid the calling from God on his life. With help from his brother, Aaron, to compensate for his speech impediment he returns to Egypt, warns Pharoah repeatedly to let his people go before each plague comes, and ultimately delivers the Ten Commandments to the people in the face of their idolatry in the Sinai Desert. Frankly, it is a much more coherent story than the knockoff we are offered by Ridley Scott. It depicts God as He is – loving and committed to sinners.

I am not telling anyone to see or ignore this movie. It has its points and it is reasonably good entertainment. There is even reason to wonder if Moses – in the gradual relaxation of his militant atheism and journey to a clearly reality-based faith – is a kind of surrogate for the producer/director's own search for the really real. But whether readers see the film or not, read the real story. Compare it to the knockoff. Think on it. Pray on it. There is pure gold in the real thing.

THE PASSION OF MEL GIBSON

2014 marks the tenth anniversary of Mel Gibson's *The Passion of the Christ*, and of Mel Gibson's own passion. Although a sober Christian for more than a decade before Passion, Gibson's rep was as a hard living action figure until he made a film about Christ. The industry to which he brought billions of dollars has never forgiven him for breaking the stereotype. His own outrageous behavior–fueled by alcohol when he broke his own recovery justified the condemnation in the minds of those who condemned him. This top box office draw before Passion has not found employment with a major Hollywood studio since its release.

There was his 2006 arrest for drunk driving when he shelled the arresting officer with a torrent of anti-Semitic invective, and the tapes of abusive phone calls to the girlfriend for whom he left his wife and other children. That he was reacting–as an alcoholic and not as a rational man–to the relentless attacks he received from the Jewish community over what they perceived as anti-Semitism in the Passion is no excuse. (The film accurately depicts the Roman occupiers as the executioners of Christ.) That the tapes of the calls–in their entirety–show an ongoing shakedown of a wealthy movie mogul by someone skilled at pushing the buttons of an alcoholic way off the wagon does not lessen the fact Gibson has a violent temper–when he is drinking. But it has been ten years. He has held countless meetings with Jewish leaders and groups attempting to reconcile; he has donated millions to Jewish causes and concerns. He has been sober again these past seven years. Is forgiveness and a second chance on the horizon, or is his the unforgivable sin?

According to Allison Hope Weiner, a print journalist who wrote some of the most vitriolic material against him before she got to know him, it is past time to forgive.

I met Gibson a few weeks prior to Passion's release. I was part of a focus group of about seventy people–one of many groups invited to a screening of a rough cut of the film in multiple cities–and Gibson showed up, took questions, and gave us a couple hours of his time over and above the screening time for the film. I saw a visibly shy man who had already absorbed massive amounts of criticism for a film no one had yet seen. Although we were all Christian leaders and expected to be at least sympathetic to his efforts, he seemed fearful that we too would open fire. I saw also a man who believed–despite his clearly expressed faith in the Lord who had rescued him from alcohol and self-destruction twelve years earlier–that he could prevail over his personal crises on personal strength alone. That is a recipe for disaster, and especially in a recovering addict.

But I keep remembering that screening and picture a man so humble on the one hand and so committed to making a film that glorified his Lord on the other that he sought–and accepted–recommendations from the audience for improving it. One strategic scene in particular was seriously modified for the theatrical release as a result of our input; there may have been others. At the same time his grim determination to tough things out makes him more a slave to pride than he is to alcohol. But which one of us is free from that addictive demon? His fall should serve as a lesson.

Mel Gibson is an amazingly talented and committed man. I love films like *Braveheart* and *Signs* and *The Patriot*–where he portrays strong but conflicted characters battling their personal demons and seeking the face of God as the only and ultimate solution. I loved *Gallipoli* and I hate films like the *Mad Max* and *Lethal Weapon* franchises–because the latter are–to me–all action and no struggle for truth and abundant life. If Mel Gibson is anti-Semitic in his heart and not just a man who struck out blindly and stupidly in an alcoholic rage one night I am Santa Claus. And if he is anything but a flawed human being who wants to be better than he is and often blows it, I am Rudolph the Red Nosed Reindeer. He is certainly not the Pharisee in Luke 18 who thanks God he is not like other men and goes away self-satisfied and self-congratulated. He is more like the tax collector who cries out for the mercy of the Lord and finds it in Jesus. And it has been ten years.

THE LAST SHIP

Americans of all stripes love to put down the entertainment industry. It is too violent, too politically correct, not violent enough to be realistic, not politically correct enough. We still watch. We flock to movies based on comic books and we make a television series like Modern Family a mega hit even though anyone who thinks it a realistic depiction of family needs to actually spend time in one. Then along comes a hit based on heroism, patriotism and faithfulness and it is panned by critics. I refer to the just completed first season of the TNT series–*The Last Ship*.

A US Navy destroyer is on a mission in the Arctic when a global pandemic breaks out. By the time they hear of the disaster eighty per cent of the population is estimated infected or dead, they are under attack by rogue Russian forces, and they have lost contact with their chain of command–which appears to no longer exist. Their new mission is to use the samples of the original virus collected in the Arctic as raw material by which the Centers for Disease Control doctor on board and on secret assignment can create a vaccine or antidote or both. As entertainment it celebrates the highest incarnation of the American character–including our traditional and dynamic reliance on God to draw out the fullness of our humanity.

The cries of non-credibility are expressed in terms of "no crew is that heroic or patriotic in the face of such a disaster;" or "no captain is that iron jawed;" or even "the performances are wooden and one-dimensional." Inasmuch as these are clearly NOT the main objections, let me knock down the straw men quickly.

Crew members–from officers to ratings–show plenty of ambivalence about their mission and continued service in the face of the total breakdown of civilization. A score decide to leave the ship because their enlistments are up, but change their minds and re-up as a body. The show presents American military people as the flawed but utterly dedicated human beings the vast majority of them are; they are why I am so proud to be an American in the face of the savagery our people encounter on many battlefields without losing their humanity, or the exceptionalism of our inception. The captain has his moments of ambivalence–and errors in judgment–but he always comes back to accept responsibility for his mis-steps and have another go at it. Most of the time he is a great example to his crew; in that he is doing his job, and nothing more nor less. The performances range from adequate to awesome with almost every character exhibiting–one way or another and sooner or later, after internal struggle–that heroism Ernest Hemingway defined as grace under pressure.

My own credibility rant would focus on the captain being a part of every foray off the ship. The captain is the least expendable crew member and ought to be minding the store. But we accepted this in every captain in every *Star Trek* from original to sequel to prequel and just went with it. It's still a television drama. Why not give Captain Chandler the same break we give Captain Kirk? Why not is because of the references to God. Really.

The master chief tells the captain and others he has been placed on the ship by God and for his purposes. Numbers of the crew are observed praying in varying circumstances from the worshipful to the critical. In at least two episodes miracles occur and there are other events open to that interpretation. The captain has not yet revealed his faith or lack thereof; it is pretty clear the XO is a believer. As one would expect, there are varying degrees and visibilities of faith – and plenty of characters who exhibit none whatever. The crew is a mixed bag, just like the culture in which the rest of us live – in the real world. Nobody recoils in horror when the master chief prays for a miracle, reads his Bible, or says yet again that God has placed him on this ship for His purposes. In other words, faith is portrayed as a potent feature of everyday life.

My prayer for this most excellent program is that it neither descend to a televised Bible study nor blow away into the winds of politically correct New Agey nonsense. I pray the writers and producers maintain their integrity and their commitment to excellence. And I pray when the new season begins in 2015 millions of Americans tune in to TNT at 9 PM Sundays.

WHEN THE GAME STANDS TALL–FAITH WITH EXCELLENCE

As a college student in my pre-Christian days I was mega moved by the film, *The Loneliness of the Long Distance Runner*. A breakout role for British actor Tom Courtenay, the story depicts young juvenile delinquent Colin Smith sentenced to a reform school run by a tyrannical thug of a governor whose passion is marathon running. After several attempts to break Smith the governor discovers his talent for distance running and offers enticements if Smith will run for the school. It is all about the governor's vanity and nothing to do with the welfare of any of his charges. When Smith realizes how thoroughly he has sold out for a few privileges he stops in the grand race just before crossing the finish line. In this climactic moment he refuses victory to assert his independence and to spite the authority figure who has used him. His gesture is all about the power to say NO when all other options are cut off. He considers his NO a victory though he returns to the bottom in the reformatory culture with an extended sentence.

When The Game Stands Tall is currently in theatres with a similar climactic moment whose meaning is–and makes–all the difference in the world. A primary subplot involves a fictional running back–Chris Ryan–whose father is abusively obsessive about the son breaking the all time scoring record for California high school athletes. Ryan ties the record in the last game and is poised to carry the ball into the endzone in a walk near the end of the game. He too stops–and runs out the clock–after making sure his team wins the game. But his act is not defiance; it is submission. He says in the huddle–before taking a knee on the next two plays–that he is a member of a team and not interested in it being all about him. He has all the glory he needs already; he gives his tribute to the team and the coach who brought him all the way to where he is.

Chris Ryan is the only fictional character in the film. His story is truer than the facts–because fiction at its best tells the truth more clearly and more fully than mere facts. Every other character and incident is true and correct. The Ryan subplot simply draws the whole truth from the history in more living color.

This is no one-dimensional march to athletic glory as a reward for clean living and dedication. The story actually begins after the one hundred fifty-one game winning streak ends and a new team must discover how to live post-streak. Meanwhile, every character is flawed or struggling or both–like real life. TK spends his young life trying to climb out of the ghetto and wins a scholarship to the University of Oregon together with his lifelong friend, Tayshon. The latter continues to party with gangster wannabes in the ghetto and goes into a tailspin when TK–the innocent and responsible one–is randomly gunned down by a gang member while picking Tayshon up from a place where he should not be. Their coach delivers the eulogy and confesses that–while he will continue to love and serve his Lord Jesus–he has no answers and nothing but despair over the senseless killing. The coach himself has hidden flaws that bite him, his family, and his team.

He secretly smokes. Hardly a ticket to hell, but Coach is so image conscious he is living a lie–and that is a character issue. His smoking leads to a near fatal heart attack, being unavailable to his team for several critical months, and the exposure of his hypocrisy. He is already less than available to his family, and the confluence of consequences leads him to authentic repentance across the board.

He will become a better husband and father, a better coach, and a better man. He does this not because he is so good but because he chooses–repeatedly–to live a life referred to God and to the ones he is called to serve. His choice is all the more important when it is clear and consequential that some of his past choices have been poor ones.

This movie is well written, directed with vision, and tightly edited. The performances are crisp and natural. That makes it an excellent piece of work and one all of us can enjoy. But it also presents a powerful depiction of a prophetic community, a 1 Corinthians 12 culture, in which every one has a pivotal role and no one is expendable. See it.

TIME FOR MEN TO STEP UP TO THE PLATE: A TWENTY-YEAR-OLD MOVIE PROPHESIES THE WAY

I found myself watching an old film, *Six Days Seven Nights*, on a recent morning when I did something I don't do mornings–watch television.

I have seen this movie before and it is entertaining as is; a career woman vacationing on a Pacific island with her fiancé flies to another island for a work emergency while her intended stays behind. The plane crashes and Robin (Anne Heche) is marooned with the crotchety Quinn (Harrison Ford). Over six days and seven nights they must depend on each other to survive, lose the pirates chasing them across the island, and make the plane flyable again. During that span they move from sniping and carping non-stop to respecting, cooperating with, and loving each other with honor for her prior commitment. Frank the fiancé–using his fear (she has been missing but days) that Robin is dead as excuse–sleeps with Angelica the very sexy island beauty over whom he has been drooling since day one. When Robin returns alive he tries to make the island girl responsible for his moral compass by telling her–repeatedly–that he has been "bad...very very bad" and waiting for her to convince him he is not. When that does not make him feel better he confesses to Robin, who breaks off the engagement. With her commitment to Frank blasted by Frank himself, she and Quinn come together. Before my most recent viewing I enjoyed the film without realizing how prophetic it is.

The film features two partnered men and women. (Angelica has a casual relationship with Quinn at the beginning.) Both men and both women are seriously tempted to sleep with the one who does not belong to them. Quinn and Robin acknowledge their feelings–and the likelihood their stay on the island is forever–and yet remain honorable simply because their word means something to them. Angelica and Frank do what feels good at the moment, albeit one amorally and the other with guilt. The film ends with Angelica and Frank alone, while the pair who honor commitments come together and–presumably–live happily ever after.

In both cases it is the men who cast the deciding vote. Angelica offers herself to Frank as he stands in the open door to her room. He leaves, citing his commitment to Robin, but wakes in her bed–admitting he cursed himself each of the multiple times he made love to her the previous night. He is the one who has chosen. Likewise Robin admits her longing for Quinn, who tells her he will not dishonor her or her commitment–and that settles the matter. It does not come up again while they are on the island because he has chosen. It does come up again when she visits him in the hospital, and he chooses the path of honor for both of them again.

Men and women are made to complement one another; neither is subordinate and this is clear from Genesis to Ephesians. The Hebrew word we tend to translate as "helpmate" to describe Eve actually conveys "one who can look him in the face;" a more egalitarian meaning is not conceivable. The narrative about mutual submission of wives and husbands–not limited to Ephesians 5–offers simply gender appropriate ways to submit, one through obedience and the other through sacrifice of self interest. Conceptually men are made to protect and support women; women are made to nurture and encourage men. There is nothing in scripture or human nature to preclude women from accepting whatever calling–at whatever level of responsibility–they are given. But it is the men who are called to be responsible for choosing and implementing a healthy covenant between themselves and their wives. That is why Adam comes across as such a jerk when he lamely excuses his defiance of God in the Garden by saying, "The woman made me do it."

Six Days Seven Nights depicts a man who shoulders his responsibility despite lacking a conceptual framework for it; he is endowed with a God-breathed conscience and wills to flow with it. It also depicts a man endowed with the same conscience who chooses to wimp out when something exciting crosses his path with a come-hither wink. The story ends well for the one who steps up to the plate; not so much for the wimp.

I write frequently about God's promise of renaissance–a Great Awakening–in this nation and others. I am just as vocal on His call for a season of repentance in His Body the Church as our part in welcoming His promise. By repentance I understand a progressive re-focus of our attention on God and away from self and self-gratification-because-we-can. For men that means stepping up to the plate and being men, and not just for fidelity's sake.

GOOD SPORTSMANSHIP MAKES FOR GOOD SPORTS

When I played Little League ball I was good at everything–fielding, throwing, stealing bases–except hitting. When I finally made upper division I didn't get a hit the entire season. The humiliation was hellish; I would have done anything to avoid it, but it made me strong. And I can promise it would have been doubly humiliating had a rule been laid down that pitchers had to lob the ball to players like me for our self-esteem. Yet the powers that be in youth sports have discovered the supposed immorality of permitting one team to dominate another–whether in football, baseball or soccer–without sparing a thought for the emasculation of players given a forced pass when the score reaches a certain point.

Men–and boys–need to compete to be who they are created to be. They do not need to be cruel; they do not need to bully, but they do need to seek and contest a prize. Each quest carries the risk of loss. Each one carries the potential for learning to cooperate, growing from the experience of victory or defeat, and the value of going after victory again with the benefit of lessons learned and skills honed. What is not needed–or helpful–is a bunch of adults grimly determined that defeat will not be tolerated even if victory must be artificially limited. A growing body of research is beginning to show that a principal way in which irresponsible boys become responsible men is for parents and other authorities to back off when they make risk-embracing decisions that can result in skinned knees or severe defeat.

The rationale advanced for forbidding lopsided scoring is that such winning teams bully the lesser skilled. I am not supporting absentee parenting, much less school authorities who look the other way when the kids in their charge are being bullied. I have no use for bullies of any kind and I have fought them as a boy, as a man, and as a parent. But my father taught me to stand up for myself and I taught my son to stand for himself. When my son did stand up I backed him all the way to the superintendent and got justice for him. In another school when there was no administrative relief for an unfair punishment I sat in detention with my son before telling the headmaster I was pulling him out of the school–with my son's concurrence. He learned the world is not fair at the same time he learned he was not alone in it. Yet in this season coaches are threatened with suspension and fines if they allow a game score to pass a certain point.

Do I hate it when children are on the wrong end of a lopsided score? I hate it as I hated that hitless season when I was twelve. But that is when a parent or other authority figure comes alongside the child and bears his burden with him–if he is an authentic parent or authority figure. It is not the time to artificially shield children–through rules rather than relationships–from burdens they must carry with or without preparation as adults.

Jesus knew this when he sent His twelve principal disciples out with neither bread nor money nor extra clothing (Luke 9:1-6) to do what they had seen Him do, like healing the sick, casting out demons, and proclaiming the Gospel no secular authorities wanted to hear about. When that first foray worked out well he sent seventy-two–armed with his authority and His message. On Pentecost Sunday His Spirit sent out the whole Body and here we are two billion plus disciples later.

Efforts to shield children from pain and embarrassment are commendable on their face. But in this case the shielders weaken one group while bullying another. What the kids need a whole lot more than shielding–when we are not talking about serious injury–is relationship with adults who love them enough to stand with them, to help them pick up the pieces, to demonstrate their real value that transcends a bad day at the ballpark. I had no one to stand with me when I was twelve, and I still came out stronger for the experience. I learned how important it is to stand for and with others, and that the things that hurt my pride are not the things that kill my person. I received the most important redemption for this time when I met a God who will always stand for me and with me a decade later. Rules–however well meant–teach none of these things. Only relationship can do that.

WHAT GOD CALLS IS BETTER THAN WHAT WE CALL

In the tenth century BC–during the reign of King Solomon–the region of Galilee in Israel was designated a dirty place, a wasted place. It all stemmed from the gift of King Solomon to King Hiram (of Tyre) of twenty cities in the region to pay off a debt. Hiram was not pleased with his payment and named the whole region Kavul or Cabul; it refers literally to a swampy place, a repository of rotting plant matter. Why all the minutia? Because words have consequences and this name was still in force at least through the time of Jesus on earth. That is why Nathanael, one of His first prospective disciples wondered out loud if anything good (Jesus came from Nazareth in Galilee) could emerge from that place.

When Jewish colonists began re-settling the Galil around 1880 they found nothing but malarial swamps. Many died from disease while others tried to figure out how to drain the swamps and grow crops that would pay. In the meantime they turned more and more to their God–we call that process repentance–and they began to remember that God had called that land a place of milk and honey. As the process of repentance continued over the decades leading to Israeli independence the consequences were both spiritual and pragmatic. (And let's remember that not every Israeli practices the faith of his fathers; only a critical mass is required.) The colonists began to think more in terms of milk and honey and less in terms of kavul. They imported eucalyptus trees to help drain the swamps and used other innovative means that are the fruit of vision–I call it divine intervention–to make Galilee what it is today–the heart of Israeli agriculture, the garden spot of the nation, and the chief source of foreign exchange currency for the past eighty years. One might say that what God–in His far seeing–calls a thing is more accurate and certainly more valuable than what we–in our short sightedness–call it. One might also note that this repentance thing is a lot more about Whom we are turning toward than about what we are turning from. It is certainly more about seeking destiny than about mourning dysfunction.

The same process is going on in our own city of Redding, California. In the late nineteenth century the community we call Redding–through a misspelling of an early inhabitant's name–was first known as Poverty Flats. It was the only place in the region where no gold could be found and the first settlers were disgusted enough to grunt out a name as negative as Cabul ever thought to be. When the courts decided the spotted owl–a non-native non-threatened species–was more important than the local economy it destroyed our principle source of jobs in the timber industry and it looked like Poverty Flats was an apt name for an economic swampland. But people of prayer discerned God's name for Redding–Abundant Springs–and it turned out the city sits above one of the largest aquifers in the world. They began praying for the community under its authentic name and business people began to band together and use the creativity only God can give–alongside the dedication and effort only we can supply.

A prayer effort that began in Redding witnessed the breaking of drought in 2010 at about the same time hotel owners acted to fulfill a prophetic revelation about cooperative action along Hilltop Drive beginning to break the economic drought in the city. New industries and employers are coming into the city and the timber industry is at or near the same sales levels it enjoyed in the 1990s–although there are many more people in the city looking for work than lived here then. A local church established a holding company that leased the failing convention center so that a Redding landmark has once again become prosperous and the small Christian liberal arts university is becoming one of the top teacher prep schools in the state while preparing itself to be a major university power. Most encouraging is that Redding was recently designated one of the ten most generous cities in the USA. Poverty Flats? We live in and through an Abundant Springs mindset and the rest of the fulfillment of our name is on the way, just as it was in Israel's Galilee.

This is the fruit of a culture of repentance–turning toward the source of our identity instead of looking back on our self-generated identity of dysfunction. God just knows us better than we know ourselves.

CHAPTER 5:

CHALLENGING THE BODY POLITIC

On our weekly conference calls for the California Governor's Prayer Team–the Governor referenced is, of course, the Father and Governor of the world rather than of our state–we pray for several items concerning the political powers in our state. One is a Damascus Road experience for every leader in California–beginning with we who are on the call–and the other is that leaders would fall in love with their limitations.

The Damascus Road is–of course–the place of encounter between Saul the fire breathing vigilante determined to capture and kill Christians by any means necessary so as to prevent them from polluting the purity of Judaism and the Jewish homeland–and the Lord Jesus who puts Saul in his backside before asking in all gentleness why he feels such a compulsion to persecute the One who died for him. It is the beginning of Saul's journey to becoming Paul. It is the model of encounter with the living Christ for all of us who choose Him freely after the energy falls out of our desperate efforts to fight off His love and we collapse into His arms.

The Damascus Road is not a political concept. Yet we do live in the world. The world is a political place and the Damascus Road cuts right across its right-of-way. When we have spent our time on that road we can begin to understand the privilege of falling in love with the limitations–acting a lot like gravity–inasmuch as they enable our activities by pulling our feet onto the ground. (Before the Damascus Road limitations are only an irritant; after it they become a gift.) Political limitations on behavior are found in the Constitution and laws of the land. Spiritual and human limitations on the same thing are found in the Word of God. When we pray for this love affair with limitations to begin we also ask God to include ourselves.

Christians are called to live not as products of this world–we are a new creation in Christ according to 2 Corinthians 5:17–but as stewards of it. We have authority to bless and pastor the world and that includes addressing, correcting, and confronting the world. When we do this we had better have tested the spirits beforehand and know with confidence we are speaking for God and not for our own pet agenda. At the same time, when we know God has a word for this world–for what some call the body politic–we had best not wimp out with something smarmy like, "I have my attention set on heavenly things," or "I really don't pay much attention to politics." Jackson Senyonga is famously quoted as calling out the condition of society as the report card of the Church. We do not confuse the Gospel with the political make-up of our society, but as keepers and sharers of the Gospel we have big-time responsibilities to well represent in our communities the God who requires that justice and mercy flow like a mighty river.

The first essay is aptly titled, "Falling in Love with the Limits." Others take up topics like authentic healthcare reform, rendering to Ceasar, and there are three separate pieces on the connection of constitution to covenant. There are several postings that concern contemporary and historical miscarriages of justice–not so as to rabble rouse but so as to describe the gravity of the responsibilities that are uniquely placed on the shoulders of the Body of Christ.

Every social and political institution Americans celebrate–on national holidays and in high school civics classes–finds its first articulation in the pulpit of a New England church during the colonial period. This holds from the separation of powers (in government) to the federal system to the limitations placed on democratic rule and every right guaranteed in the Bill of Rights and the Fourteenth Amendment. Every American can (should) understand we are endowed by our Creator with unalienable rights; government guarantees but does not confer them. The other side of this coin is that every American has responsibilities that correspond–one to one–with our God given rights. Christians are uniquely called to appreciate and act accordingly; the revelation does–after all–come forth from us. And so this chapter–while not the most important–belongs squarely in the midst of this book about a Kingdom in pursuit of the people God loves and restores.

God loves each and every one of us–including political leaders and voters–just the way we are. He loves us so much He has no intention of leaving us in the condition in which He finds us. The believers in both groups need to come to grips with the reality we are expected to love one another–individually and collectively, believers or simply the citizens of the communities in which we live together–in the same way and with the same passion. After that we can rejoice that He perfects His strength in our weakness in this world before we ever approach the next.

FALLING IN LOVE WITH THE LIMITS

On our weekly conference calls with the California Governors Prayer Team we always ask the Lord to cause our elected and appointed leaders to fall in love with the limitations placed on them in law and constitution. Clearly we have not prayed enough. The lawlessness of government itself becomes more brazen and more frequent with every passing month. It may even be that we need to pray for us ordinary citizens to fall in love with the limitations placed on our freedom. By that I mean citizens need to re-discover the price of freedom–which is not just vigilance, but action to maintain and reclaim it.

In local matters a candidate for office in Escondido, California, placed a campaign sign in his own yard and was ordered by officials to remove it. He claimed his right to free speech was violated but liberal and conservative leaders alike told him he must obey the rules of the city even if they were unconstitutional. In the meantime the music group Live Nation planned a concert in Los Angeles and–after they arranged the venue–were told by city officials they could hold their concert only if it were deemed a "good fit" for the neighborhood in which they would hold it. Since when are Americans required to pass a culture test administered by bureaucrats before we can play music? And where does it say in law or constitution we should obey rules that violate that constitution? Is it not the responsibility of lawmakers to make their laws consistent with the constitution and the responsibility of citizens to defy laws that are not?

The 2010 Citizens United decision of the US Supreme Court held that arbitrary limits on campaign contributions by corporations begged the question that corporations are governed and funded by US citizens covered by the First Amendment. In the follow-up McCutcheon case–decided this year–the court said restricting citizens to $2600.00 in total campaign contributions–per the McCain-Feingold Act–is an unconstitutional restriction of free speech. Yet that same court was perfectly comfortable saying a citizen may contribute a maximum $2600.00 *each* to as many candidates as they like. Can only dissenting Justice Thomas see this is still an unconstitutional restriction of free speech?

Now Californians are denied our right to a referendum on unjust laws–a right enshrined in the California Constitution. The legislature passed AB 1266 in late 2013–the so-called Bathroom Bill–to mandate boys using girls' restroom and shower facilities and vice versa. Outraged parents and citizens mounted an effort to place this issue on the November ballot, something we have a right to do in California, and vote it down if they could. When the petition drive began Secretary of State Debra Bowen falsely claimed the law was in effect during the drive–state law states clearly that it is not. She refused to accept signatures from at least two counties until ordered by a judge to do so. She then asserted the petitions were 130,000 valid signatures short. When Pacific Justice Institute attempted to do an independent count–as is their right under state law–Bowen refused to turn the petitions over because–as she put it–there were privacy concerns for the signers of the petitions.

The Institute sued in state court and the judge ignored the law to find in favor of the secretary of state. Left unanswered is the question of how a person signing a political petition–the very essence of public speech–retains a right to privacy, especially when the people wishing to review the signatures are the very people the signers are attempting to help. But a more important question is answered by implication. Citizens do have a responsibility–an obligation–to assert our right to live under law rather than under the whims of powerful men and women. When government consistently denies us that right we have an obligation to rise up–non-violently–and deny government. We need to deny government in such a creative way that our political NO becomes a cosmic YES. AB 1266 is a case in point.

When this gross invasion of students' right to bathe and use the toilet unmolested and un-oogled takes effect parents should–on a wholesale basis–keep their kids at home until the law is overturned. Schools depend on your child being in school every day; funding is determined based on average daily attendance–ADA–and thousands of kids staying home hurts budgets. Hopefully it hurts budgets enough that school boards, administrators, and teachers unions will join the clamor for this law's repeal. But it is not a creative YES to merely keep the kids at home.

We homeschooled our children for three years, as do thousands of families in California; it is perfectly legal to do so and nowhere near as time consuming as many seem to think. Homeschooled children tend to do better on achievement tests than their public and private school counterparts; they cut through college entrance exams like butter. They have been demonstrated to experience no loss in terms of socialization. Any parents who want to consider this option can google the Home School Legal Defense Association. However, parents should beware of one thing: Even when the schools bow to the pressure and stop using our children as social science lab animals those parents who began to home school during this period may find they and their kids like it so much they won't be going back.

Jesus says He came to set the captives free. But He never said freedom was free. He told the man in Mark 2 to rise and walk, not be lifted up and floated away, after healing him of his paralysis. He says the Kingdom of Heaven is taken by force in Matthew 11–not the force of violence but of the rising assumption of responsibility. That is falling in love with our limitations as citizens.

RENDERING TO CEASAR GIVES WAY FOR RENDERING TO GOD

Radio waves have recently been saturated with commercials paid for by an outfit called the California Endowment. They feature voices claiming to be young and vulnerable undocumented immigrants who want only to receive the same healthcare coverage now available to all other Californians. They point themselves out as our neighbors, school classmates, co-workers and co-shoppers in any California community. The commercials end with an encouraging call for us to realize that healthcare for all depends on all of us doing our part to accept and support each other. The trouble is that the whole campaign is based on layer after layer of lies.

I began teaching in California public schools before the seventies began. By the time they were well underway school authorities were already forbidden to ascertain the immigration status of children seeking to enroll – even confirming addresses was verboten. And hospital emergency rooms have been required by law to offer free services to those who cannot pay for longer than I can remember. These voices have been classmates for decades because government forced their acceptance and they have never been cut off from healthcare. As a certificated reading specialist I was compelled to teach Spanish speaking students to read Spanish before I taught them to read English – the short-lived theory being this would make English instruction easier later. It was short-lived because it turned out most of the undocumented could read no better in Spanish than in English and the effort only compounded their confusion.

Two decades ago Californians adopted ballot initiatives by large margins that denied basic services from schools to welfare to people in this country illegally. The courts threw these elections into the trash heap, declaring the results unconstitutional. This is how millions became our classmates and neighbors in need and seeking only to normalize their lives among us.

BTW – there are no undocumented immigrants in California. There are legal and illegal residents. Anyone with any decency should have a broken heart for poverty-stricken people seeking a better life in this land of immigrants. But after taxpayers have been forced to pay for programs as hare-brained as they are illegal, while repairing their own vehicles after collisions with drivers as uninsured as they are undocumented, and dealing with other crime that emerges from any large group of people living in shadow, that compassion is wearing thin. And then we come to the biggest lie of the California Endowment and their little propaganda campaign. They are themselves a creation of the insurance giants Blue Cross and Blue Shield.

These companies are so-called non-profits. That means they cannot pay dividends to stock holders. It does not mean they must hold their costs down; they have unlimited license to pour their surplus funds into anything they deem in the public interest. Like radio campaigns to mainstream illegals and obtain for them paid healthcare into the bargain. And for those who ask what difference it makes if these illegals are already entitled to free access to care, the answer is simple. Those who receive free healthcare are not paying insurance premiums at this time. But when everyone in California has health insurance the companies rake in more billions–whether from rate payers or tax payers is of no concern to them. The insurance companies–both for and not for profit–are and always have been the biggest beneficiaries of Obamacare and Covered California. But there is more money and more power over human lives to be had. And so the radio.

Compassion for people in need is a Christian virtue. I have never turned away anyone in need over immigration status–or even asked about status before helping. But I do get tired of the lies, the fraud, and the bullying we are subjected to by government and corporate people grimly determined to mind our business at our expense...and to their considerable advantage. So what does the God who sent the Son expect of us?

His word–spoken by the Son–calls us to render to Caesar what belongs to him and to God what belongs to Him. Our constitution tells us exactly what we owe to government–Caesar if you will. We owe the support necessary to carry out all constitutionally designated functions from national defense to building highways, from providing a viable currency to making a level civic and economic playing field. We owe everything else to God–from defining justice to understanding and exercising compassion.

Healthcare for all falls under compassion; it is not a government function. Truth is also a God responsibility. He knows how to deal with those who speak true and those who lie.

AUTHENTIC HEALTHCARE REFORM

A close associate of mine got a 5% cost of living raise effective January 1. The trouble is it will not be enough to cover the hike in her medical premium–not near enough. The same story is repeating in multiple versions all over the country as the Obamacare disaster infects greater and greater multitudes. We have heard about the now six million Americans cancelled by their insurance companies because their policies no longer meet government standards–and the standard official line that these cancellations are good for their victims because they are forced to buy new policies that include pregnancy care for men and gender adjustment treatment for the 99.5% of Americans who do not want it. But this is only in the individually mandated market, where government is counting on massive purchases of unwanted insurance to pay for the treatments of those who need them.

Anticipating the delayed coming of the business mandates companies have cut back large swaths of their workers to part-time status so their employers will not be forced to buy all or part of their insurance. That means employees have less income to buy much more expensive insurance when government blithely tells them to just go to the exchanges–the ones that do not operate in the first place due to technical incompetence. And when government legislates that fewer hours will now constitute full-time, the employers simply cut hours further to get under the lowered bar.

What if we insisted on authentic healthcare reform? To what would we awaken?

The first awakening would be to the reality that authenticity in an American context requires freedom. Even if we believed the inflated figure of thirty million Americans without health insurance–not healthcare, for free healthcare for the indigent and impoverished has been law on the books for decades–forcing the entire nation onto government-run exchanges to attempt to benefit less than 10% of us is madness. Yet Obamacare depends for its survival on forcing enough healthy people to pay for the sick that we remain solvent on their backs. A healthcare reform plan that reduces the freedom with which we have obtained healthcare in the past is not reform at all.

The second wake-up call would remind us we built the best healthcare system in history through healthy competition between competent professionals. In a free market economy incompetence is punished by failure and competence is rewarded with success. Competition is what keeps the game honest and a level playing field is the guarantor of competition. That would mean the insurance companies are not permitted to penalize people for the "sin" of having a pre-existing condition, as these things in no way harm the actuarial tables by which the companies live. It would mean companies would be denied their own protected market territory because policies would be portable from one job to another and across state lines. It would mean companies had to do business across state lines in order to stay in the game. And it would mean tort reform to reduce the crippling weight of malpractice insurance. Patients should be compensated fairly for a loss and doctors who repeatedly prove themselves incompetent or unethical should face permanent loss of their license. When government knows its sole responsibility is promoting competition it can stop tinkering with the system–from which nothing but unintended consequences ever comes.

The third heads-up would be to those who say critics offer no alternatives to Obamacare. That has always been hogwash. Congressman Tom Price, for one, offered a promising alternative at the same time Obamacare was first advanced. The Price Plan had all the advantages claimed by Obamacare–from competitive exchanges to eliminating penalties for pre-existing conditions–and none of the coercion. Unfortunately Price belonged to the party of no power (2009) in either house and his plan was never considered by the very leadership that condemned his party as "the party of No." Is this problem too complex? To the only nation that has landed on the moon?

The Biblical Galatians declares Christ set us free for the sake of that freedom found only in Him. I bring this up only because it seems freedom has been the primary object of the abundant life He brings from the beginning. It is difficult to imagine a good gift that summarily cancels the best gift we've ever been given. This might be a good time to pray our way back to the drawing board–democratically and legally displacing those blocking our path–and act on the fruit of that prayer. I bring this up only because it seems not to have been tried.

THE CONSTITUTION AS COVENANT

Covenant as both concept and reality has its origins in the people of the Old Testament. The earliest recorded covenant is between Noah and God the Father. God promises to bless Noah and his descendants and to never again flood the earth; Noah promises to serve God all his days. A later covenant is between Abram–later Abraham–and God the Father. In it God promises to bless and prosper Abram and his descendants and the patriarch promises to serve God to the exclusion of all others. He commits to circumcision as a sign of his belonging to Yahweh–God. The covenant with Moses is more elaborate, spelling out ten standards of behavior that will indicate human faithfulness to God while He gives them the promised land, Eretz Israel, and blesses and prospers them in the land. By the time of the Mosaic Covenant other nations and cultures were entering into such agreements, but the Hebrews were unique in claiming their covenants were with the One God and originated with Him.

Covenants are agreements between two corporate parties, one of whom is clearly the senior and stronger partner. They state rights and responsibilities for the protection and blessing of the weaker by the stronger and the service or obedience to be rendered by the weaker to the stronger. Covenants differ from contracts in that they are open ended–more like a cornucopia than a closed container. Within the parameters of the Covenant–the Ten Commandments in the case of the Biblical Old Covenant–both parties are free to expand. God can do more than He promised and the people can offer more profound service, but neither is free to give less than originally promised.

The first American covenant–as opposed to a charter or contract of incorporation–is the Mayflower Compact of 1620. The Pilgrims pledge to give all glory to God and advance the Christian Faith as they establish a human government for making such laws as would facilitate their divinely ordained purposes and the general good of the people. In other words, the people themselves are the senior and stronger party; they create and commit to blessing government in order that it might serve them. Other American civil covenants–such as the Constitution–follow this pattern.

The point here is that most people think government the senior and stronger party because it has the backing of armed forces and agencies. But the genius behind our Constitution and the laws created to implement it is that the people are sovereign. We created and bless a government–but only so long as it serves us as the stronger and senior partner to whom it owes allegiance and submission. That is why we specify which powers government may wield and state that any powers not specifically granted are not its property. That is why we have a Bill of Rights for the protection of the people and nothing for the protection of government.

Truth is we have never lived up to our end of the covenant with God; I refer here to Old and New Covenants that–in Christ–apply to all peoples everywhere. The beauty of the founding of America is that our first leaders understood and proclaimed this reality. Some periods have been better than others, the Great Awakenings coming immediately to mind. But the sovereignty we hold over government was a gift of the sovereign God to Whom we owe all we have. Instead of serving Him we have all too often exercised the sovereignty we were given to enslave some and slaughter others. We have ceded power to government it was never meant to have. We did all these things because of what we thought emergencies–as though God failed to foresee the westward expansion, the Great Depression, or even the War on Terror, and we had to step in and do what He could not. This is idolatry–worshipping ourselves and our intellect in the place of God. And the fruit is in the bin.

Today we have massive unemployment, fifty million Americans on food stamps in the richest country in history, a government spying on us and threatening our right of religious liberty, free expression of ideas, and the responsibility of parents to seek appropriate medical aid and education for their children without government interference. Even our children's diets are under supervision.

There is a way to address this impasse in a potent way, but it will require a lot more than some massive get-out-the-vote drive and educating the population regarding our origins and destiny. The next posting of this blog will begin that address.

RESTORING THE COVENANT WILL RESTORE THE CONSTITUTION

We human beings have never been really good at keeping the covenants we make with God or with each other. Noah had a drinking problem and Abraham passed his wife off as his sister out of fear of a pagan king. Americans declared all men created equal and then pretended blacks and Indians were not really people in order to justify enslaving and brutalizing them. In each case the people sinning were doing what they thought they had to do in the absence of a God Who is anything but absent. The good news is we can know and serve a loving God who permits and even encourages do-overs. The do-overs are called repentance.

Repentance means to turn about. It includes turning away from our covenant breaking ways, but it centers on turning toward – re-focusing – on God and the promises we and He have exchanged. Part of the reason God never abandoned us over – for example – slavery is the reality that a substantial minority of Americans saw it for the evil it was and worked tirelessly to replace it with the authentic vision of equality expressed in Declaration and Constitution. Even the Founders who write in Blacks as only three fifths of a person did so in order to one day gerrymander a Congress that might outlaw slavery. It is axiomatic that God never abandons a city or nation for its evil, but only when there is no critical mass of righteous ones with whom He can work. Check the stories of Sodom and Gomorrah, Moses bargaining with God for the preservation of apostate Israel in the wilderness, or even Elijah complaining in his little cave.

There exists a grassroots ministry called The National Day of Repentance. Less than two years old and launched by word of mouth and a fledgling (at the time) web site it is now operating in more than forty states and thirty nations. The sole purpose of this ministry is to encourage Christians to re-focus our attention on God and His covenant with us – as though that were more important than restoring our constitution and nation – because it is. We also happen to believe wholeheartedly that this re-focus on covenant will lead to restoration of constitution and nation one way or another. That is the way things happened in the Bible. That is the way things happened in American history as well, from the first Great Awakening that enabled the American Revolution and the documents that framed it, to the second that enabled the end of slavery, to the third that brought the success of the Civil Rights Movement and the advent of Morning in America under Ronald Reagan's presidency.

The next scheduled National Day of Repentance is April 30 – the anniversary of George Washington's First Inaugural Address. In that address he literally commended the fledgling nation into the hands of the loving God. The date is also the anniversary of Abraham Lincoln's 1863 Day of Prayer, Fasting and Humiliation. (Funny how two of our founding fathers most associated with no real faith – by some foolish scholars – are the most pronounced in their calling on God for His mercy over the nation.) The web site – no longer fledgling – is www.dayofrepentance.org. Any who wish to participate need only engage some act of corporate re-focus on God on that day, or beginning on that day. Those who represent a Christian ministry of any sort are invited to go on the web site, accept the incredibly generic statement of faith, and post their activity in case others might take inspiration from knowing about it.

In California the current drought is being addressed by the Rain and Reign Coalition, a gathering of thirty-six ministries that cross denominational lines and pray for the growing of repentant – re-focused – hearts across the state. We repent – turn away – daily of the shedding of innocent blood, the idolatry of human reason, sexual infidelity and perversion, and the breaking of covenant from treaties to families. We repent – turn toward – daily for God's mercy in breaking the high pressure ridge that holds back the rain and the highly pressured hearts that hold back the prosperity and joy that is His promise for California. Any wishing to participate can begin to pray daily as we do.

Some – perhaps many – see this as pious tripe. Good enough. How have our efforts worked out for us the past decade or so? In Jeremiah 31 God promises a new covenant written on every human heart that turns to Him and to bring all of His blessings to bear through those hearts. He makes the same promises in Isaiah 59, Ezekiel 11, and Joel 2 and 3. They are always preceded by a period of repentance – that we might be enabled to receive Him. It is the same with every American Awakening. What have we got to lose?

COVENANT AND CONSTITUTION CONNECTED

When President Abraham Lincoln called for a day of Prayer, Fasting, and Humiliation April 30, 1863, people prayed only in the North, the South being at war with the North and disinclined to do anything at the behest of Lincoln. Now I would never contend that God was on one side or the other in a war; His aim is always that we come onto His side. But He does have a habit of responding to heartfelt prayer, and He surely hated slavery. Two months after this day of repentance the two sides fought the Battle of Gettysburg and the tide turned permanently in favor of the Union.

Some would say, "Well, if God hates slavery would not the tide have inevitably turned," and the answer would be a resounding, "No." God hates lots of things that abide in our world. But He has a habit of responding to heartfelt prayer.

April 30, 1789, our first president, George Washington, took his oath of office and gave his first inaugural address. Washington led the members of government onto their knees in prayer. He dedicated the fledgling nation to God, like his New England forefathers building a biblical "city on a hill." Some would say, "Just a minute; Washington was a Virginian and everybody knows the Virginia colony was a commercial venture with plenty of exploitation of black slaves and native people." They would be right about that, but they would be wrong to ignore the reality of Washington's life – a life bathed in prayer, worship, and repentance as a lifestyle – a life that shows his spiritual forefathers to be the Pilgrims and the Puritans of Massachusetts Bay, men and women who introduced the concept of covenant to the Americas.

Washington led a nation that was weak, disorganized, and virtually bankrupt. Steeped in prayer and dedication to God, it survived and prospered to become the greatest nation on earth and the one most blessed by God after Israel.

This year National Day of Repentance officially links arms with National Day of Prayer, one day later on Thursday, May 1. NDP's theme is One Voice United in Prayer; it comes from Romans 15:6, in which Paul calls the Body to be One in prayer and praise to the Lord Jesus. We link arms unofficially with Washington: Man of Prayer, an event set to occur in the congressional Statuary Hall one week later, May 7. All three observances will focus on loving God and answering His call to repent – re-focus – on Him. We do not believe God will reward our humility by lifting us out of the national quicksand in which we seem trapped. We believe, rather, that He has never abandoned us, but that we must return to the shelter of His wings if we would give Him the kind of access to us that permits His blessing and healing to occur. That is what He says in His own Word and American history supports as His pattern.

In California alone we have seen two kinds of drought healed through prayer-led action. The last drought in California – prior to 2012 – began in 2008 and hundreds – a critical mass for that time – prayed daily asking God to break it. Prophetic words were uttered in the state that God would break the drought in its third year if people prayed – and that is precisely what happened. In a man-made drought a federal judge – relying on bogus science – threw the state into economic chaos by closing the pumps in the Sacramento River Delta and costing some forty thousand jobs. Suits were brought and presentations made – and again prayer was offered daily that hearts might be softened. After some eighteen months Judge Oliver Wanger announced he was unimpressed by the science for closing the pumps and the water again began to flow in the delta.

At this time God is calling for a thoroughgoing repentance in His Church for California's history of leading the nation in shedding innocent blood, covenant breaking, sexual sin, and idolatry. He does not want a pound of flesh from us, but He does require a ton of re-focus. In the National Day of Repentance we are calling on all churches – across the nation – to set aside May 4 as Repentance Sunday. The day can be observed in any way each congregation and ministry desires – but as one Body. Let this prayer be the beginning of restoration of Constitution and Covenant. Let us repent not because it "works" but because it is right. Let God be the one who works as we get out of His way.

TRADITIONAL MARRIAGE VERSUS THE LARAMIE PROJECT: TRUTH OR DARE

If a single event galvanized the movement toward recognizing homosexual marriage it must be the brutal murder of Matthew Shepard in October 1998. Shepard encountered two men in a Laramie, Wyoming, bar and left with them. They later pistol whipped, tortured, and lashed him to a fence. Death came six days later in a hospital; his murderers serve consecutive life sentences. His case became–and remains–the catalyst for anti-hate laws protecting gays; it is the spiritual catalyst for re-defining marriage. The narrative is that Shepard was killed by heterosexual rednecks venting homophobic rage; it says we must guarantee it never happens again. Films, theatrical and book projects have told the story–the most famous being The Laramie Project. Trouble is, the narrative is a lie from start to finish.

The torture and murder of this 21-year-old man was certainly as brutal and criminal as it is portrayed to be. But Aaron McKinney–the principal killer–was Shepard's sometime lover. His motive for the crime was to steal some ten thousand dollars worth of meth-amphetamine from Shepard. McKinney has admitted in interviews that he fabricated his anti-gay rage defense; he has also admitted the drug theft was his motivation. Although some law enforcement people deny Shepard was a drug dealer police investigator Ben Fritzen declares drugs and money were the motivation for the attack. As horrible as was this crime, it had nothing whatever to do with Shepard's sexual orientation, his being a sometime male prostitute, or any sort of intolerance.

Yet judge after judge–in defiance of law and constitution–and now some state legislatures–decide for "tolerance" and "marital equality" in an effort to prevent a repetition of what never happened in the first place.

Principal battlegrounds right now are federal courts of Australia and the Supreme Court in the US. But legal experts argue that–even should our Supreme Court rule for the people of a state to define marriage in the several cases before it–states like California in which the Court refused to review the lower federal court decision overturning that state's marriage law would have to re-adopt such a law by popular vote or accept justice permanently denied.

Some argue the facts don't matter. Tolerance and acceptance–they say–is a good in itself and we should continue our national march in this direction regardless of its sources. (Never mind the legalized bigotry practiced against business people who wish to operate their businesses in accordance with traditional and even Biblical values. This list lengthens on a daily basis.) But this logic presupposes the kind of tolerance/acceptance expressed in authorizing gay marriage is good for all concerned. Reality is it is bad for all concerned.

In every nation hosting gay marriage long enough for studies to be conducted the gay marriages are documented to be inherently unstable and short-lived–with noteworthy exceptions. Homosexual fidelity is (usually) found to mean returning to the relationship after adultery; authentic monogamy is rare. Domestic violence occurs at much higher rates than in the heterosexual community. Worst–in my view, but difficult to document–is the reality that gays imagine they will find peace in marriage but–when nothing changes–a deeper despair than before. Their problem is not intolerance.

Heterosexual unions also suffer. Straight couples become less likely to marry when marriage definitions are neither stable nor reality-based. Married couples become more likely to divorce. Children of hetero homes, subjected to a drumbeat of politically correct propaganda, are more likely to become relationally confused and de-stabilized. This is much more prevalent for children in gay households. Nobody wins.

Do we want to subject our children to a game of cosmic truth or dare? Of course not; nobody–gay or straight–wants that. But given the flight from reality inherent in the debate over marriage–all over the world–and the outright lies most media report as truth while suppressing the facts of such pivotal cases as the Matthew Shepard murder, there is little that reason can accomplish. This can only lead us–I hope–to contemplate the bankruptcy of our fallen reason against the wisdom of the King of the universe. He says He perfects His strength in our weakness. Let us fall on our faces and beg Him to do just that.

The National Day of Repentance is observed annually on the Jewish day of Yom Kippur. Repentance is neither more nor less than the re-focus of our attention on God and away from our binding dysfunction. Today the question of what marriage is–and how committed Christians are to it– is at critical mass in Australia and the United States–and perhaps other nations as well. Would all who honor God on this day pray for the resurrection of authentic marriage in heaven and earth? Would we re-commit to practicing it in the grace of the Lord Christ, with neither malice nor vengeance in our hearts? That would be a two-pronged act of repentance.

Our God provides a road to abundant life. Time has come to be walking it to the exclusion of all others.

SCORE ONE FOR FREEDOM BUT OBAMA'S WAR CONTINUES

The Supreme Court has decked Barack Obama in recent days. They decided by a 5-4 majority that requiring Hobby Lobby and Conestoga Wood Products to provide abortion services–clearly violating their faith–defies the 1993 Religious Freedom Restoration Act (RFRA) and the First Amendment. They likewise declared states and localities may not bar free speech from public walkways in front of abortion clinics–or anywhere. Leftist talk show hosts mock the decision they say permits citizens to nullify federal law. Truth is the decision forbids government to nullify State and Federal Constitutions. Others claim an American launching a business must play by the rules and not by his conscience. Truth is the First Amendment prohibits rules that trump religious conscience. (Standard constitutional understandings permit such rules only in the case of what the courts call a compelling government interest–like forbidding snake handling around children, polygamy, or the amputation of body parts from thieves just because the Koran requires it.) These decisions are a big home run for freedom of faith, albeit decided in a very narrow context; the Hobby Lobby decision applies to "closely held" or–in English–family owned corporations.

This is not a bad thing. Courts traditionally limit their decisions to matters and interests actually brought before them. Future decisions in subsequent cases should follow the line of thinking in the Citizens United case–decided in 2010–so eventually no company will be forced to violate the faith of founders and owners to satisfy a law attacking the Bill of Rights.

The Court uanimously rolled back the Obama appointments to the Federal Labor Relations Board absent senate approval, another score for freedom. The separation of powers doctrine forbids one branch of government to ride roughshod over another; that riding is how dictatorships, monarchies, and caliphates are established. But the president, in a dizzying display of arrogance, simply announces his next bypass of Congress and dares the rest of us to stop him. His war against the nation that gave him all he has continues.

All this was done a year before he dictated the legalization of five million illegal aliens because–as he said–he has a pen and a phone.

The man who would be king announces if Congress will not enact the immigration reform he wants he will continue to bypass them. In other words, although the Supreme Court has told him he is not the supreme law of the land, he declares he will continue to act as though he is. He refers to a range of actions/inactions from declaring amnesty for illegals here long enough to suit him to assassination of American citizens abroad to declining to rescue American citizens being abused in foreign lands. Marine Andrew Tahmoressi was held prisoner in Mexico without presidential comment until public outcry forcing the Mexican government to release him is one example; that one of the murdered Israeli teens that triggered the 2014 Gaza conflict was an American citizen is another He dared Congress to sue him while speaking in the Rose Garden.

The subtext of this presidential bullying is the notion that if no one else will do the right thing he will. His attitude pre-supposes he *is* right and *he alone* is authorized to decide the right. He depends on the reality that challenges to his arrogance take years to percolate through the courts. In a nation of laws none of this will wash; in a culture of entitlement that worships at the altar of feel-good it does. Both left and right have periodically worshipped at that altar; today it happens to be from the left.

What do we do?

Dinesh D'Souza says in his new film, *America*, we do not have a Washington, Lincoln, or Reagan at this time; but we do have us. I would add to that, "We Americans have always had us and we have always had the Lord Jesus Christ, His Abba, and His Spirit–when we acknowledge them. They made Washington, Lincoln and Reagan the heroes they became; they will make us the men and women we are called to become."

Jesus Christ Himself says if His people acknowledge Him He will acknowledge–uphold–them. This implies a continuing commitment to play by the legitimate rules–to not become the travesty we oppose. If this looks like an exercise in futility, I remember an exercise in personal futility some time ago. I was called by God to protest the consecration of an apostate bishop. I knew I would be alone and ridiculed. The rules gave me the right and the responsibility to read a statement; the rule keepers denied me that right. I left the building wondering why God insisted I make such a wasted gesture. I wondered until my statement–unspoken during the service–went virile and rounded the globe on the internet. People still approach me respectfully, saying, "So you're the guy who..."

We are called by our God to stay in this game for the long haul. It is a marathon and not a sprint. And our God says He will never leave us. Do we believe Him? Is there anyone or anything else worth believing?

DRUNK WITH POWER

Toronto Mayor Bob Ford is an alcoholic whose addiction is ruining his career. (He admits he smoked crack during "one of my drunken stupors.") But alcohol is not the only thing on which to get drunk. Former San Diego Mayor Bob Filner got drunk on his own power to abuse scores of women both employed by his administration and simply colleagues he met as he exercised his power. The scandal when his victims finally obtained a hearing eventually forced him from office, admitting all that he had done but denying to the end there was anything wrong with it. In the case of Barack Obama we find a whole administration drunk with power. His attorney general first covers up an arms debacle that costs American lives, then blames a previous president, and finally just stonewalls a congressional committee. His secretary of Health and Human Services tells American citizens she does not work for them. His IRS leadership lies repeatedly about agency persecution of political opponents and the illegal release of confidential materials. And the president himself lies about murder in Benghazi, spying on American citizens, his own involvement in the IRS scandal, and what Obamacare will do to citizens who already have health insurance. If that is not enough, he routinely re-writes legislation such as his signature healthcare law in blatant defiance of the Constitution as cooly as he deliberately mis-quotes the Gettysburg Address to remove references to God. This president is so drunk with power that when the House of Representatives adopts – legally – a bill doing the same things the president illegally decreed to correct his own insurance cancellation nightmare, he threatens to veto the legislation.

No good thing ever comes from drunken-ness and nothing ever will. But the greatest damage comes from being drunk with power.

Intoxification with power – and the vindictiveness that accompanies it – spreads to lower officials and civilians as well. Recently fake blood was spattered on peaceful life advocates in Albuquerque, New Mexico, by so-called pro-choicers. I say "so-called" because these people have no interest in the freedom to choose in – say – an election. AG Eric Holder has no problem with voter intimidation by gangsters in Philadelphia at the same time he accuses legitimate poll watchers of suppressing the vote in that same city, demonstrating his soul brotherhood with the gangsters. (In a city in which multiple precincts cast zero votes for the president's opponent – not one; is that statistically possible – whom would a reasonable person expect to be guilty of vote suppression?) A man was recently arrested for murder after shooting an armed man who broke down his door at 2 AM and charged him. In Washington DC the insurance commissioner was fired by Mayor Vincent Gray for agreeing with a proposal to ask insurance companies to restore cancelled policies, and a low level Obamacare employee named Elaine was fired for answering the questions she is charged with answering when the questioner happened to be talk show host Sean Hannity. Right here in Redding it turns out our own Mercy Hospital helped write the protocols for Obamacare; I learned this because my radio program was sponsored by Mercy. When I blogged against Obamacare Mercy summarily dropped my program with that explanation. It is about intimidating–not debating–opponents.

The Bible has a wonderful passage addressed as Ephesians 5:18. It instructs readers not to become drunk with spirits–including the spirit of power–but rather be filled (drunk, if you will) with the Holy Spirit. Becoming intoxicated–filled–with God is how we come to authentic sobriety. Confirmation occurs as people change behavior–and the fruit of it–sometimes over time but sometimes quite rapidly. The recently concluded Forty Days for Life campaign reports sixty abortion clinics have closed since 2007 as they prayed and blessed outside clinics with appointment cancellations as high as 75% when they are praying; these drunk in the spirit types do nothing more aggressive than prayer. The Rev. Martin Luther King led a civil rights movement for fourteen years–until his martyrdom–fueled by nothing but the Holy Spirit, according to King himself. Former House Majority Leader Tom DeLay personally told me how he remained at peace through seven years of trumped up indictments on perfectly legal behavior, criminal conviction, and eventual acquittal-on-appeal of felony charges. He said he went to Congress not knowing his Lord and became filled with Him while there; he had no other explanation. Like former power broker Chuck Colson, DeLay now knows real power. And he knows not even the halls of government can forever freeze God out.

The Bible also says His strength is perfected (2 Corinthians 12:9) in our weakness. The Christians who took down autocratic governments in the Philippines and throughout Eastern Europe had no resources other than prayer and forgiveness without giving up their convictions. I don't say our present government does or doesn't need taking down. But like King, Colson, and DeLay, I recommend being drunk in God's Spirit. It is the only authentic sobriety, and the only real power.

TOKYO ROSE AND AN ANOINTING FOR INTEGRITY

Iva Toguri is Tokyo Rose to most Americans, our most notorious World War II traitor. Born in America in 1916, she died in America in 2006. She was the victim of one of the most horrific injustices in American history because Harry Truman wanted re-election.

Iva Toguri traveled to Japan in the weeks preceding Pearl Harbor to visit her seriously ill mother. The last ship for the States departed without her on the eve of war and she was stranded in a land in which she had never lived and toward whom she felt no loyalty. The Kempetai – the Japanese secret police – forced her to renounce her American citizenship but permitted her to work for a radio station as a secretary. They later insisted she begin a regular broadcast as Orphan Annie; the nickname Tokyo Rose was bestowed by American servicemen. Toguri did what she could to undermine the Japanese propaganda effort. She read her scripts with tongue-in-cheek, refused much she was told to include, and – by some accounts – managed to pass coded strategic information to American forces. She was promptly arrested by the US Army following the Japanese surrender.

She was held and investigated for a year before the army released her because they found no evidence she betrayed her country. When syndicated columnist Walter Winchell heard of her release he launched a months-long tirade against her and those who were "soft" on traitors. President Harry Truman, fighting an uphill battle for re-election, ordered her re-arrest and transport to the United States – as a stateless person. Her whole political arrest and trial got Winchell off Truman's back and Truman back into the White House. She was convicted of treason in 1949 and sentenced to ten years in prison. The jury was denied access to transcripts of any of her wartime broadcasts. Every witness against her admitted to perjuring themselves years after the trial and the prosecutor committed suicide. She was released in 1956 and President Gerald Ford pardoned her in 1977. She never again saw her husband because he was unable to come to America.

What about her constitutional rights? What about the presumption of innocence and the right to a trial free of government misconduct? Reality is that when the entire weight of a government – even a supposed constitutional government – is hell bent on making a scapegoat there is nothing one or a few can do to stop it. The juggernaut can only be stopped – and reversed – by the application of equal force. That equal force comes about in a democracy only when an informed, alert and relentlessly skeptical public remains on watch and demands integrity from officials – and from a media that is supposedly anointed itself for integrity. There is no room for "growing weary in well doing" as the Bible puts it. There is no room for a "we fought the war; now leave us alone" mindset, because the war for what America stands for is never over until we lose our freedom or King Jesus comes back and His Kingdom comes with Him in power.

But why bring Tokyo Rose up now? Because we are living in a time of public exhaustion now. We live in a time in which Martha Stewart, Scooter Libby, and Congressman Tom DeLay are convicted in federal court not of criminal wrongdoing, but of insisting they were innocent after the government decided they were guilty. In DeLay's case it took seven grand juries to indict; the prosecutor kept impaneling new juries until he got one to say what he wanted to hear. Delay's conviction was thrown out by an appeals court ordering a not-guilty verdict rather than a new trial. But the years lost to these people, and their shattered reputations and careers, are unrecoverable.

The Word of God says when–and only when–we acknowledge Him Who is Truth before men He acknowledges us before His Father, teaching in that very hour what we are to say and do. He says when we seek Him first He will supply all we need in this world and the next.

In practical application that means we are relentless in seeking truth regarding government agendas from Benghazi to IRS persecution to NSA spying and the assaults on the First and Second Amendments. It means we recognize and repudiate the insanity of polls showing 68% of us applaud as good and necessary the revelations of Edward Snowden about the NSA while 56% want him tried for treason. It means we seek an anointing for integrity for ourselves and demand–relentlessly–that persons in power seek it for themselves before prosecuting Snowden for the "crime" of exposing them.

CHAPTER 6:

CHALLENGING THE FAITH OF SCIENTISM WITH AUTHENTIC SCIENCE

God loves and honors science and scientists. When He created our world He recorded it in Genesis as a story told from the point of view of a martyr–Greek for eyewitness–literally a participant observer; this is how He makes it all about His revelation. The creation account is told from the perspective of an observer watching from the surface, which is why the order of events seems off kilter to anyone realizing the earth is one of the later events of the process. But–from its viewpoint–the account is startlingly accurate.

Genesis 1 records the earth as under a great darkness, for example, before God spoke light into existence. Science now knows the earth was covered by light-shuttering clouds in its early days–as Venus is now. The earthbound observer would have experienced the formlessness of the planet and its waters in darkness until God released the cloud cover with His word about light. And we can still take it to the bank that the Big Banger uttered that word about light long before there was a world to release from its own self-produced darkness. Science should have no quarrel with this perspective.

Where science does take issue with revelation one of two things is always true. One is that science has not yet observed and measured what God has already reported–the scientists of one era thought the earth flat, the center of the solar system, and winds moved in wall-front patterns. The truth of a round earth and heliocentricity was never doubted in the Bible and discovered by scientists before Columbus set sail. That winds operate in cyclonic rather than wall front patterns was known only to scripture until the nineteenth century and scientists discovered this to be the method of cleaning the atmosphere much more recently.

The other and more insidious truth is the competing religion I call scientism. There is nothing scientific about scientism. Its adherents claim scientific veracity but believe what they want to believe – must believe – in order to avoid accountability for what they wish to do. California voters approved a six billion dollar bond measure to fund research into the use of embryonic stem cells to cure conditions from Parkinson's Disease to catastrophic brain and spinal injuries. There was never a shred of evidence that such cures were possible then or now; the clergy of scientism – who call themselves scientists and have the credentials to prove it – rationalized their harvest of the victims of elective abortion with the promise these things would come to pass because of the capacity of embryonic cells to morph into other kinds of cells. Yet nothing has ever come of their efforts – nor of human cloning experimentation – but a few products of mutation that quickly died. On the other hand, experimentation in the use of adult stem cells has resulted in more than one hundred successful treatments and the field continues to grow. The only fruit of embryonic research has been wasted billions and desensitization of our culture to the butchery of unborn human beings.

The same silliness is expressed with grim determination by the clergy of evolution. Evolutionary theory turns on the notion that life forms mutate in order to evolve. Yet in nature we have not a single record of a mutation that survived, let alone thrived. And the mathematical odds against the thousands of successful mutations that would be required to assemble an eye capable of vision when each step in that chain would actually reduce chances of survival until the evolutionary chain is complete are beyond imagining.

This chapter celebrates science as it debunks scientism. Essays address real science and real social science. It considers the so-called science behind elective abortion and a feature film touting an old and exhausted evolutionary theory that looks good only with state of the arts special effects. It continues with the truth – the scientific truth – about healthy families, climate change, and intelligent design. It concludes with a plea for all of us – scientists and lay people – to operate out of the courage of our convictions and not from the fear of the prophets of scientism that seeks only to intimidate since it has little to show of reason.

My prayer is that readers will encounter this chapter – and take away from it – a healthy irreverence toward all emperors who have no clothing. Even more

I pray readers will discover something of the wonder of God's revelation. Let us remember that authentic science – including the scientific method – was invented and advanced by Christians from Augustine to Francis Bacon and Sir Isaac Newton. The most exciting scientific work today is being done by faith-filled believers such as Astrophysicist Hugh Ross and others in the faith-filled medical community. Travel to the moon has only convinced most of the astronauts who flew there of what a wonderful universe the Lord has created and what a wonderful way – science – He has given us for its discovery.

REAL SCIENCE AND REAL LIFE: SCIENCE VERSUS SCIENTISM

A famous line from the original, *The Day the Earth Stood Still*, is uttered by Professor Barnhart, the scientist and voice of human reason. "We scientists are not always listened to." Scientists ought to be respected and obeyed when they function as scientists and ignored when they function as clergy. This is the difference between science and the religion called scientism. One deals with facts and realities; the other simply worships false gods.

Facts and realities are what they are. Mankind does not navigate to the moon, or circumnavigate the globe in ships, or cure diseases and build roads and bridges, without the blessing of hard science. There is this thing called the Scientific Method–invented by people of Christian faith–that sets parameters for accurate and reliable perception of scientific truth. When scientists follow their own rules the rest of us are blessed. When they step outside their own structure out of a need to believe this or that the rest of us are assaulted with mythology at best and harmful practice at worst.

The dichotomy is not between science and faith, but between science and the false faith of scientism. The Bible is not a science textbook, but when it speaks in opposition to scientism it has never been wrong. For example, the secular community first posited a flat earth and wall front patterns of terrestrial winds–the one until the fifteenth century and the other into the mid nineteenth century. (The Church, to its discredit, bought these myths for a time.) But the Bible describes a round world and a cyclonic pattern of wind action that actually cleanses the atmosphere; a view now universally accepted because it is true. Facts are facts. Reality is reality–whatever the source.

There has been tremendous controversy in California over allegations from scientists that pumping water from the Sacramento River into thirsty Central Valley farmlands threatens the delta smelt. Reality is that non-native striped bass are the biggest killer of the smelt, and even the courts see this now. Environmentalists and scientists got it wrong when they attacked and permanently crippled the NorCal logging industry to protect the spotted owl, a non-native species–versus the native barn owl–and which the clergy of scientism now want to attack directly because they see its resurgence as a threat to their spotted owl. And the medical orthodoxy of the forties and fifties was that a scientific formula was better for infants than mothers' milk until they actually analyzed human breast milk and found it exponentially healthier for human babies. Who knew?

We can see the same disastrous consequences from faithful adherence to the mythical promises of embryonic stem cell research as literally billions of dollars were diverted from the actual promise of adult stem cells–which even now boast some one hundred different successful therapies against zero for the embryonic prophets. One can only speculate how much farther along real science might be if facts governed decisions from the beginning.

The front page news a few weeks ago was about climate scientists' efforts to convince an increasingly skeptical world that climate change is a reality–and man-caused–in the face of no rise in temperature for over a decade. Of course the politically correct line is that this is a wrinkle in a trend known since 1951, but the really inconvenient truth is that the climate community was predicting a new ice age from the fifties into the nineties. Even more inconvenient is the fact that Greenland was a good deal warmer just a thousand years ago than it is today. Climate–like wind–operates in cycles that have nothing to do with human activity. One can only speculate about how much human life could have been improved in the past two decades if scientists spent their time doing science instead of seeking grant money and power through prophesying climate hysteria and punishing their colleagues who dissented from it.

But the real responsibility does belong to the Body of Christ. For too many decades we have gone along in order to get along. We have resisted accountability to God and to His Word ourselves. We have pursued our own private concerns and programs rather than risk ridicule and opposition in the public square. We have called our faith a private affair–finding God only in politically correct gaps in so-called knowledge–which is just what the practitioners of scientism demand. God's call to repentance is indeed about the positive re-focus of our attention on Him. But we have an urgent need to clear our own decks before re-setting our course toward His Kingdom.

REAL SOCIAL SCIENCE IS STILL SCIENCE VERSUS SCIENTISM

If we believe the conventional wisdom touted by most social scientists today, Attention Deficit (Hyperactive) Disorder is endemic to our culture. If a boy shows any aggressive tendencies – which are often difficult to distinguish from initiative and/or a sense of adventure – we medicate him in order to control his behavior. We recognize AD(H)D as a disability in adults and expect employers to walk softly. The trouble is that under such circumstances the man (or woman) concerned has scant incentive to adjust his behavior to compensate for the challenges of his condition – or to explore the special blessings that go along with it.

The symptoms of ADD are easy distractibility, difficulty staying on task, and poor impulse control. Add the H – for hyperactive – and you have a person with difficulty sitting still and paying attention to the teacher while simultaneously messing with his neighbor. The blessings are enhanced creativity, an ability to see the world globally, and a love of thinking and acting outside the box. If Steve Jobs was not ADD, neither am I – and believe me, I am. Instead of depending on medication that suppresses symptoms, and the creativity gifted with them, we learned to compensate for the symptoms and enjoy the blessings. We did not believe the propaganda – because it was based on conjecture rather than research within the scientific method – that ADD vanishes in adulthood; it does not. We did not accept the conclusion – based solely on frustrated parents, teachers and doctors – that it was a deal breaker for success; it is not. Famous people with ADD include Albert Einstein, Bill Gates, Walt Disney, Michael Jordan, Tom Cruise, Bill Cosby, Whoopi Goldberg, and Babe Ruth.

If physical science must be based on facts and realities so as not to stray into the land of fables that is scientism, it is that much more necessary to live in the real world when we promulgate social science principles. The consequences of delusional thinking can be catastrophic for the multitudes affected by it.

California has adopted several laws in the recent past that do great damage in their pursuit of the false faith of social scientism. Assembly Bill 777 and Senate Bill 48 – both enacted into law in California – require that homosexuality be treated as a normal condition in public school curricula at all levels, and that social science curricula lionize figures like politician Harvey Milk and composer Aaron Copeland, even though Milk was a minor local leader and Copeland was (in all probability) not homosexual at all. Yet research trends indicate the condition is primarily a result of childhood trauma and/or dysfunctional relationship with same gender parents. The Kinsey Report – based on skewed samples and falsified data – has been debunked for decades. The doctor who removed homosexuality from the list of psychiatric disorders says he was wrong and geneticists deny any biological basis for it.

Senate Bill 1172–California law–forbids therapists to assist young people reporting gender confusion and seeking help. These laws attack academic and professional freedoms guaranteed in the Constitution at the same time they paint a false picture that therapy given upon request is abusive to victims battling social stigmata surrounding their sexuality–refusing it is the real abuse. While it is true that much research remains to be done on the topic of healing for homosexuality, the evidence gathered so far indicates cure rates about equal to those for chemical dependencies and there is no evidence whatever that this therapy is harmful to those receiving it voluntarily.

Assembly Bill 1266 mandates that gender confused children may use the restroom or locker room that corresponds to their gender identity at any particular time. (This law–along with the No-therapy-Law–remain under court challenge.) The rationale is that transgendered children have been traumatized by school bullies and that freedom of restrooms will ease their pain. But existing research shows them among the least likely to be bullied. The record is that accommodation does nothing to ease their pain. Although no studies exist to document the damage done normal children forced to share facilities, abundant anecdotes of humiliation and bullying–of the overwhelming majority of the population–should be self-convicting. Science shows transgendered people are a small fraction of the less-than-two-per-cent who declare themselves homosexual. Once again blind adherence to the pseudo faith of scientism can only damage gay and straight, adult and child.

But responsibility still rests with the Church. Nearly nine of ten Americans claim Christ. Most favor life, marriage, and science. Yet when our values and viewpoint are attacked with fraudulent claims we wring our hands instead of doing our homework and expressing truth. It is time to step up; there are too many of us to ignore and too much at stake.

INTERSTELLAR: HOW TO DISCONNECT FROM REALITY

When I was an undergrad at San Diego State my roommate and I went for a walk one evening. A strikingly beautiful woman approached us; she passed within a foot or two of us and only then did we realize she was actually a man–a female impersonator. My roomie stared at his passing and intoned, "Well, it's quite an accomplishment...but nothing to be proud of."

He could have meant the recently released film, *Interstellar*.

Lavishly photographed; well written, acted, directed and produced, and with special effects creating a spectacle and simultaneous microcosm of the universe beyond anything I have seen before, this epic is an incredible achievement. From a cinematic viewpoint it is awe inspiring. It also features more plot holes than a swiss cheese. Astronomically gargantuan plot holes gape from the screen. One depicts a man, protected only by a space suit, successfully transiting a black hole–a celestial phenomenon featuring gravity so intense it crushes stars and even light itself–hence the name. Another places the man inside a tesseract–a geometric form not found in nature–from which he shares mathematical equations that enable intergalactic colonization with his daughter across time so she can teach him when he is a young man before leaving earth. Later the tesseract squirts him back to home and his daughter–now fifty years older than he; it just happens. A movie bursting with such magical thinking is impossible for this cowboy to see as anything but conceptual rubbish.

But some will say this is all covered by Einstein's Theory of Relativity. Don't mention it to Einstein unless you really want to offend him. Others will cite the new and "innovative" theories of Astrophysicist Kip Thorne as rationale for what the film dramatizes. This too is rubbish.

Albert Einstein defined insanity as doing the same thing again and again while expecting a different result. The producers of *Interstellar*–and especially Executive Producer–the very same–Kip Thorne should take note. His theories are about as new as propeller driven aircraft. They are a rehash of a sub theory of evolution that says if there are enough universes or dimensions or timelines–take your pick–the mathematical impossibilities in the notion of creation by random chance are eliminated. The theory stubs its toes against first causation, as do all its brother and sister theories. The Big Bang doesn't help; it implies a Big Banger and we know Who that is. But if Thorne and his friends dress it up with enough stirring music and compelling visual presentation they appear to think they can sell what the physics community rejected many decades ago.

The plot of Interstellar begins with earth in apocalypse – but God is nowhere in it. An un-named blight destroys a different food crop each year and the dust storms make the Dust Bowl of the 1930s look like a Sunday picnic. The air is going bad and Mankind will perish within a generation unless we can re-locate to another planet – at least some of us. Farmer and former astronaut Cooper – who never reached space (Matthew McConaughey) – conveniently stumbles into a top-secret NASA facility just down the road. He re-connects with Professor Brand (Michael Caine), who recruits him to command an expedition for which he has not trained through a newly discovered worm hole – into which astronauts were sent ten years back to discover an earth-like planet in another galaxy. Brand tells Coop a million people can be saved – including his family – if he goes, although he might never return. Brand is lying; he doesn't have the equations to construct the rescue; he can only send thousands of frozen embryos. He excuses his dishonesty by favoring species over persons. Coop discovers the deception and attempts to return to Earth, but is caught in the black hole and learns that the ghosts who communicated with his daughter when she was ten are really his own future self signaling from inside the tesseract.

What it boils down to – they keep repeating that it is all about evolution – including future anticipated evolution – is Coop eventually discovers we – the collective we – are God. The film is simply another attempt to evade accountability of any kind to a real God – that is the rub for atheists who, like alcohol addicts, need people to approve and perhaps share their dysfunction. It's the warmed over Buddhist, Hindu, and Taoist philosophy – dressed in cinematic splendor – I outgrew as an undergrad. It is ultimately mega manipulative. I don't like manipulation; I do prefer the really real. His name is Yahweh, His Son is Jesus, and His Spirit is the manifestation of His love on earth.

CREATION VERSUS CHANCE IN CONVERSATION

At the ripe old age of thirteen I spent a dream week at the Emerald Bay Boy Scout summer camp on Santa Catalina Island. My helmet diving adventure was the high point. We lived out my favorite cinematic fantasy–*20,000 Leagues Under the Sea*–with a working deep sea diving helmet–our swim trunks and tennies made the rest of the dive outfit–and a guy on the raft above pumped oxygen into our helmets while we walked the floor of the bay some twenty feet down. I was chosen to go first and was having the adventure of a lifetime when I noticed the air was stuffy enough to move me to pull the lifeline. When I surfaced the guys were laughing. The airhose had broken loose and floated to the surface. The divemaster said, "Should we tell him?" before assuring them I had at least thirty minutes' air already trapped in the helmet and we were only allowed a fifteen minute dive.

My question–then and now? If I had plenty of good air independent of outside supply, why was that air so stuffy I called for help? If life is independent of the Lifegiver why are we born trailing an umbilical?

Michael Crichton–the novelist–is my favorite writer who believes in evolution. I enjoy him for more than the spell-binding storytelling for which he is justly famous. He is an honest evolutionist–passionately committed to his point of view without being either shy or defensive about addressing the obvious–to anyone–flaws in the theory. For example, in *The Lost World*, he acknowledges what creationists have pointed out for years about irreducible complexity. He says there is simply no way that random chance can account for all of the mutations needed to occur in a coordinated manner to account for the development of visual organs. He writes–on page 310–"a single fertilized egg has one hundred thousand genes...switching on and off at specific times to transform that cell into a complete living creature...Just when the organism needs a circulatory system, the heart starts pumping. Just when hormones are needed, the adrenals start to make them...It's incredible." He adds that there is no way to randomly assemble a working machine from the parts in a junkyard, yet he stands his ground as an evolutionist.

The character–Malcolm–functioning as the voice of reason still rules out creation–as even a participant in the conversation, because he deems it impossible. Then he posits a combination of crystallization and self-organizing behavior as subjects (although not conclusions) for conversation. Crichton overlooks the reality that crystallization must have a cause beyond chance, and that terms like self-organizing–applied to animal behavior–are oxymorons. But he does stick to his story, and his honesty–as far as it goes–only adds to the enjoyment of the story.

Laminem is a protein molecule so small it cannot be seen without an electron microscope. It is found only in the shape of a cross and it literally holds organs, skin, bone and tissue together; that's why it is called an adhesion molecule. It paraphrases the Word of God found in Colossians 1:17, that "In Him all things hold together," which was written two millennia before the electron microscope was invented. What are the odds?

The Wild Horse Nebula is more than thirty million light years from earth and invisible to even the largest terrestrial telescopes. It became visible only when the Hubble Telescope was orbited beyond the atmosphere. Inside the nebula is a black hole millions of miles across and shaped like–you guessed it–a cross. It confirms Psalms 19:1, that, "The heavens declare the glory of God," written three millennia earlier. And, by the way, had some ancient civilization orbited a Hubble the nebula would have remained invisible to it because the universe had not yet expanded enough to provide sufficient contrast between light and darkness to reveal it. What are the odds?

Occam's Razor is a philosophical construct that pre-dates Christianity by centuries and says–simply–that the simplest explanation for a phenomenon is likely the correct one. The simplest explanation for life functioning as well and in as coordinated a manner as it does is that it is Someone's idea presented as a gift to the rest of us. Random chance is so complex as to be inconceivable, even for an honest evolutionist. A combination of crystallization and "self-organizing" behavior really doesn't fare much better. I choose to believe life is a gift–and to do my best to worship, obey, and proclaim the Giver. That's my story and I'm sticking to it.

LIFE AND DEATH IN THE BACK ALLEY

One of the principal arguments for legalizing abortion was that it would eliminate injury or death for desperate women driven to back alleys and amateurs for their abortions. In fact the statistics are virtually unchanged since Roe v. Wade; organizations such as Planned Parenthood have made it so difficult to monitor safety conditions and the numbers of incompetent doctors staffing facilities has seen to that. But those stats will change now that Governor Brown has signed new legislation regulating abortions. SB623 was originally created to regulate the boating industry. Amendments and deletions have recreated it to permit abortions to be performed by non-physicians – what we used to call back alley practitioners.

Allegedly the law releases restrictions on a government funded program operated by UC San Francisco to train midwives, nurse practitioners, and physician assistants to perform abortions. The training is co-sponsored by Planned Parenthood and has brought in nearly four million dollars – from the state – with another three and a half million promised. It is justified on the grounds that there are not enough doctors to meet the demand for abortion in the state. Unmentioned is the fact that more and more doctors refuse to perform abortions on grounds of an awakened conscience. Downplayed is the fact that Planned Parenthood and the university refuses requests for independent review of patient files (with identities safeguarded, of course) or even information on how many have received this training. Reality is the old fashioned back alley practitioners had as much training as these folks get, and the same secrecy. Reality is that only doctors of veterinary medicine can abort your pets but anyone who has undergone this program can abort your daughter.

Naturally – before he signed it – I was hoping and praying the governor would be inundated with requests to veto this barbaric bill. But I hope and pray for more than that now that the bill has become law. I ask the Lord our God – and people of good will across the state – to finally engage in a meaningful dialogue about issues of life and death in California. For the record I have been seeking and waiting for such a dialogue – one centered on when human life begins and the social, legal and cultural ramifications of that for thirty years. Without exception I have been told by the other side that they don't want to talk to a troglodyte such as myself, wait my turn while the other side tells its story – my turn has not come in the past three decades – or, yes, we want to talk and we'll call you – but the phone never rings. My personal opinion is that all the evidence – medical and otherwise – points to human life beginning at conception, but I would love to see someone actually challenge my viewpoint instead of just insulting me for holding it.

The spiritual jury is in–and that is indisputable. The Bible is shot through and through with God's attitude toward everybody–including all babies and all mothers–from 2 Peter 3:9's assertion that none should perish to Jesus' own declaration in John 10:10 that He came that all might have life and have it abundantly. In Luke 1 the baby John the Baptist leaps in his mother's womb at the entrance of a Mary pregnant with Jesus, so demonstrating the biblical view that pre-born children are capable of human relationships that spring only from human personhood. (Science has confirmed this repeatedly.) The Christian movement was unique in demanding that the Roman and Greek cultures in which it grew would hereafter respect pre-born human life. (Jews shared this pro-life attitude but did not challenge Greeks or Romans with it.) This respect for life became a hallmark of western civilization that saw no serious challenges until I was a teenager.

I do want to see our state enter into serious dialogue about the arguments for and against being the national leader in providing abortions. I want to know why we perform a quarter of the abortions in America while accounting for a tenth of the population, and I want to know why taxpayers fund thirty thousand of them regardless of the conscientious objections so many of us hold. And yes, I want the mothers who genuinely fear a crisis pregnancy to be given assurance that all of us are willing to be of help and without judgment. But for starters I will be happy if the state's lawmakers reverse this bill so that these mothers are not sent back to the back alleys. Let the governor sign that one.

HEARTS OF THE FATHERS

The Pew Research Center study released just in time for Fathers' Day contains both good and challenging news. The good news is that fathers in traditional families spend 250% of the time they spent with their kids in 1960. The challenge is that those in nuclear families are below fifty percent of American households. The good news is that men who have chosen to make and keep a commitment to family are doing just that. The better news is that–in repeated studies dating from the Reagan through Clinton years–their kids are less likely to become involved in crime, drugs, poverty, and broken families themselves. They are more likely to enjoy success in many dimensions of that concept. The bigger challenge is that fewer men seem willing or able to make that commitment in the first place, and the consequences of non-commitment are just as well documented.

The study knocks a few stereotypes into a cocked hat. One secular myth is that the more educated a person the less likely he will hold traditional values. But the reverse is true. From within the fairly narrow parameters of the study it is revealed that only 13% of college educated men are siring children out of wedlock. The figure climbs to 51% for the high school-only educated, and to 65% for school dropouts. Three quarters of fathers aged twenty to twenty-four have children out of wedlock while that percentage drops to 36% for those aged thirty-five to forty-four. (Well, DUH! If you are a father under twenty-five in this culture you are probably not married!) Another secular myth is that most people know how other people are thinking and behaving. Yet this study shows the public about evenly split between thinking the average dad is more or less involved with his kids than in the previous generation. We need to get out more and discover everybody is not just like us–on both sides of the equation.

Traditional biblical families–at least in paradigm–really are the best equipped to produce healthy, productive, and well socialized children and adults. Studies of co-habiting before marriage were conducted at the Universities of Wisconsin, Houston, and others twenty-plus years ago. In near identical results they demonstrated the risk of divorce or termination of relationship in couples who co-habited before marriage was four times that of couples who lived together first as husband and wife. Meanwhile multiple studies authored by liberals and conservatives from that era and earlier made it proverbial that the best way to avoid poverty and crime, and assure healthy social adjustment, academic success, and prosperity in children was for their parents to marry before their birth.

Don't get me wrong; the Bible is full of dysfunctional families. David is no paragon of parental integrity after the rape of his daughter, Tamar, by one of his sons. On top of that the King of Israel is a polygamist who has one of his best friends killed because he lusts after the man's wife. But the model held up in scripture and commended by God is both consistent and insistent that a man should leave his father and mother and cleave to his wife (Genesis 2:24 and Mark 10:6-9) that they may become one flesh. The Lord commends the permanence of the marriage covenant in Malachi 2:14-15 and again – through Jesus – in Matthew 19:7-9. The formula for a happy marriage grounded in mutual sacrifice expressed in Ephesians 5:21-33 is just as foundational for covenant living between God and mankind. The measure of the Word of God has never been how well we measure up to it, but how consistently God adheres to it when He speaks. But things really do go a lot better when we aim at the target instead of at whatever we would like to believe is better.

As marksmen say, aim small and miss small – aim at the target and expect to hit somewhere near it. On the other hand, aim at nothing and expect to hit it every time.

We live in a season dedicated by the Lord – in the words of Luke 1:17 – to turning the hearts of the fathers to the children prior to His return – whenever that may be. Not everyone is able to live in a nuclear family, and there should be no judgment on those who don't – whether the cause is divorce, widowhood, or poor decisions – whether fault or no fault. But our culture is clearly poised to recover to its roots, and just as ready to keep doing what it has done the past half century while expecting a different result. It is up to us with eyes to see to cheer, facilitate, and choose the culture of life that is our birthright if we will receive it. King David turned to God and so can we.

OF SUCH IS THE KINGDOM

(Author note: This post appeared in late 2014. The bill discussed below was expected to pass with a wide margin by political insiders. It failed after a massive prayer effort as legislative committee members who had dismissed testimony about its dangers to children did an about-face, began listening to witnesses–and said as much.)

The Yuba College Faculty for early childhood education is staunchly opposing a bill making its way through the state legislature with so little noise one can wonder what all the silence is about. The bill is Senate Bill 837 and it forces four-year-olds around the state out of state funded pre-schools into so-called transitional kindergartens. It increases class sizes and expels their former teachers unless they hold a state teaching credential. The problem is these teachers have degrees in Early Childhood Education while most credentialed kindergarten teachers lack any training in ECE. That means college professors with doctorates would be unable to work except as an aide. But it also means jobs and union dues for unionized teachers in the push to monopolize our schools.

Although I have no proof, the old looks-like-a-duck-and-quacks like one school of thought indicates the silence is about unions scratching political backs and vice versa. But whatever the reasons, this bill is a bad bargain for kids and families. And–like so many state policies–it works by coercion where it cannot work through persuasion.

Early Childhood Education longitudinal research began in the 1960s with Project Head Start and the Perry Preschool Project. More than half a century of solid data backs the concepts and methods of ECE. SB 837 falsely states this research supports the transitional kindergarten model; in fact this model did not exist until quite recently and has never been tested. It is a whole different approach to educating young children, but its methods and models already appear to contradict the findings of ECE programs over the years. The evidence–the science–supports Early Childhood Education and its methods, not Transitional Kindergarten.

837 places four-year-olds in classrooms with five and six-year-olds, and on campuses with children more than twice their age. By and large they are not ready for such interactions on a large scale, and these interactions will be largely unsupervised; there are just too many kids on a campus and too few teachers to watch all of them, the bullies and their victims. Early Childhood Education

schools operate under safety regulations that are neither present nor feasible in large elementary schools.

The children will be forced into learning modalities that are appropriate for grade school students but harmful to pre-schoolers. And their natural energies can virtually guarantee many will be labeled ADHD and put on heavy psychotropic drugs like Ritalin, or equally inappropriate medications like Strattera. The latter is intended only for children six or older and its most prominent side effects are suicidal thoughts and serious liver damage–in that order. Yet it is well known that schools and doctors are increasingly willing to drug the child who is too much in motion rather than attempting to deal with him in an age and learning-style appropriate way. This is an epidemic in our present culture.

Perhaps the worst feature of this bill is that it denies parents the chance to choose ECE for their children, a choice they have been able to take for granted up until now. These parents will be forced to place their children in the care of teachers who are credentialed, but completely untrained and unqualified for the children they will be asked to teach. Let me stress, not one unit of early childhood education training is required for a credential that includes kindergarten. But those trained in ECE and lacking state teacher credentials will simply find themselves unemployed if this bill passes. Meanwhile California parents and their children will once again be expected to bow and suffer at the altar of one size fits all. The value added horror is that if this thing goes forward in California it will soon be the pattern for the nation; that is the national trend for the past half century and more.

The bad news is the unions will be the big winners. More jobs and more educators will come under their control.

The good news is just what Jesus famously says about the little children being the stuff of the Kingdom of Heaven, as He recommends we become more like them instead of insisting they become more like us. He is not saying children are smarter or more socially advanced than adults. But they are more simply and more purely the persons they are, without masks and layers of dysfunction to hide behind. Defeating this bill makes a chance to leave the children to develop along more natural lines than crowded classrooms and hard drugs can ever permit. This posting will come out too late for the vote in the senate; contact your assembly member to voice your concern. Then spend some time playing with your children.

GLOBAL WARMING–STILL CRAZY AFTER ALL THESE YEARS

(Note: Newly elected President of California's State Senate Kevin DeLeon declared in his first speech his top priority–leading the fight against climate change.)

What do you call it if you mix documented facts like no–none, nada–increase in the average surface temperature of the earth in the past eighteen years, or the reality that there has been no loss of Arctic ice in eight years while Antarctic ice covers more ground than it has in forty, with environmentalists like Al Gore? With apologies to Paul Simon–still crazy after all these years.

The University of Illinois' Polar Ice Research Center found Arctic ice stopped losing ground between 2005 and 2006. They report Antarctic ice grows–compensating for any loss–as it has for decades. Patrick Michaels directs the Cato Institute's Center for the Study of Science. Their research shows global warming stopped in the mid nineties, about a decade before Gore and friends boarded a train already out of track.

In the midst of hysterical demonstrations–the People's Climate March recently paraded through two thousand worldwide locations–more and more scientists recognize they bet on the wrong horse. Dr. Steven Koonin was Barack Obama's undersecretary for science in the Department of Energy before publishing a Page One story in the Wall Street Journal's Weekend Review on the topic. He says climate science and conclusions about global warming are anything but settled from his new position as director of the Center for Urban Science and Progress at New York University. He warns the prevailing groupthink–his term–achieves nothing but the stifling of serious discussions leading to rational policy decisions. Koonin notes the repeated claims of consensus on the subject, but says there is just no such thing. He adds, "The climate has always changed and always will."

Koonin happens to believe, by the way, that human action does influence climate, although he does not call it the principal dynamic in change. In fact, he maintains, human action can at most cause shifts of one to two per cent. And he admits that while human contributions to carbon dioxide levels have risen by twenty-five per cent in this century the surface temperature is not increasing–as the computer models worshipped by the Gore school say it must. He acknowledges the shift–from Arctic to Antarctic regions–rather than a net reduction in ice mass, as well as the fact sea levels are not rising any faster today–if at all–than they did prior to 1950. And then we get to John L. Casey, President of the Space and Science Research Corporation and former White House national space policy adviser.

Casey goes a lot farther than Koonin. In his book, Dark Winter, he calls the climate change hysteria "the greatest scientific fraud in history." He contends the sun – a far more potent influence on climate than any human action – has entered a cyclical period of "solar hibernation' that will alter climate within the next two decades. He does not call it a coming ice age, but he says global crop damage will come and we are totally unprepared for it. Why? Because the politics – not the science – is all about warming and how much government should restrict human free enterprise in order to combat something we did not cause and cannot hope to control. We can only – if we are crazy enough – control one another right back into a human caused stone age.

Casey points out that science in the former Soviet Union is far more open to free inquiry and experimental verification – wherever the results lead the discussion – than is the United States today.

Some will ask how our president does not know of these findings coming from his own present and former advisers. Why does he keep making speeches to international bodies claiming human caused climate change is the foremost danger in the world today? Perhaps a president who misses three in five of his national security briefings is just as inattentive to his science briefings.

And the polar bears headed for extinction due to human excesses? Their numbers have increased by about twenty-five per cent in recent years.

The good news is that there is a God Who not only creates this world but lovingly maintains it and calls us into partnership with Him. There is no Biblical excuse for wanton pollution or irresponsible use of resources. Scripture says the heavens themselves declare God's glory; a house build outside this revelation cannot stand. The Son of God tells us to let our yes be yes and our no be no. Only with honesty and humility can we discover and act on truth, and that always leads to good decisions for living. The only alternative is to remain crazy. And deadly.

A LONG TIME AGO IN A GALAXY FAR FAR AWAY

It is now a decade since the Body of Christ lost a battle in Pennsylvania–a battle that made headlines all over the country–a battle that was lost before the first reporter asked the first question of the first source–and long before the federal judge issued the ruling that is regarded as a black eye for the proponents of intelligent design.

The school board in Dover, Pennsylvania, issued a policy in 2004 that required science teachers to read a statement before teaching on the origins of life to the effect that evolution as a theory had more holes in it than a swiss cheese and that a theory called intelligent design offered an alternative way of looking at things. Teachers were then forbidden to mention alternatives to evolution following that preliminary statement, although students were encouraged to do their own research and were provided with information on alternative textbooks if they wished to follow through on seeking multiple explanations for the origins of life. The school board was voted out of office by the people of Dover before the case ever came to trial, and the judge ruled that their policy constituted an "inanity" that amounted to a thinly disguised injection of illegalized religion into science instruction. The judge pointedly declined to consider the truth claims of intelligent design; his scathing prohibition on its mention in public school classrooms was grounded solely in what he called its religious origins.

I maintain that the Body lost the battle long before the judge issued his ruling because we chose the wrong issue on the wrong battlefield. Even the most arrogant of courts will not seek to rule on something so far outside their expertise as "where it all comes from" in the world. They will only rule on whether or not a given theory or body of work can be legitimately introduced into a publicly funded school system. The expert testimony on the veracity of intelligent design has merit in such a case only as a secondary issue to the question of whether or not local school boards are entitled to establish curriculum that meets scientific muster as well as evolution. An even more fundamental issue is that of academic freedom for teachers–are teachers credentialed by the state free to teach what their research and training tells them to be rationally verifiable concepts and precepts–or are only those viewpoints acceptable to a court permitted as acceptable speech? The case should have been decided solely on the constitutional rights to free speech and local control of the defendants–rights which were trampled upon by the court in Pennsylvania.

The issue here is not whether either intelligent design or evolution is a theory that can hold its own against reality checks. Reality is that every critique of intelligent design put forward by the judge–that it cannot be experimentally verified, that it does not account for extinction of species, that it leaves great gaps in terms of the age of the universe and that there are other ambiguities–is even more a feature of the theory of evolution. The so-called scientific view of creation has never produced a shred of experimental evidence–which would have to amount to observed instances of evolution–and it cannot account for the transitional species it posits because none has ever been discovered. Its hypotheses on extinction of species are revised on a regular basis and are never subject to laboratory verification. It posits a fairly consistent age of the universe by simply backdating from its own assumptions on just how long it would take for worlds and species to evolve. It cannot make up its own mind on such basic topics as whether or not dinosaurs are related to birds or reptiles and even on whether the brontosaurus ever existed. Reality is that it requires a lot more faith to believe in evolution than to accept a theory of intelligent design–but this is not and never was the reason for the controversy.

The controversy remains a pitting of those who respect and practice science against those who are faithful adherents of the religion of scientism. In the latter faith and a need to believe a theory of "it all" that requires no accountability on the part of the believer trump evidence for a Designer Who claims we belong to the One Who Creates us and really ought to–as they say–dance with the one what brung ya. The obsession with not being accountable to an authority greater than man drives some to be as fanciful as George Lucas when he began the Star Wars saga with, "A long time ago, in a galaxy far far away…"

One of my favorite memories is of a friend of mine who has a doctorate and believes in evolution. It is one of his missions in life to convince me I am foolish to believe my God made everything. One day exploring some buildings dating to colonial times he pounced. "Do you believe there was ever such an animal as eohippus?" he asked. I said I did; we have their fossils. "Well," he continued, "everybody knows eohippus is the first horse. He evolved into the modern horse over millions of years."

"Have you conducted DNA testing?" I asked. "Does eohippus have horse DNA?" He was appalled at my unfairness; nobody can obtain DNA from fossilized prehistoric animals. He repeated that everybody agrees eohippus evolved into horses. "You tell me you can prove evolution through this forerunner of a horse, but without DNA you cannot prove this little guy is even related to the horse," I said. "Fact is, eohippus looks more like a fox than a horse; he has no hooves, and his legs are of such disparate lengths from front to back that he bounces like a pig instead of running like a horse." I ended with a question, "What have you got besides bones resembling tiny horse bones and speculations from generations of paleontologists? What science have you got?"

Reality is my bones resemble pig bones as much as eohippus bones resemble those of a horse. Yet nobody imagines I evolved from a pig except people offended at my unbelief concerning evolution. Reality is without DNA I cannot pass a paternity test for my children but wealthy and powerful people can demand we scratch the idea of a Creator without DNA evidence.

Don't get me wrong. Science is a great gift; it is a double gift having content–things observed in patterns of activity and therefore known to and how existing–and structure, the structure we call scientific method for learning by experimentation. Praise God for the men and women who devote themselves to scientific disciplines–with discipline being the operant word. When we discipline our minds to accept what can be proven, to hold in tension what has not yet been demonstrated, and to let go of what simply does not emerge from facts in evidence–no matter how much we want or need to believe them–we are practicing science. When men and women with a lot of letters after their surname ask to be believed not for the evidence they present but for those letters following their name there is nothing scientific occurring. Such people are simply the mullahs of materialism.

The Wild Horse Nebula is about thirty million light years from earth, so distant it was only discovered after we orbited the Hubble Telescope. Within the nebula is a black hole about four million miles across. It is shaped like a cross. Psalms 19:1 states, "The heavens declare the glory of God". These facts–astronomical and scriptural–are verified observations and thus science. The laminem molecule is what we call an adhesion protein. So tiny it can only be seen through an electron microscope, it literally binds the cells in our body together. It is the catalyst that makes a body possible. Colossians 1:17 declares, "In Him (Jesus) all things hold together." The laminem molecule is shaped like a cross. Again these facts are observed–the molecule and its description and the corresponding Biblical declaration. This is science.

Where it gets dicey is in the conclusions. Have I just proved beyond doubt that an all-powerful God designed the Wild Horse Nebula and the laminem molecule, planting those verses in the Bible so we get His point? Actually, no. There is nothing compelling–although it looks, quacks and walks like a duck–about the connection between scripture and these celestial/physiological phenomena. I have no need to compel belief, nor to stifle debate. (Unlike the evolutionists who go to court to ensure Creationist-believing teachers cannot speak to impressionable children on school campuses.) But I would rather take my chances in honest and spirited debate than to rely on the arrogance of those who think themselves above scientific proof for their positions. DNA anyone?

Evolution offers precisely what George Lucas presented in *Star Wars*, an impersonal and unloving force holding us and ours together without expecting us to love and obey. God offers Himself, and His Son Who comes that we might have His life and love abundantly. He is not afraid to take His chances in the marketplace of ideas. The question becomes whether we want the really real, or a fantasy that begins, "A long time ago, in a galaxy far far away…"

NEEDED: THE COURAGE OF CONVICTION

It is mega predictable in today's political climate. Every time new research demonstrates increasing support for pro life convictions in the US–such as a recent Gallup Poll–someone claiming to be a peacemaker goes public with a plea for all of us to play nicely together and go silent on those pesky and divisive social issues such as abortion. The Gallup poll shows just shy of 60% of Americans now want elective abortion eliminated altogether or restricted to cases of rape or incest. (If law were changed to reflect that reality the numbers of abortions would be small fractions of current totals.) More than 70% want abortions of convenience prohibited, and nearly 80% oppose public funding of abortion–like the three hundred sixty million dollars that subsidize Planned Parenthood clinics without directly paying the doctors. Now that such clear majorities of all Americans take conservative positions on abortion–and other social issues in many cases as well–California Republican donor and activist Charles Munger is waging war to force the state Republican Party platform to delete clauses addressing them. He says the GOP can only win elections with a more nuanced position–read silence–on them.

He and the political establishment see their views as science–political science.

The trouble is that when majorities of Americans saw themselves as pro-choice the cry was for the pro-life minority to sit back and honor the rule of the majority. Now that the majority has shifted in a pro-life direction these same folks want the majority to stifle itself in the interest of unity around the economic and infrastructure issues they see as more winnable in that silence over the pre-born baby holocaust. They want most of us to look at the big picture, take the long view, and bring in a government that ignores the issues that split us apart as a people. But former California Republican Assembly President Mike Spence says the passion is in the social issues, such as abortion. "No one's ever walked a precinct because of above-ground water storage issues. Core issues are what motivates our base and our volunteers," according to Spence. He thinks Munger and his ilk naïve at best. I think we can respect the will of the majority or try to change it by prayer and debate. But we do not tell the majority to silently make way for the will of the minority.

There is a fundamental issue of perspective that is even more basic when applied to candidates by voters. Should we be one-issue voters who only care about whether an elected official would vote to fund Planned Parenthood when he becomes an elected official? Of course not; there are many issues before our legislative bodies both state and national. A single litmus test is short sighted at best. But the other side of the coin is that pro-abortion people tend to have a worldview that says we need to be told what to do and manipulated into a position in which we will do it, not being smart enough or courageous enough to get there without their assistance. Pro-life people tend to have a perspective that–in general–respects not only the fact of life but the features of freedom, humility before God and mankind, and the individual responsibility that square with a Lord Who came that we might have life and have it abundantly.

There is nothing magical or automatic about a life-oriented approach–that is why we should not be single issue people–but more often than not people who favor death to any undesirables see life as a limited opportunity poker game in which some must win while others must lose. There is not enough on the table to let everyone have some of the pot. They think they are just playing the hand they are dealt. People who believe everyone has at least the basic right to life, liberty and the pursuit of happiness tend to see life as an unlimited opportunity game in which we can always ask the dealer for a new deck–and He loves us enough to deliver to all if we just get out of His way by being more willing to give than to take.

In any case, as the tide of public opinion turns more and more toward a culture of life than a culture of death, we need the courage of our convictions and the confidence to laugh at those who would compromise us at the end of a good day's work. St. Paul says over and over throughout his writings to stand firm, to do all things necessary and then stand firm. This is especially true for us and especially now.

And it is science–if we understand science as the observation and measurement of what is existentially real. Like scientists from Aristotle to Einstein understand it.

CHAPTER 7:

CHALLENGING THE CHURCH

Revivals differ from Awakenings in scope, as we discussed in the first chapter. The former begin in the churches – or perhaps one pioneering church – and their fruit is good. Many are healed, led into life-giving relationship to the Lord of Life, and the life of the Body is re-energized in many dramatic ways. I can think of no phenomenon that has impacted my own life and ministry to a greater degree than the Toronto Blessing outbreak of the nineties. I was healed and transformed across the breadth of my being both personally and professionally – as were countless others. But the city of Toronto is not different from what it was before the outpouring began. That is a tragedy.

The latter – the Awakenings – begin in the fields, in the streets, on the beaches and banks of rivers, and in forest carpeted wilderness. They roll out from God's magnificent and infinite heart. They too are characterized by eruptions of healing, massive numbers of people propelled into the abundant life of Christ, and the fresh new winds of the new thing God is doing in any who will receive it. But they are not contained within the walls of the Church. They begin outside and they enter as many churches as will receive them – however late in the process they accept them. The biggest news is that the communities in which they come to be are changed for the better. Jails empty, families are united, economic activities are re-invigorated, and medical professionals must look for sick people to treat because so many are healed. The Jesus People was the most recent Awakening in America and it spread throughout the world.

I had never yet heard of the Jesus People when I came to Christ in 1970, yet I owe not just my friendship and servanthood with Jesus to them; I owe its very shape and its every angle to the reality they impacted the air I breathed in their friendship and servanthood.

The Revivals and the Awakenings differ in scope and impact but they have much in common. One of the features they share is the tendency of churches to reject them as strange, foreign, weird. "We don't do it that way here," constitutes what some jokesters call the seven most sacred words of the Church. What is really up is the spirit of religion, as opposed to the Spirit of the Lord. When Jesus confronted the Pharisees with their devotion to religion superceding their attention to God they tore their hair and their clothes; how dare this carpenter with no advanced education challenge their faith!

One of the saddest episodes in the Gospels is the story of the fig tree cursed by Jesus in Mark 11 as He is about to enter Jerusalem. The fig tree symbolizes Judaism to the Jews. It stands for all that they understand about King Yahweh and His covenant with His still-to-this-day-chosen people. Jesus encounters such a tree outside the city gates and notes that it bears no fruit–even as He acknowledges it is not yet the season for figs. It doesn't matter to the Messiah–not a fig does He care–that it is not the season according to the calendar. His attitude is if religion cannot bear fruit simply by standing in the presence of God it is useless for bearing fruit at any time. His so-called curse is nothing but His promise that this tree will never again deceive by producing fruit that cannot confer life.

How many times have we heard pastors, elders, or anyone in authority say–when confronted by vision–"This is good, but it is not the right time," or "not yet the season," or "Our people are just not yet ready for this; we must prepare them, and that takes time." They will quote from Luke 14 about counting the cost, and the scriptures do indeed warn us about failure to look ahead with clear eyes before we leap. But the last verse in that passage says quite clearly that any who are not willing to give up–to sacrifice–all they have are not fit to be His disciples. We are wise to prepare for becoming neuro surgeons, plumbers, and even theologians. Becoming active and fire-breathing disciples is a decision–always–for now.

This chapter addresses first the Prophetic Community called for in Old Testament prophets from Jeremiah to Joel and in New Testament letters (especially) Romans, 1 Corinthians, and Ephesians. It encourages humble and trusting discipleship–for leaders and rank and file alike–distinguishing magic from miracle. It confronts the bullying that is all too common in the Church, and exhorts pastors to be fearless in their pulpits. It reminds Christians that the condition of secular society is a judgment on us. It seeks to identify the really real in our churches and in our streets; Jesus says if it is not of Him it is no more real than the enemy's effort to seduce Him into ruling the world outside of relationship to the Father in the wilderness temptation. But if we cling to our sense of orderliness over and above leaving our boats and going where He leads we are just as pathetic as the rich young man who went away sad because he had many possessions.

The good news is God honors repentance whenever it occurs. Those churches and persons who reject the Great Awakening that is already underway, preferring the secured shade of their favorite fig tree, will be welcomed into the vineyard just as were the workers who come at the eleventh hour in the parable. But why in the world would anyone want to waste time examining the Gospel when we could be living in it?

GOD'S PROPHETIC COMMUNITY

I had been invited to preach in a small church on California's north coast. As the team led us in worship I felt a sharp pain in my right ear. There was nothing wrong with my ear and I decided it was the Lord's way of signaling His plan to heal somebody else. I approached the senior pastor and told him what I thought. He took the microphone when his last praise song ended, asking if anyone in the congregation had a problem with the right ear. When a man in the back raised his hand, the pastor asked four men sitting near him to lay on hands and pray. Within seconds the man with the ear shouted praise and said that his ear was healed, while the rest of us gave God glory.

This is a textbook description of the prophetic community described in 1 Corinthians 12, Romans 12, and Ephesians 4–to name a few places in scripture–in which every part of the Body performs a necessary and valued function in the operation of the Whole to the glory of the Head. In this case I had the word of knowledge, the pastor orchestrated the operation, the man with the wounded ear presented himself, the four men prayed, and the rest gave the glory and honor to God.

Few of us realize that this model is not a goal to be sought, but a description of the proper functioning of an organic design for here and now–on earth as it is in heaven. Even fewer recognize that this design is not limited to the local congregation, but is just as intentional and just as essential for the gathered albeit scattered Body of Christ.

God predicted this phenomenon through multiple prophetic voices in the Old Testament. He tells us–in Isaiah 59–that the spirit He has placed on the prophet will remain on all of the children of Israel, and on their descendants, so that all will have His words in their hearts. He speaks–in Jeremiah 31–of a new covenant in which He will write His Law on each of our hearts so that men need no longer teach each other because all will know the Lord intimately. He declares–in Ezekiel 11–that He will replace the heart of stone in the whole people with a heart of flesh that will enable all to follow His dictates and decrees. Finally there is the most famous statement of all–in Joel 2 and 3–that in the latter days He will pour out His Spirit on all flesh so that all may prophesy and so make their contribution to a composite revelation of the Lord our God that literally erupts from the midst of us–the place where Jesus said His Kingdom resides.

In the Old Testament God created a community to worship and serve Him. He provided prophets to come in and instruct the community on what God was saying, as He promises in Amos 3:7. But in the New Testament, as a result of the Pentecost explosion that births the church in the wake of the King's death and resurrection, He gives that community a prophetic identity in its own corporate life. From then until now He sends prophets into the community in order to coach and release the community's own voice of prophetic revelation–in thought, word and deed. That is why Paul can write (in 1 Corinthians 14:26 and following) that when we come together one is given a song and another a word and still others revelations and tongues and interpretations. He goes on to instruct the Body in the orchestration of these unfolding gifts, but he also appoints pastors to preside over these occasions–not to quench the Spirit, but to release the Spirit in decency and in order.

Two concepts must be firmly grasped and one caveat embraced if we would function in terms of this Biblical model.

The first concept is simply that the pastor is a gatekeeper–among other things–but a keeper of the open gate as opposed to the closed gate. The pastoral function in this context is to sit at the gate during its hours of opening–as did Mordecai in the Book of Esther–and dispense liberating wisdom. This is what the pastor did in that little church on the coast. He saw his function as releasing the Spirit, not judging it and not judging whether or not the congregation was ready for the coming of the Lord. Had my word of knowledge been false no one would have raised a hand and no one would have been healed–the fruit for good or ill would have been obvious. The pastor did conduct events, but to enable rather than to inhibit. He exerted real authority–but only in order to open the gate to those called to enter in and verified by their fruits.

The second concept is that this biblical model is intended for the extra congregational Church–the one that crosses denominational as well as parochial lines. The New Testament never speaks of any church body smaller than the one in the city–albeit that one may consist of local congregations just as our bodies consist of cells and even organs. But it is organic systems that conduct the bodily functions and transformative revivals and–like Paul's letters–are addressed to cities and regions rather than to congregations–even mega congregations. There is no guarantee that every congregation to whom the Spirit makes overtures will accept the invitation to catch fire, but it is clear that the called-out ones–the Ekklesia, or Church–wait until everybody is on board before moving out at our peril. What part of "go" do we not understand?

That brings us to the caveat. There simply is no viable alternative to embracing the Prophetic or Kingdom or Servant Community model. (What we call it is not important.) It is the model called for in the Word of God. Every revival or transformative movement in history has begun as a grassroots move of God in which institutional norms and procedures are bypassed by the Spirit.

Some say we must take extreme care that none be offended, but Jesus says (Matthew 11:6) we're blessed if we take no offense, not if no one offends us. Every such movement requires pastoring and administering in order to keep it on the rails–but God Himself sets the pace at which that train moves, just as He supplies the power and the fuel to turn those driver wheels. Stopping to redesign the process before engaging it is not recommended.

We live in a season of unprecedented favor for miraculous interventions and decisions for the Lord and His Kingdom. It is summarized in Luke 1:17 that we should go forth in the Spirit and power of Elijah, to turn our hearts to the children, to prepare a people for righteousness. He is on His horse and on His way. All aboard!

MAGIC VERSUS MIRACLE

When the Toronto Blessing broke out I "knew" this wasn't the Lord's doing. It did not fit my understanding of Scripture that people fall to the ground and twitch for extended periods of time, much less break out in prolonged laughter and claim God was healing them in it. I called myself a Spirit-filled Christian–steeped in tongues and healings alongside the sacramental worship of my Anglican denomination–but this was not the way God did it in my experience. It turns out God wanted me to bust my own paradigm for reasons of His own, and He had His own methods for making it happen.

In July 1995 I attended a Congress on the Holy Spirit in Orlando, Florida, with some twenty thousand Christians of every denomination and style. I was having a wonderful time when Jack Hayford–one of my heroes–busted my chops saying Toronto was clearly a God-breathed event. I was so shocked to hear that from the mouth of this leader I gasped to God that if He wanted me to change my view I would have to discuss it with Dr. Hayford personally–knowing how impossible that would be to arrange as I stood behind a thousand people who wanted a moment of his time in front of me. Yet when his talk was finished I watched as the crowd literally parted and I was able to walk up and talk with Hayford–a talk which led me to take my family to Toronto and see for myself. The crowd parting under those circumstances can only be described as a miracle. I witnessed other miracles in Toronto, including a deep inner healing I did not even know I needed.

One was in the finances. To take my family to Toronto would cost $900.00 and change. Though I had never before just called on God for a particular amount, I had no way to afford the trip without His intervention; I prayed for the exact amount and asked no one else to help. Over the course of a week unexpected gifts came that totaled what I needed to the penny. I can only call this too a miracle.

What is the difference between magic and miracle? In an age in which we think spirituality a catch-all in which any variation is thought life giving that's an important question to ask, but the answer is pretty simple. Magic is our effort to intervene in the life of God. Miracle is what happens when we permit Him to intervene in ours.

Even in the churches we practice positive thinking and confessing what we want until we get it. We visualize having the things we seek and devise strategies to manipulate both circumstances and people. We watch movies like *Harry Potter* and *Lord of the Rings*, failing to discern that one is about seeking power and the other is about surrendering it. In business we attend seminars designed to unleash the power person within us. Only a few years ago a book and film series called *The Secret* made a splash amongst Christians and New Agers alike in which the author made the incredible claim that Jesus was just a guy who knew how to visualize and then obtain what He wanted; it was nothing but a rehash of the practice of conjuring and no more compatible with Christian faith than a ouija board. But we can only recognize the dichotomy if our heart is to accept God instead of manipulating Him.

What was that? We can only recognize the disparity if our heart is to accept God instead of trying to manipulate Him.

The Christian scriptures tell us we will do the things Jesus did – and greater things than these – when asked for in His Name. But the clear meaning of "in His Name" is in accordance with His will for us. I received my chat with Jack Hayford and the funds to act on his advice because God had plans for me and I chose to want what He wanted. The fruit was a life re-shaping experience grounded in a season of repentance that looked a lot like progressive surrender to my God. It was great fun into the bargain.

I have watched limbs grow out, cancers and heart conditions healed, and the dead raised. I have prayed wildfires out, droughts broken, and monsoons ended. I have never thought these things happened because I wanted them enough, and never spent a moment thinking I somehow possessed the power to do these things. I have also experienced the complete success of my manipulations – only to stand jaw-dropped before the unintended consequences of having my way. I've tried magic and I've tried miracle. I recommend miracle.

Our God is a God of miracle – of intervention. Truth is, I recommend God.

ADDRESSING BULLYING IN THE CHURCH

Many years ago I pastored a so-called pastor-killer church. Of the two pastors who preceded me, one was so frightened of the elders he would throw up Sunday Mornings before preaching; he literally dropped dead of a heart attack one day. The other had a series of nervous breakdowns until forced to resign. These elders were so dedicated to controlling their pastor they forbade publishing the minutes of board meetings without their approval. When they got a draft copy they would delete any item revealing their abusive behavior. When I would publish the minutes with those items re-inserted the rumor would go around that I was to be fired at the next meeting in retaliation for defying them. But like clockwork about sixty members would show up for the meeting and–under their steely gaze–no move would be made to fire me.

Bullies prefer to operate in darkness. The last thing they want is to come under observation, much less report. Secular dictators from Hitler to Stalin to Mao expended great effort to keep secret their treatment of their people. Church leaders do not sink to that level, but there is plenty of bullying in the churches–at all levels–and daylight is usually the thing the bullies fear most.

In another church I pastored there was a tradition of men exercising all leadership functions. When the elders asked if I favored this way I responded that I did not. I said, however, that I did not intend to force them to change–to sighs of relief–provided we continued to discuss it until they came around to my viewpoint or I to theirs–to sighs of distress. Reality was that neither the Bible nor church tradition–let alone reason–supports their position. I simply kept shooting holes in their reasoning until they demanded we end the discussion. When I reminded them of our deal they collapsed before the daylight I splashed on their mythology. But bullying is not limited to elders versus the pastor.

All Americans–Christian or not–have been shocked and disgusted by the revelations of cover-ups of predatory perversion on the part of priests and pastors over the past few years. (This is by no means limited to the Roman Catholic Church; in fact, the instances found in that denomination–the world's largest–are not proportionately greater than in any other branch of the Body.) This is as clear an example of bullying by clergy as could be imagined, although most are smaller–albeit every bit as abusive. I know far too many women who have dated church members or leaders who proved abusive and taken their pain to the pastor, only to be told it would be too disruptive to the congregation to act on the information. Early in my own ministry as an associate pastor I became aware of a man in the church stalking a single woman. When I confronted the stalker–after being assured by the senior pastor and our bishop that I would get no support for this–I was forced to bluff him and–thank God–it worked. But I have given only a few brief examples of a sick situation that must be addressed in order to be healed.

I will never forget the member of the California State Assembly who addressed us at the first Line in the Sand event in 2011 with these words, "If you would see the state house healed you must first heal the church house." That is why I am so dedicated to God's call for repentance in the Church as a pre-requisite to the Great Awakening He promises.

The good news is as I said before. Bullies prefer to operate in darkness; they dread the light of day on their activities. The challenging news is that leadership–including anyone with ears to hear, eyes to see, and a mouth to speak–needs to turn the light of day on bullies in the Church–and outside it. The Lord our God would say–because He defends the defenseless by His very nature–this is a big part of acknowledging Him before men. Only when we do this can we expect the Son to acknowledge us before the Father.

But the even better news is that our God permits do-overs at any time and at all times. Repentance is a privilege, not a punishment. The moment we repent; the moment we stop sinning–whether by our own aggression or our silence in the face of it–and face Him, we embark on the first and best day of the rest of our life.

PULPIT FREEDOM SUNDAY

(Author Note: This piece was first published in 2012.)

The first Sunday in October has been designated Pulpit Freedom Sunday by the ministry bearing the same name. Begun in 2008 by the Rev. Jim Garlow, it attracted a handful of pastors. The number has grown steadily and several thousand are expected to speak out in 2012. They will declare the right to express their faith is a gift from God, not government. They will state that the Johnson Amendment–added to the IRS Code in 1954 to forbid tax exempt organizations from endorsing candidates–violates the First Amendment and is non-binding. They will express their views on any issue they believe can be addressed in faith–including who is best qualified under God to hold political office. They will mail their sermons to the IRS.

This blog posting will express my God-given right–and responsibility–to speak as I believe God speaks. No one is forced to agree with anything I say, but by the God I serve no one will tell me when or what to speak.

The Johnson Amendment is named for its sponsor, Lyndon B. Johnson. It pre-supposes that because religious operations are permitted to pay no taxes to government they should also have no say in the choosing of those who would lead that government. Early Americans gave the vote only to tax-paying property owners, but Americans came to believe that citizenship alone is the only criterion for voting. No citizen is denied the right to influence public policy because they may pay no taxes. It should be no stretch to conceive of the religious exemption for tax free institutions.

But even if the conception does stretch some minds, the First Amendment states clearly that no law shall be made restricting the free exercise of faith. Anyone who passed high school American Government knows the power to tax is the power to control; taxing faith-based ministries is restricting free exercise. And anyone who has read the Declaration of Independence knows Americans are endowed by our Creator–not our government–with our constitutional rights.

I have never endorsed a candidate for office in my life, and I won't begin now. My function as a Christian leader is to establish principles within which people may–if they choose–operate as they choose their leaders. That said, if anyone reading this post and the questions I pose in it thinks I am implicitly endorsing a candidate for president that is their problem and not mine, for if I do in fact endorse it is my constitutional right.

First Question: The Bible says for freedom we are set free in Christ. Of the two main candidates for president, which one believes citizens should freely choose their healthcare plan and which one made his signature achievement the imposition of a national healthcare plan that was opposed by some 70% of the population? Which one says regulations on business should only level the playing field and which one says no business was ever built without government investment and influence?

Second Question: The Christ of God instructs us to let our yes be yes and our no be no; truth telling should be our default. Which of the two main candidates for president tells the truth about recent events in Libya that took American lives and which one keeps changing his story and blaming others for the changes? Which one declares himself a staunch ally of Israel while refusing to meet with her leaders and telling other leaders how he despises them? Which one visits and stands with Israel? And while we are at it, which one releases–through his staff–secret information about the military tactics that killed Osama bin Laden and tells the leader of Russia that he can be more flexible on defensive weapons programs after he is re-elected president?

Third Question: The Word of God says that human life is a self-authenticating gift from God that is best shaped in the context of traditional marriage between a man and a woman. Which candidate adopts this view of both life and family? Which one defies it–and every legitimate study ever done on either issue? And for that matter, which one claimed the government as the source of our rights and which one the Creator in the recent presidential debate?

Readers who claim the Name of the God of the Bible–and any who find these Biblical principles make sense whether or not they believe this God–are invited to make their choice in alignment with Him. Any who reject this model for our existence are welcome to do as they think best. I'll not question their right to do it.

THE REAL ST. PATRICK AND WHAT HE MEANS

Aside from green beer and corned beef, the shamrock, and allegedly running the snakes out of Ireland while dressed as a leprechaun, who is St. Patrick really? He is a man who understands that God in Christ provides everything he has–from life to freedom to the privilege of enjoying beer and beef and things that grow from the ground. He is a man who considers it a privilege to keep re-focusing his life on that God; we call it a lifestyle of progressive repentance. He is a man who dedicates his life to saying, "Thank you," to God in tangible ways for all that He has given and will give.

Patrick did not begin life that way. He was born to wealthy Roman parents in the British Isles when they were a province of Rome. He lived a life of leisure and earthly privilege; servants took care of anything that mattered; he hung out and was cared for. At age fourteen he was kidnapped by Irish pirates and fitted with an iron collar to denote his slavery. He was placed in a pasture with a flock of sheep; it was cold and he was always hungry. He had no one… until the Voice.

Raised in a nominally Christian home, neither Patrick nor his family took their Christ seriously. They had everything they believed they needed without Him. But in the pasture Patrick welcomed the Voice like a man lost in the desert welcomes a spring of clear water. They talked each day and Patrick never asked whether the Voice was really the Holy Spirit or just his desperate imagination; he asked only that the Voice never leave Him. The Voice was faithful and Patrick came to respect the Authority it carried.

One day the Voice told him to go; his ship was waiting. Without hesitation he left the sheep and walked two hundred miles through territory in which every inhabitant could collect a reward for killing an obvious runaway–the iron collar a dead-on reveal–and no one ever bothered him. He went where the Voice said and not where the Voice did not. When he reached the eastern coast there was indeed a ship with a captain willing to take him–for a fee. Patrick said he would return. He came back days later with the required price but had no idea how he obtained it. The captain took him to France where another ship returned him to his home and family.

The problem was that he found home unutterably boring. The Voice was not present, though every comfort he remembered was there in abundance. One day the Voice re-appeared. The Holy Spirit instructed Patrick to return to Ireland and share the Truth and the Presence of God in Christ with his recent tormenters. He tried–without success–to explain himself to his uncomprehending parents before heading to the mission field for which his two-year captivity had prepared him. They thought themselves reasonably good Christians who saw no reason to go overboard in their faith. They wondered why Patrick could not be content with a good thing. They did not comprehend that the good is always the enemy of the best. This is nowhere more true than in the Body of Christ.

The rest of his life Patrick ministered–with power–to the Irish. He was frequently hungry and cold, threatened with ugly forms of martyrdom, and often in serious danger from folks who did not think being their former prisoner necessarily qualified him to offer them new life in Christ. But his faithfulness paid off; the Gospel took root and spread like the clovers of Ireland. A century later spiritual and lineal descendants of disciples of Patrick returned to Scotland and enabled the people to know the Lord Jesus. Their work was accompanied by the power Jesus promised to those who followed Him, just as it had been for Patrick. They too cherished the Voice of God more than any gifts of power and plenty He might give. Patrick and the Voice taught them.

I pray the Body of Christ in America will not be kidnapped by pirates and forced to suffer captivity in a cold and hungry place. But truth is we have highjacked ourselves with our grim commitment to doing things decently and in order–according to our ideas of decency and order, not His. The nation has simply followed our lead, truth to tell.

The God who has nothing against plenty–He is its source–will cheerfully use pressure and lack to get our attention if that is what it takes. Let us not be like the fig tree Jesus encountered outside Jerusalem that declared itself not ready to bear fruit when He approached. The time to bear fruit is when He comes, not when we decide we are ready. In the words of Robin Mark's famous praise song, The Days of Elijah, "Behold, He comes, riding on a cloud, shining like the sun, at the trumpet's call. Lift your voice..." Let us lift our voices and re-focus our attention–now. And let us rejoice that His strength is perfected in our weakness.

THE CONDITION OF SOCIETY IS...

The twin decisions of the US Supreme Court on marriage are as clear as mud; they resolve none of the issues that drive the marriage debate in California or the nation. But let's talk about what they do–and what they do not do.

With respect to DOMA–the federal Defense Of Marriage Act–they strike down only the section of the act forbidding federal benefits to same sex couples even where states recognize their marriages. The Court upheld the primary intent to protect states' rights to recognize only marriages that accord with their laws. The Court reaffirms the right of states to enact their own laws and definitions of marriage. California's Proposition 8 is the action of a state defining marriage, although Prop 8 is not mentioned in the DOMA decision.

With respect to Prop 8 the court did not overturn the measure. It did rule that the defenders of the law lacked standing to defend that law in federal court; it overturned the decision of the Ninth Circuit Court of Appeals declaring Prop 8 unconstitutional, which means the case is sent back to the federal district court which also declared the act contrary to the US Constitution. Here it gets really muddy–the California Constitution states clearly that state laws can only be overturned by appellate courts–state or federal. No such overturn of Prop 8 has taken place now that the Ninth Circuit decision is voided.

The Alliance Defending Freedom–which defended Prop 8 in the courts–joins Focus on the Family's Citizenlink, the Family Research Council, and SaveMarriage.org–led Andy Pugno–in claiming the measure remains the law of the land. The media have misreported these decisions across the board. Pacific Justice Institute–with which I am most familiar and connected–calls the odds on maintaining Prop 8 very long. California officials have a long history of flouting the law and the federal Ninth Circuit Court of Appeals–whose jurisdiction was eliminated by the Supreme Court ruling–has ordered the resumption of gay marriages in California in direct violation of the rule of law which provides twenty-five days for petitioners to seek a re-hearing from the Supreme Court. Gay marriages have already commenced in California.

Let's be clear. A federal court having neither jurisdiction nor authority with no case before it ordered California to violate its own constitution by sanctioning these marriages. Lawless officials–governor, attorney general, and mayor of Los Angeles–acted on the supposed strength of this order.

Ugandan Evangelist Jackson Senyonga famously said, "The condition of society is the report card of the Church." When the Church is healthy the society is healthy. When the Church is mired in bondage of her own making the society is likewise bound. Where is the Church now? Where are her pastors and other leaders?

Many leaders do speak and act from within the liberating parameters of God's Word and the laws and constitution of our state and nation. But when nationally recognized leader Jim Garlow calls for pastors and leaders to assert their freedom to speak under the First Amendment less than half of one percent of the pastors answer from their pulpits. When a local church was viciously attacked in our local paper I could not find one local pastor to publicly assert with me that church's right to its own identity. This is not okay.

When King David engineered the murder of one of his own officers to cover the affair the king had with his wife Nathan the Prophet publicly confronted the king. It was the same with Elijah and other biblical prophets. When President Lyndon Johnson worshipped at Bruton Parish in Williamsburg, Virginia, in early 1967, the pastor confronted him about his lies and lawlessness in conducting the Vietnam war without a congressional declaration of war and without congressional oversight. The pastor's sermon –preached in the President's presence – began the process leading to Johnson's decision not to seek re-election. Courageous pastors, bishops, and business owners are challenging the Obama Administration on forced abortion coverage provided in Obamacare. Will the Church rise up to confront government about its abuses of power across the board – and especially now in the issue of forcing a state to adopt same-sex marriage when its people have said yes to traditional marriage? Will the Church set its own house in order at the same time?

My next posting will feature recommendations – exhortations really – on how this should be done. But whatever we do as a Christian community let us actively recall that we do not place our trust in the human protectors of constitution and community – how has that worked out on Obamacare and traditional marriage – but in the One who creates them both.

THE REPORT CARD OF THE CHURCH

When California's governor and legislature attempted to gut open meeting and freedom of information laws there was an immediate uprising on left and right. The government backed down. One can only wonder what would happen if left and right were equally horrified by the lawlessness of the state's secular authorities and the Ninth Circuit Court in pushing forward gay marriages when they have neither the authority nor the jurisdiction to do so. As things stand the issue is no longer homosexual marriage, but rather elected and unelected officials acting contrary to law because they can. That should send chills of both fear and outrage up the spines of freedom loving people regardless of their opinions on gay marriage. What government can do to gore the ox of one faction it can do to the ox of another on another day.

That fear and outrage is not manifesting at this moment. It is left for people of faith and common sense to stand or fall because – as Jackson Senyonga famously said while visiting California, "The condition of society is the report card of the Church." The implication of the biblical story of the paralyzed man healed after his friends lower him through the roof to lie at Jesus' feet stands in to symbolize the present situation in the Church in California and across our land. Until the healed paralytic stands and walks – testing the new muscles he has received – he is not really and fully healed.

My last post mentioned how prophets of Bible times confronted kings with their wrongdoing from David to Ahab and Herod. Daniel confronted the emperor of Babylon. They risked their lives each time they confronted rulers; yet they were convinced that life was not worth living outside of service to the God who had given them real freedom and real life. In fact, as three of Daniel's friends prepared to be thrown into a super-heated furnace they declared that – although they expected God's rescue – they would not change their decision to serve Him in truth even if he did not deliver them from evil. When the disciples are hopelessly confused by Jesus' hard statements and some begin to walk away the Lord asks Peter if he too will go. Peter asks, "Where would I go? You have the words of life." What have such stories to do with ordinary Christians in California in the face of governors and attorneys general who refuse their duty to defend state law – and defy the courts when they don't get what they want?

We can excuse ourselves all day long by saying we are not Elijah and we are not John the Baptist. Or we can repent – re-focus on God as our life source and life model – and reflect that since the first Pentecost we of the Body are a prophetic community. We need not make the Nathans in our midst the surrogates for what we ought to do – and are enabled to do. The good news of the Supreme Court decisions and the lawless response to them is that we can finally know – I hope – that putting our trust in men and institutions to do the right thing is a fool's bargain. Trusting in and following God wherever He leads is the only game in town. But what ought we do?

We ought as the Body of Christ to enter into a serious season of repentance – re-focus on God – with practical consequences as direct and visible as that man walking in a village in Judea two thousand years ago. That means we respond to Jesus' statement in Matthew 10 that He will acknowledge us before His Father only if we acknowledge Him before men. It means we call, e-mail and speak – throughout the state – demanding that government officials obey the law and perform only their lawful duties while we obey only their lawful orders. This is an act of supreme repentance for those of us who have remained silent and imagined our faith a private matter.

Even more we ought to pray as never before for government leaders, for leadership in our churches, and for those with whom we disagree on the values and shaping of marriage. We pray a Damascus Road experience for all leaders – beginning with ourselves – in which we like Paul are confronted with the overwhelming love of God on Whom we have turned our backs even while imagining we served Him. We ought to pray every day that leaders would fall in love with the limitations placed on their power in the Constitution and in the Word of God which inspired it. I can guarantee our grades will rise on our next report card – for all concerned – if we do as we ought.

THE JESUS PEOPLE AND THE THIRD GREAT AWAKENING

They came rocking and rolling into the end of the sixties and changed the personality of Church and nation–as Great Awakenings do. They had encounters as intimate as they were dynamic with the Living Jesus in places like the beaches of California–and Oregon. They met Him in the deserts and in the state and national parks. They praised Him in high schools and lakeshores around Bakersfield, and in the coffee houses of Hollywood and San Diego–and Boston and Chicago. Their notoriety peaked in the nineteen seventies but their impact was dynamic through the end of the twentieth century and their influence is felt today.

They launched the short-term missions movement and the faith-based recovery movement. They broke the gifts of the Holy Spirit out of the church basement and contemporary worship movement into the sanctuary and top-40 Radio. They planted the Messianic Movement in Israel–and around the world–along with the Calvary Chapel and Vineyard denominations and a mainstream Christian music and media industry. The artistic types among them include bestselling authors, producers and screenwriters like Bodie Thoene, James Scott Bell, Michael Phillips, and David McFadzean–names that may or may not be familiar to readers but who shaped much of our current book and film culture–the parts of which we can be proud–because they created high quality family friendly television–like the *Home Improvement* series–and a slew of books from legal thrillers that pray to historical fiction that honors Israel to a re-discovery of old masters like George McDonald. They sparked every revival of the past half century from Toronto, Ontario, Canada; to Redding, California. And they remain the most hidden and ignored phenomenon of the past three hundred years. They are the Jesus People.

Like the people of Great Awakenings before them they did not fit into the church box. God took leaders like Lonnie Frisbee and Richard Twiss where he found them–the former high on LSD in the desert and the latter on heroin on a beach in Maui–He brought them down and introduced Himself to them the way He approached Saul of Tarsus on the Damascus Road. He did not make them conventional Christians after that; He made them explosive servants of His Kingdom, filling them with His Holy Spirit and the gifts that so often accompany the Spirit–healings, prophecies, miracles and such.

God also took more conventional leaders like Chuck Smith, James Dobson and Jack Hayford–and leaders somewhere in between–like John Wimber and Todd Hunter–and used them to structure and pastor the movement past its beginnings in an upper room the size of the US western coastal states. These leaders struggled with each other and with the tension that always exists when God does a brand new thing on the one hand and declares His word that the new creation has a shape consistent with what He has done before. They redeemed the vision of the peaceable Kingdom the hippies thought came from the Age of Aquarius and the Jesus People discovered came from the authentic God. They waited in the wings when the anarchical good intentions of the hippies collapsed with the deaths–from overdose and exposure at Woodstock and from violence at the Altamont Speedway in late 1969. They proclaimed and acted as though the Word of God were indeed living and true–in the midst of our rioting and unraveling world–if we would have Him.

The impact of the Jesus People is still felt in our culture–from the arts to the amazing numbers of young people who engage in service projects both domestically and abroad to the spirit of collaborative leadership that is now normative in our culture from schoolroom to board room. But it is just as true–as Ed Underwood points out in his excellent book, Reborn to Be Wild, that we of the movement all too often allowed ourselves to be housebroken. Add to that the unremitting drumbeat that the Boomers were nothing but a bunch of self-indulgent yuppies who abandoned their children and their social responsibilities and it is easy to see why the Awakening God gave us Boomers is so largely forgotten and ignored.

Reality is God never repeats His movements into the world anymore than He repeats the design of a snowflake. Yet every snowflake looks enough like every other snowflake to be recognizable as what it is. The Boomers have a calling–to pass the baton to the next generation while we are paving the straight highway in the desert for our God–see Mark 1:1-4 in the Bible–so they can walk it while we are still building it. But if we would recognize and appreciate the Great Awakening that is coming in our time we–all of us–must recognize and appreciate the one that came to the Jesus People.

RIGHTEOUSNESS IS...

The traditional season of Lent is approaching quickly and I want to say something meaningful about it. To do that I have to tell a story. Maybe several stories.

As we spent the day in worship and prayer in a little house dedicated to that purpose in Ronkonkowa, New York, God spoke. There were seven of us–three from the Long Island location where we met and one from Pennsylvania with a ministry in New Jersey, representing the tri-state region; two from New England with regional ministries and representing that region; and a guy from California (me) who thinks God wants to bridge the nation with His Holy Spirit. When we asked God for a vision He showed one of us a meandering river and a road being supernaturally built upon its bank. When I wondered why an unadjusted meandering route seemed more favored than a straight pathway God spoke, and I was the one privileged to share, "Righteousness is a question of alignment, not direction."

When Jesus turned toward Jerusalem His friends faced a walk of several days. They spent many months on the journey, not because their leader couldn't follow directions, but because the Son of God knows righteousness to be a question of alignment rather than of direction. During this time–which is chronicled in Luke's Chapters 10-19–the disciples have already confessed Jesus as Lord, witnessed more miracles than can be shaken at by the proverbial stick, and gone on their own first missionary journey that featured similar acts of the power to bless and heal. They have begun to see and anticipate their inheritance as heirs of God's grace and glory, but they have a long way to go before growing into it. On the road they will learn to pray and to sustain prayer, they will comprehend that their job as gatekeepers is to open rather than close the portals of the Kingdom, and they will discover the difference between religion and relation to the Most High.

They will find out what is important and what is trivial–unlike the religious leaders of their day–and they will come to marvel at the privilege of repentance and sacrifice. They will come to know that a history of sin–like that of Zaccheas–is no more a barrier to Kingdom life than a history of poverty a barrier to wealth–like the woman putting two pennies in the temple treasury or the man given five talents for investment in the Kingdom. They will make another mission trip and practice the principles (Luke 10:2-9) of blessing before all, followed by hanging out with people, meeting their needs (as God provides) and witnessing for their faith–in that order.

Their journey to Jerusalem turns out to be a lot more than time elapsed in the covering of the ground between where they began and where they arrived.

The months on the road have become a question of progressive alignment rather than direction.

More than twenty-five years ago God gave me a spoken word. He said, "I want you to go to Galilee." Although I wanted to journey to Israel then and have been there since, I was pretty sure at the time it was not all about that kind of trip. In the intervening years God has been teaching me the very same things He taught the disciples way back when–and being unbelievably kind when it became clear I needed remedial work in lessons supposedly already learned, in tests supposedly already passed. Whenever I pronounce myself now ready for Jerusalem He gives me another opportunity to repent–to re-focus on Him–and so come to see myself in a more accurate light. The time in Galilee has turned out to be the greatest privilege I can imagine and anything but the irritating rehearsal for the good stuff I once imagined it to be. I am pretty sure my experience is mainstream in this regard.

During Lent Christians traditionally practice giving up something they are likely better off without. They often take up a practice that benefits their walk and others' welfare. These are good things, but God help us if tokens of sacrifice and ministry are all we take to advantage in Lent. It is about intentionally seeking a closer walk moment by moment. It is about telescoping our earthly pilgrimage into a better idea–and a taste–of the heavenly one. Repentance–turning toward God and away from self as the center of existence–is the greatest privilege and the longest process we will ever be given. That is true whether we begin across the land or right where we are.

Righteousness is about alignment more than direction. It is about Whom we are with more than where we are going.

A CULTURE OF REPENTANCE

God is the sole source of truth and His Word the most comprehensive and reliable deposit of revelation, but not the only such. I have recently read Francine Rivers' *Sons of Encouragement* and Mike Frank's *Prosperity With Purpose*. Rivers writes a biography of Jesus in the climactic section of her book and Frank tells his own story of transformation from practitioner of prosperity to one who knows his identity in Christ is a lot more important than what we can get from Him. I happened to read both books just at the moment I most needed their witness.

In Rivers' portrait Jesus must contend with the people who think Him a rock star and treat him as superficially as we treat rockers. I can almost hear them saying, "That was a great miracle; do some more," and Rivers attributes just such sentiments to the crowds during His early ministry. We are in the most prolific season for miracles (and decisions for Him) of all time, but many are so insatiable for the spectacular manifestations of Holy Spirit that we seem to be watching a performance and expecting the star to top each act with a bigger one. Beyond that the tendency–in Rivers' fiction and in much of our experience–is to wait passively on the Lord until He manifests a new one instead of accepting responsibility for the stewardship of what we have already been given. People then–and people now–tended to fall away when the topic turned to their own repentance. This is especially so when repentance is viewed as a lifestyle rather than a one-shot to clear the conscience on the one hand, or a single dynamic act of taking up our pallet and walking on the other.

Frank's book chronicles his meteoric rise through the ranks of several corporations becoming a multi-millionaire through his gift for seeing and developing leadership in colleagues while missing the blooming of his own wife and children. God led him through a progressive repentance as he first began to make his wife's dreams a bigger priority than his own. He found himself making even more money than before. He fathered a daughter with a fatal birth anomaly and left the company he helped to found in order to devote himself to her–and she died virtually in his arms. He began the hard slogging work of re-meeting and reconciling with his other children while dealing with the grief and disillusionment of losing Lexie. In the meantime he was still battling the lie he had received in childhood that he was not–and would never be–welcome in the company of men. His story is like that of so many men–and many women–who heroically fight the symptoms of their spiritual bondage without recognizing that surrender–to Jesus–is the price of victory.

Jesus spoke clearly about both kinds of bondage–and their antidote–in Mark 8:14-21 when he warned the disciples against the leaven of the Pharisees on the one hand and that of King Herod on the other.

The Pharisees' sect began with the warlike followers of Judas Maccabee, but had become thoroughly passive by the day of the Christ. Although they wielded great political power their prevailing philosophy was to keep themselves ritually and legally pure and await God's judgment that they were indeed the best that Jewish culture could produce. Jesus' primary complaint about them was that they kept demanding new signs while failing to act on the word and power they had already received, and forbidding others to go where they chose not to tread. Many in the Body today are crazy for more miracles and new prophecies–but lusting after these things for their own entertainment and justification. They need to take repentance at its true and dynamic meaning.

The Herodians were self-made people. Herod himself was one of the most effective kings in all Jewish history. He brought high employment, undertook many public works projects that made life better for his subjects, and was skillful enough in diplomacy to play competing factions off of one another and keep the Romans off his and the country's back–so long as taxes were paid and the peace was kept. Jesus primary complaint against them was that they feared neither God nor man–like the unjust judge of the parable in Luke 18–and they were completely unscrupulous. Many in the Body today do not believe the Word of God which promises a Gospel of power and not of mere words. They look down on those of us weaker and more vulnerable and believe that only the strong–as they understand strength–are fit to survive even in God's Kingdom. They too need to take repentance in its true and dynamic meaning.

Repentance is a process of turning away–abandoning–the things we have created as substitutes for God–from man-made laws and traditions we say please God (they don't) to acknowledging and believing only those portions of scripture that accord with who we already are. Caleb and Joshua say–in an earlier portion of Rivers' book–that the people escaped from Egypt while bringing Egypt with them. God has spoken to us through The Call, Sacramento; the Response, Houston and Baton Rouge; and A Line in the Sand, Pasadena and Los Angeles; that we need to leave Egypt in the hands of the Egyptians and seek God with all of our hearts. This call goes not to the un-churched, but to us in the Church. The promise is that He has plans to give us and our nation a hope and a future under His reign. The challenge is that we must keep seeking His face–not our own comfort zone–if we would find Him. Our continuing surrender is the price of victory.

We brought Egypt with us. It is time to leave Egypt behind and re-focus–as a lifestyle–our attention on Jerusalem and Jerusalem's God.

CHAPTER 8:

WITNESSING IN THE PUBLIC SQUARE

Jesus famously says in Matthew 10:32-34 that whoever acknowledges Him before men will be acknowledged by Him before the Father; He adds that He comes not to bring peace, but a sword. This is opportunity coupled with obligation.

Jesus speaks of being noteworthy in the Throne room; when we make public our witness He makes public His witness for us. But He makes it just as clear that this public witnessing is not an option to be taken up or cast aside. It is what we were born for.

How many times in scripture does the Lord say – one way or another – that He brings the sword of decision into our midst? How often does He tell His people He does not know them if they fail to do as He says and as He does? When He says He is unaware of our good works outside obedience to His commands He means there are no good works outside of obedience. The word we translate as "witness" is the Greek "martyr" and it means "participant observer." It refers to one who can report accurately and faithfully not just because he saw but because he did alongside what he saw. The Christian Gospel – per the public witness of Paul the Apostle – is not a thing done in a corner. It is in full view of anyone caring to see. And although it is true not everyone is required to sacrifice their physical life for Christ and His Kingdom, all are expected to let go of any claim to that life as a condition of inheriting life everlasting.

That means anyone reading these words must know that any idea of faith in Christ being a private matter between the reader and the Lord had best get shed of that notion before going any further. Every one of us is required to give an account of our faith on earth well before we ever get near Heaven.

How do we witness in the public square?

Part of it is sharing our personal journey with God in Christ whenever opportunity presents itself. We are not let off the hook – by the way – because we don't think ourselves very effective at telling stories, or well versed in the scriptures, or whatever excuse we may offer. For one who has not met Christ – in scripture or in the world – we may be the only Bible they will ever see. God knows this before we encounter the person with whom we get to share. He set it up – however much a mistake it might appear to be.

Part of it is doing our homework and speaking out – in whatever forum we are given – on issues that impact the life of people for whom Jesus gave His. Of course that means voting; there is no excuse for a Christian refusing to vote unless he is truly convicted that no candidate for this or that office represents a Godly choice. If that is the case in the general election remember we are accountable for our activities during the primary season when we have far more choices available. (Did we work actively to promote a Godly candidate? Do we speak out on issues like life, marriage, and free expression of our faith?) There is likewise no excuse for refusing to tell others who we voted for and why. What if they think us fools? Was not Francis of Assisi proud to be known as God's fool? Does not Paul trumpet from the New Testament that it is his privilege to suffer persecution in work and social circles? None of us can come close to his level of persecution, but we can share his joy if we will.

At the same time I knew a man once who poked napkins from his ears to ostentatiously make his protest against the "ungodly" music played in his company cafeteria. Being thought a fool and being one are two different things. We need to ask God to teach us in the very hour we need it (Matthew 10 and Luke 21) how to be winsome in our witness.

This chapter addresses seeing life from the gift of a Eucharistic – more than thankful – heart. Its essays stress our call to be ambassadors of His reconciliation, and announcers of His Kingdom with pragmatic tips on how to do these things effectively from where we are. It celebrates the rich heritage we have in America of being grounded in God's revelation and referring back to that grounding – through repentance – in a most public way. It differentiates between secular heroes and the One Messiah and declares unequivocally that only hanging in there with Jesus draws into the knowledge of truth. Finally it trumpets the Easter story – re-told and re-cast for the ears of every culture – as the same old story of a Man who is God, a Man-God who gave His life for the sake of ours. This Man-Who-Is-God is alive today on earth as He is in Heaven; His footprints and handprints are everywhere displayed in the pragmatic blessings He creates and distributes through the lives of His followers.

Thirty years ago Peter Weir made an amazing movie called Witness. It is a story of a good cop being hunted by bad cops in his department because he protects a witness to a murder they committed. He hides among the Amish–people who reject violence–and much of the film looks at his efforts to understand how people can live like that when he understands the pursuit of justice to need a lot of what his hosts call bashing the bad guys. The climax of the story erupts when the bad cops corner him. He manages to take out two of the three before the third gets the drop on him. In the meantime the Amish farmers have been sounding the fire alarm and the whole community comes trooping across the fields to stand in silent witness. The bad cop facing more than a hundred unarmed witnesses drops his gun and sinks to the ground in defeat. God has perfected His strength in the weakness of the witnesses.

Whether a given issue should be addressed by violence or not is a judgment call. But there is no substitute for witness in the public square. Jesus says, "What we whisper now must be shouted from the rooftops after." This day is the after day. We were born for such a time as this.

A EUCHARISTIC HEART MAKES THANKSGIVING MORE THAN A DAY

By December 2013 my wife and I were as close to burnout as we have ever been. Leading a parachurch ministry is always edgy; we had not seen a ministry paycheck in two-plus years. (Nor have we seen one since.) Yet by God's grace we gave thanks for all we had and for all our needs being met. Then we were shock-surprise-gifted with a fabulous two week vacation in Hawaii. The airfare was the fruit of bonus miles from ministry trips; the condo from the unexpected generosity of an old friend. While there we received one surprise gift after another – from five days' swimming with sea turtles off a beach where I had never seen them congregate before – to finding parking places much later in the day than they are ever available, to bringing home my favorite Aloha shirt, bought at a street stand discovered after a wrong turn.

All of these things are unquestionably gifts from God. But the cultivation of a mindset that believes and appreciates in advance as much as after the fact is what I call seeking a Eucharistic heart.

The word is Greek for thanksgiving; it traditionally names the Holy Communion. When we choose to receive whatever comes as gift even before it comes we come to see things through the eyes of the God Who gives them. Perspective broadens and the ability to respond to opportunities grows. A Eucharistic heart embodies Jesus' promise we'll be taught what we need to know in the very hour we need to know it. This promise is important enough to repeat in three Gospels. But such a heart cannot be grown through human effort. It comes as a gift asked repeatedly.

Truth is we are so steeped in our survival-of-the-fittest worldview we rarely think to thank. We are (too) busily tilting at the next windmill, like nine of the ten lepers Jesus heals in Luke 17:11-19. He tells the one who turned, "Your faith has made you well," though all were cleansed. This because all lost their leprosy while one gained a newly authentic life.

Jesus Himself gives thanks for having a few loaves and fish to feed thousands, for Lazarus in the tomb four days, and while dining with disciples hours before his death. He sees opportunity where others see disaster – not because He is committed to looking on the bright side, but committed to referring Himself to His Father through thanksgiving – He can then see the world through the Father's eyes and respond through the Father's heart. We are not called to achieve a new perspective, but to forge a new habit that will take a lifetime of asking and practicing to establish. This is an act of progressive repentance that goes way beyond sorrow for sin. It shows and draws us toward new life.

The Pilgrims of Plymouth practiced this heart. Their numbers cut in half by disease and starvation, they kept choosing to give thanks for the life God had given. They kept asking Him to give grace to thank and praise Him. When local tribes taught them to grow food and provided much of their first harvest feast it was natural to share and give thanks despite the dangers that still lay ahead. But it was natural only because they had been practicing simple obedience to the scriptural command. Part of the new perspective they gained was conviction to treat the tribal people as children of God. The Pilgrims were rare colonists in that they respected and appreciated their neighbors.

Last September my radio sponsor base was so depleted by the ongoing recession that cancellation was imminent. Forced to cancel a family trip by illness, we gave thanks–and gained three new sponsors.

Some say, "But what about people starving and dying of disease? Aren't they as worthy as you? Don't they give thanks?" Some thank and some don't; I'm not to judge. But we are worthy to know of Jews who covered their heads to pray while awaiting death in Auschwitz. A Eucharistic heart gives thanks for their witness and for the conviction that it must never happen again, whatever I might have to do to stop it.

I don't understand how God acts from situation to situation. As a Christian I try to serve those in need and pray that all needs will be met, not just mine. But I do know that when I operate out of a Eucharistic heart not only am I better able to see the wonders God performs in my life; I am better able to serve Him in the lives of others. Have a blessed Thanksgiving. May it be not a day but a developing lifestyle.

LIVING AS AMBASSADORS OF RELATIONSHIPS

I wrestled with God in prayer all night that night in 2006. Diana and I were in the Philippines for the World Christian Gathering on Indigenous Peoples. Unlike the 2005 gathering in Sweden, I was not scheduled to speak–and that was fine. I understood my calling this time as meeting with leaders and building relationship around conversations concerning their vision for WGCIP and how things were unfolding. Yet the Lord seemed to be prompting me to share my personal testimony as a descendant of Scottish Highlanders. My people were as abused, exploited, and massacred by invaders of their land as were the people of color and colonization who made up the vast majority of those in attendance. The only difference was that my skin is white and my people have–largely–found a way to navigate our history and prosper. But I was not scheduled to speak and I was sure the impulse to share was a product of ego alone.

Except He would not leave me alone. And so I prayed and protested all night.

I knew that if I shared it would be stories of uses and abuses to which I have been subjected by family and friends over a lifetime–on top of my Scottish heritage. It would be about my repeated efforts to forgive and move on, only to find the anger boiling up in me after some new provocation or some seemingly innocuous trigger event. At that point I would call on God to be my strength and forgiveness all over again, because He says this is both good and ultimately good for me. I would share how God convinced me his call to forgive seventy times seven (Matthew 18) is satisfied by anyone who simply stays in the game. We are required only to hang in there with Him and with each other, having another go at this forgiveness thing. We are not judged by success or failure, but by persistence. I would tell them the rules do not change even when the very Pacific Islanders I befriended and for whom I obtained employment used their new position to steal a half million dollar inheritance from me. I would acknowledge that I still struggle with this, but by God's grace I depend on and serve in His love and not through my own outraged sense of justice.

Just before dawn He described the sign that would indicate He–not my ego–was calling me to speak. My friend, Hakon Ennokksen, an indigenous Sami man, was leading the European delegation and they had charge of the program that Wednesday Night. If Hakon would take Diana and me into his delegation–appropriate because of our Scottish ancestry–I would know God wanted me to share and I would do just that. I went looking for Hakon in the breakfast room as soon as it was open, but before I could approach him he spotted me across the room and came running. As he ran he was shouting my name and saying Diana and I must join his delegation for the evening so we could offer our testimony. Message from God received.

Some will say I need therapy if I think God speaks to me. I think the Inventor of speech is quite capable of using it, and that He speaks to everyone.

What I did was controversial. Some in leadership believed that only people of color should be allowed to speak from the platform any more. Others wondered if we had broken protocol, inasmuch as we were unscheduled. They concluded that–inasmuch as we spoke only on the invitation of the evening's leadership–we were perfectly in order. And the fruit was awesome. More than forty people approached me privately over three days to say that my testimony that the Lord requires only that we stay in the game had set them free in His love.

In 2 Corinthians 5:16-20 Paul declares himself and the rest of us a new creation in the love of Christ. He says Abba has done the heavy lifting by reconciling us to Himself through the death of His Son. But the corker is his contention that we activate the new creation in ourselves by progressively receiving that reconciliation and living as His ambassadors of that reconciliation. That drives my prayer for family and friends, for people I meet in restaurants and shopping places (when they are okay with it) and the reason I can't stop talking about my Best Friend. It is why I write books like *Living As Ambassadors of Relationships*; it is why I blog and broadcast. It is how I strive to live a life of progressive repentance–always grateful for the do-overs of which my Lord seems to offer in inexhaustible supply.

THE HOLY SPIRIT AND THE ENDTIMES

I'll call her Ruth; she was our server when the extended family went to breakfast together during our last visit. I make a practice of asking servers if I can pray for them whenever I am in a restaurant, and they are glad I asked nine times out of ten. Ruth began to tell us of her fears for a grown child serving in a military hotspot, a recent death tearing her and others in her family apart, and several other things as well. We prayed for her peace and for protection of her loved ones and saw tears of relief flowing in her. She told us she was not scheduled to work that morning but her manager had asked her to help out. She added that the server assigned to our table had asked her to take it for him because he didn't want to serve such a large party. She said God clearly orchestrated the whole scenario so that we could pray for her–of all people in that city.

I praised God for what He arranged, and thought of how the only variable He did not control was my willingness to ask a stranger if I could pray for her. We all have the power to thwart God's plans by simply saying "No" to His call. But the fruit is awesome whenever we say yes. One of my in-laws visited that restaurant weeks later and Ruth was again on duty. She recognized him immediately and came over to say she was still praising the Lord–openly–for what He did through us that Saturday Morning.

Of course we never know what the Lord is up to before we become involved in it. One time I attended a school play because the daughter of some friends was in it. They introduced me to the family of her best friend and the mom asked if I would pray for her mom–an eighty-six-year-old in the late stages of cancer–who was not present at the play. I agreed and prepared to say a quick thanksgiving for her remarkable life and to wish her a peaceful transition into God's immediate presence. His word in my ear was, "Don't even think about it!" and I figured He had other plans. I took a deep breath and prayed for the grandma–in absentia–that God would heal her cancer even now. I next heard from the family about two weeks later. The grandma was completely cancer free.

For those readers who are hyperventilating over this story, I'll point out two things. One is that I do not have the power to heal; God does, and He enjoys working through willing human vessels. Two is that He invented speech; it is not a stretch for Him to speak to those same willing human vessels. Jesus called all of us to evaluate things in terms of their fruit, not their plausibility by our standards. Ruth received peace and healing for her heart; the grandma received healing for her cancer. Cases closed.

But of far greater importance is that God is calling His people–and any who desire to become His people–to expect the next Great Awakening. He launched this call the first day of 2008. He expects us to prepare for it by undertaking a season of individual and corporate repentance. By this He means–of course–to clear the barnacles from our spirits–what we call sin. But what He really wants–when the decks have been cleared–is for us to progressively re-focus our attention on Him. That means we become intentional about saying, "Yes" to whatever we hear or see Him doing, however counter-intuitive or uncomfortable that may be. It means judging our circumstances according to what we know of Him instead of judging Him by what we know of our circumstances.

It means to dedicate our lives–as He puts it in Luke 1:17–to going forth in the spirit and power of Elijah, to turn the hearts of the fathers to the children, to prepare a people for righteousness. It means to expect Him to show off when we show up, but showing up for us means to live in terms of others' needs. And it means righteousness–understood as alignment of our lives for the abundant life He brings–is the inevitable fruit of that dedication. Books like my own *The Holy Spirit and the EndTimes* are not about apocalyptic visions intended to terrify. They are both proclamation and primer for the greatest season of all time in which to serve the Lord our God.

The Great Awakening He promised in 2008 is today underway. The birth was announced in a vision of dry bones coming to life to form the skeleton of a lion–the Lion of Judah–and a man–the Lamb of God. Besides the vision I describe here there have been prophetic words and visions received all over the world. We in PrayNorthState are blessed enough to have heard confirming messages from multiple American locations and from across the Atlantic and across the Pacific–just from the friends and colleagues God has brought together in our circle–not to mention all the other ministry circles and communities of which we are not yet aware. God has begun to gather the prophesied–in John 14:12-14 and other places in the scriptures–end times harvest. And the best news of all is that the simplicity–and the urgency–of His call to His people to commit our lives to repentance while He does the heavy lifting and imposes no heavier burden than this–remains unchanged.

This the best news I have ever heard since Jesus first told me He loved me and wanted nothing more and nothing less than all of me.

AMERICAN EXCEPTIONALISM–PART 1 of 3

When I was privileged to give a keynote address at the Fourth World Christian Gathering on Indigenous Peoples in Kiruna, Sweden, the MC–a convener of the event–gave a dramatic and worldview changing response. I delivered a message that worldwide revival would begin with the indigenous peoples, but only if all of us chose repentance over redress of even justified grievances. (I am white, but descended from Scottish Highlanders.) I was coming from the Biblical concept that none can look God in the eye without first falling on their faces before Him. None are without sin, according to Romans 3:23, "For all have sinned and fallen short of the glory of God." Arild Maso, a Sami man, took the microphone when I finished my address and called for a complete change of course in the assembly. We had always concentrated on forgiving those who had harmed us; today he required us to focus on seeking forgiveness from those we had harmed. The more than one hundred tribes and nations represented spent the rest of the day in repentance.

In making my appeal as I did I was expressing one of the primary tenets of what is known as American Exceptionalism. That tenet is that all we have in the United States is an undeserved gift–for the uses of which we are both responsible and accountable. It comes from the Puritan playbook, along with the kernels of every other institution we hold dear in this country.

American Exceptionalism is the matrix of ideas summarized in the understanding that we are a people bound together not by a common history or ethnicity, but by a shared body of belief about who we are and what we are called to do. We reiterate this understanding each time we say that we are a nation of immigrants, that we are uniquely gifted to bring liberty and limited government to the world, or that we do what we do for the good of mankind rather than for a self-serving agenda. When I offered my own apology to a Filipino delegate named Pio Arce that afternoon in Sweden, I apologized for the brutality and arrogance with which we blessed his nation, but not for the fact that we are the only nation in history to conquer a land and work tirelessly to set it free in less than a generation. He agreed with me and we became friends that day. I was again expressing a primary tenet of American Exceptionalism–we see ourselves not as masters but as servants to the world.

Critics will say that imperial powers throughout history have claimed the kind of exceptionalism that animates Americans–from Rome to Great Britain and from Nazi Germany to the Soviet Union. It is true that Rome saw herself as gifting the world with Pax Romana, while the British Empire called it Pax Britannia–the peace and order of civilization as those nations understood them.

Nazi Germany claimed to offer racial purity and the Soviets came bringing so-called political purity. Rome and Great Britain stumbled on their own arrogance and sense of entitlement. Nazi Germany and the Soviets were evil and corrupt out the gate; they fell of their own bloated weight. Americans are unique – for better or worse – in believing we are called by God to bless the world with what we were given by Him – the first democratic republic in history and the first nation constituted so as to have a limited government for the release of maximum opportunity for all mankind. Of the latter reality there can be no doubt; the record of history is clear; of the former there can be no reasonable doubt when viewing the whole of our track record.

Americans as a people and culture are a flawed template for such an undertaking. We failed to make a constitution that abolished slavery, although we expressed our disgust for it in the document and the papers that facilitated its adoption, and we installed a mechanism in the document for repairing its deficiencies by amendment. We treated the indigenous peoples we found with brutality, although we address such issues with an open-ness that is unprecedented in the world. When we repent of our sins and excesses, as I did in Sweden and later in the Philippines, it constitutes not an about face but a return to our identity in Him who creates us as a work in progress.

The next installments of this series will examine our flaws and our rootedness in a hope-filled future. If we would approach thinking of our Independence Day more as a celebration of our dependence on God it seems the right thing to do.

AMERICAN EXCEPTIONALISM–PART 2 of 3

American leaders from John Winthrop to Ronald Reagan referred to America as a City on a Hill. The concept is rooted in the book of Isaiah. The Israelites saw themselves as endowed by Yahweh–God the Father–as first fruits of His intention to redeem mankind after our catastrophic fall in the Garden of Eden. Israel saw herself as uniquely blessed and uniquely charged to live and share with other nations a life with and under God. Christians see Jesus Christ as the resurrection of that vision–as well as its empowerment and re-inauguration. When Americans claim that kind of language we claim not a reincarnation of that vision so much as an adaptation of it in terms of a secular context of unlimited freedom and maximum opportunity. But to secularize the context in no way lessens the sense of giftedness from God or obligation to Him. Tragically, many of us see ourselves as somehow superior to others because of this legacy; others see only the gift and not the Giver; while still others are so conscious of the ways in which we have failed to live up to our destiny that they engage in an orgy of self-loathing whenever the topic arises.

Indeed we are a flawed template–and that is putting it mildly. It took us ninety years to eliminate slavery–we were virtually the last occidental nation to do it–and another century-plus to integrate African Americans into the American Dream. There are those who argue–justifiably–that the job is far from complete; yet the fruit of our task of making a truly egalitarian society for all of the tribes and nations greatly exceeds that of any other nation.

We have broken virtually every treaty we ever made with the Native Americans who preceded us into the land, and we have treated them with unimaginable brutality along the way. At the same time we have acknowledged and acted on their claims more quickly and more thoroughly than have our counterparts in–for example–Australia, New Zealand, or Japan. Our record includes the homesteads provided to ethnic Hawaiians–which are theirs by right–but such rights are flagrantly denied in many other lands. Although we hold territory beyond our fifty states, we have never instituted a colonial system, and we have blessed former colonies in which the so-called indigenous people treat those who preceded them in a manner fit for shame. Vietnam, Fiji, and multiple African nations come to mind. We are a flawed template, but we always return to it and the template of the city on a hill is indeed our exceptional identity.

The nation that gave the world the Monroe Doctrine–forbidding colonial nations from further operations in the hemisphere we swore to protect–practiced gunboat diplomacy when our economic interests were at stake in Latin America right up through the fifties. We subverted governments we believed dangerous–such as Guatemala when a socialist regime was elected–and we supported dictatorships so long as they were not communistic–such as Batista in Cuba, Somoza in Nicaragua, and Marcos in the Philippines. We promised backing to nations throwing off the communist yoke and then we bailed out on Hungary and Czechoslovakia when they acted on our promises.

At the same time we share the heritage of Puritan, Quaker, and missionaries of all denominations who dealt honorably with the Indians because they took their marching orders from God and the covenant they made with Him concerning their life in the new land. The treaty breaking was in the hands of those settlers and their descendants for whom manifest destiny was an entitlement rather than a calling, according to Marshall and Manuel's masterpieces *The Light and the Glory* and *From Sea to Shining Sea*.

We defended people groups around the world when they were the victims of aggression–from western Europeans to Pacific Islanders attacked by dictators in World Wars I and II. We rebuilt Europe–including the nations of our enemies–and Japan, supported freedom seekers in Southeast Asia and Korea, and defended the innocent of Kuwait and Iraq without so much as a thought to grabbing their oil resources–despite accusations to the contrary. We have supported the Jews who clawed their way out of the Holocaust, and we have supported the legitimate aspirations of the Arabs in what we know as the Palestinian territories. When we saw what domestic racism looked like on television in the sixties we stepped up to the plate as a people.

We Americans are a deeply flawed people; we are people, after all, and that comes with flaws. Yet we are a people closer than any other–except Israel, perhaps–to appreciating and activating a national relationship of corporate covenant with God in Christ and Christ in God through the Spirit who embodies the Trinity in our world. Our first Great Awakening–in the 1730s and 40s–gave us our identity in Him. Our second Great Awakening–in the first half of the nineteenth century–gave us our character as the first and foremost nation of entrepreneurs who share with others. And our third Great Awakening–in the latter half of the twentieth century–gave us our personality as a people undaunted by obstacles so long as our God is undaunted first.

We have shown more honesty and integrity than any other nation when it comes to confessing and atoning for our transgressions. Yet the good we have given the world despite our flaws is without comparison. It is our right to rejoice in all this so long as we give the glory to the One who alone deserves it.

In the final installment of this series I will look at our hope-filled destiny.

AMERICAN EXCEPTIONALISM–PART 3 of 3

Every American president until our present leader has expressed and celebrated American Exceptionalism, but John Fitzgerald Kennedy said it best. "We shall pay any price, bear any burden, meet any hardship, support any friend, oppose any foe to assure the survival and success of liberty...The energy, the faith, the devotion which we bring to this endeavor will light our country and all who serve it–and the glow from that fire can truly light the world." His address speaks to the secular context of an American dream of freedom for all–not just Americans. Yet he knew the book the Puritans tried to live by is the explicit repository of the concepts we combine into what we call our national exceptionalism. Paul–speaking for Jesus Christ and His Father and Spirit–says, "For freedom Christ has set us free." The freedom of which we speak is not a means to an end; it *is* the end of our making and creation.

Toward that end we remain unique on the world stage as a military power that acts with as much mercy as justice when we attack nations–like Afghanistan–who harbor terrorists and (into the bargain) are so hateful they prohibit women from seeking an education. We attacked Iraq because it continued to threaten its own neighbors as it threatened us. And we remain unique in that we withdraw quickly following an attack–as quickly as a popular government can take the reins and stabilize the nation, and this has always been our pattern. (To those who say Iraq was about oil, where is the Iraqi oil we allegedly stole; where is the price relief at American pumps?) We behaved in this way with the Philippines, Cuba, Vietnam, Eastern Europe, Italy and Japan; there simply are no examples of the other way around.

When we built the Panama Canal, we first liberated Panama from Columbian oppressors. When we discovered the sources of yellow fever and various other public health plagues we made our knowledge–and our resources–available without hesitation. In the wake of both world wars we fed those displaced by combat and led the way in their rebuilding efforts. When we led the conquest of space we also led the drive to avoid militarizing that new frontier, and we have made our space resources and technology available in a precedent setting movement. We drove the great wave of missionary work of the nineteenth century, and we are driving the short-term missions movement of today, with its emphasis on local indigenous control of decision making. Last but not least, our battles and our struggles have always been fought out in public, whether we debate healthcare, treatment of prisoners of war, or the spending priorities of our nation and whether unions have the right to pressure the agenda. This is because we are–at our core–a transparent people on the road of repenting into freedom.

It does not seem to matter whether our leaders are liberal or conservative in their shared commitment to what makes us Americans. Ronald Reagan said, "We have never been aggressors. We have always struggled to defend freedom and democracy. We have no territorial ambitions. We occupy no territories." Yet Bill Clinton said, "America remains the indispensable nation. America, and only America, can make a difference between war and peace, between freedom and repression, between hope and fear."

When I taught in the public schools in the seventies and early eighties I distilled the American Dream for my students into the opportunity for all to make twenty thousand a year and live in a forty thousand dollar home. Those numbers today would look more like one hundred and two hundred thousand respectively, but the reality has not changed. Added to that opportunity is the chance to practice our faith–whatever it may be and none if we prefer–and work out our lives to suit our own understandings. Many will say that such opportunities exist around the world today–and so they do. But they never existed before America and we are the drivers of such a vision today. Others will ask if the French Revolution and the Soviet Revolution did not lead to the same thing; reality is that their legacy was the Reign of Terror and the subjugation of millions until their defeat. Reality remains that we–at our best and so long as we serve our founding vision–are the nation that understands that so long as we trust in God for freedom we are set free–and not for ourselves alone but for a world to whom our Guiding Light gave His life, and then returned to welcome us into His Kingdom.

HEROES AND MESSIAHS: IN WHOM WE TRUST MATTERS

The tag line for the latest Captain America film is, "In heroes we trust." That supposedly clever play on the national motto, "In God we trust," is pathetic. Heroes – both real and of the comic book variety – are of great cultural value. Real heroes are role models and God-sends for each of us. Yet gods they are not and messiahs they are not. Heroes are rare and wonderful, but there is one Messiah.

Even so, God the Son is always looking for heroes who will acknowledge Him before men so He can acknowledge them before the Father. He has inspired a great model of what He seeks in last summer's film, *God's Not Dead*.

The plot line offers a university course in Philosophy. The professor begins the first day of class with an arrogant declaration that there is no God and only a fool would think otherwise. He passes out a sheet of paper to every student and demands that they write, "God is dead," and sign their names – in order to save the time in which they might debate the question. One student says he cannot sign it; he believes Jesus is His Lord and he will not dishonor this Lord. The professor challenges the student to defend God's existence in three twenty-minute segments over the next couple of weeks and flunk the class if he fails. The student – reluctantly – accepts the challenge. When the professor later confronts the student privately he admits that he hates the God who did not heal his mother of cancer and promises to destroy the student's career in retaliation for daring to take on the professor.

There have been many complaints about this film and its alleged lack of realism from many secular quarters. They are straw men and should be dismantled one at a time – hopefully without spoiling the surprises in the film for those who have not yet seen it.

Atheists say real atheists do not deny God's existence because they hate Him; they simply do not believe He exists. While I don't presume to speak for all who deny God, I know too many atheists just like the professor to accept this as anything but self-justification. Politically correct zealots project anti Islamic bias because a Muslim girl is brutalized by her father when he discovers her secret faith in Jesus. Again, I know former Muslims of both genders who face death if their families should discover their whereabouts. And the real grief of the Muslim father over what he believes his religion compels him to do discounts the view Muslims are presented as unfeeling brutes in this movie.

Amateur psychiatrists ridiculing the dementia patient who gains her faculties just long enough to speak eloquently to her wayward son about God's love don't know many dementia patients; such things do happen and I have seen them. Conservatives who think business tyros like the Dean Cain character are not that crass are obviously unfamiliar with the muck at the top of many pyramids. Progressives who claim students have rights to free speech on campus and professors would not hold students hostage to pet issues should review the dozens of cases cited at the end of the film–these are just pending cases of the Alliance Defending Freedom, one of many non-profit legal foundations who defend the First Amendment as their principal activity–or they could check in with me. I experienced this kind of discrimination–bullying–at San Diego State University more than forty years ago and it is much more prevalent today.

Anyone who finds the moment-of-death conversion to faith in one of the atheist characters non-credible should talk with me–or any Bible believer who has tended many people at this moment. And some of the pious among us should get comfy with the reality these people really do go to heaven–whatever they have done on this planet.

Only one aspect of the film struck me as unrealistic. When the student puts his proof to the test of democracy–per his agreement with the professor–every student in class stands to affirm their conviction despite the possible consequences to their class grade. The truth is most American Christians lack the courage to make such a gesture, and there are real consequences for cowardice. Jesus says He will acknowledge before His Father those who acknowledge Him before men; those who deny Him will be likewise denied per Matthew 10:32-3. But the consequence of courage is joy and peace in this life and an incomparable retirement plan.

God already sent the only Messiah we need. But He is looking for heroes and our culture needs the kind depicted in *God's Not Dead*.

THE TRUTH WILL SET US FREE

Lawlessness and bullying go hand in hand in our world. One of the most ghastly examples in history is remembered a few days after Christmas–the massacre of every boy under two years of age in the town of Bethlehem by a king as paranoid as he was tyrannical. King Herod would stop at nothing to eliminate a baby he understood to be the rightful king of Israel as a rival to his reign of terror. The irony is Herod was elected by the Romans, not the Jews, to be the Jewish king; he lacked even the requisite (for that day and culture) ethnic qualifications to be a legitimate candidate. He spent his tenure suppressing that truth in brutality that engulfed even his immediate family.

On a much smaller scale–so far–we see lawlessness in our government today and bullying on the part of politically correct plutocrats that is designed as much to suppress truth as to enforce conformity to their views. An administrative law judge in Oregon ordered Aaron Klein to make a wedding cake for a same sex couple or face fines; Klein shut down his business rather than violate his faith. A federal judge in New Mexico ordered wedding photographers Elane and Jonathan Huguenin to make their services available to homosexual couples in response to a 2006 lawsuit after the Huguenins cited religious conviction mandating their refusal. Gay marriage was not legal in Oregon or New Mexico at the time and the Alliance Defending Freedom is appealing the Huguenin case to the US Supreme Court. In Colorado baker Jack Phillips was ordered by a federal judge to service a gay couple's wedding even though gay marriage remains illegal in that state. In constitutional America faith trumps government–especially where consumers are free to patronize other businesses who share their views. Ideas become law when enacted by a legislative body, not because a judge decrees it. Judges who behave as these judges have are just as much criminals–under color of authority–as are others who flout the law.

On the plutocratic scale we have the recent specter of ESPN–lest readers think gay activists have cornered the market on bullying–refusing to run Christmas ads for a Catholic hospital that names Jesus as the reason for the season. More recent is the controversy over the A & E Network's *Duck Dynasty* star Phil Robertson. Robertson was suspended indefinitely from the show for comments he made to GQ Magazine having nothing to do with the show but yet disagreeing with the gay lifestyle and agenda. Personally I grow increasingly testy over the constant cries that gay people are being bullied when most instances of bullying over homosexuality making news feature gays as the bullies. After a public opinion uprising both ESPN and A & E backed down. But it will keep happening and the only question should be about what decent people ought to be doing about it.

By decent people I mean people who respect law, constitution, and the right of others to live as they will so long as they do not violate the rights of others. The advice I give is for everybody, but I suspect only professing Christians will find the inner strength for its sustained activation.

The first thing is to spend our sympathy on those who are being bullied, not on the bullies themselves. That does not mean privately deploring the injustice; it means vocal and public support from each and every one of us who loves decency and fair play. Phil Robertson ought to have the biggest fan club in the nation; Jack Phillips ought to be doing a land office business. It doesn't matter whether we agree or disagree with their views; we defend their right to express their convictions. If they express themselves poorly, as the Robertson family acknowledges he did, the right remains intact.

Public outcry is potent. Cracker Barrel Restaurants has apologized to their patrons for removing *Duck Dynasty* products from their shelves; the products are back. The public uprising over Chick fil A resulted in a bummer for the bullies.

The second thing is to not waste our sympathy by indulging in hatred ourselves. I sat near a grandfather filling his grandson's head with homophobic jokes in a restaurant yesterday and–frankly–if all I knew about it was what I heard from this moron I would be out marching in favor of the gay agenda myself today. I have always taught congregations I pastored that if we would speak on this topic at all it should be from the standpoint of a heart broken for wounded and suffering people; otherwise we do well not to speak at all. If we are not part of a solution both truthful and compassionate we are just part of the problem.

The third and climactic thing is to actively believe the words of Jackson Senyonga, "The condition of society is the report card of the Church." That means what goes on in the world–for better or worse–is the responsibility of those carrying the Spirit of God. Jesus said, "Render unto Ceasar what is Ceasar's and to God what is God's." The Church–led by Her pastors–should become a mighty (albeit non-violent) army taking a cue from the groups of veterans and truckers who marched peacefully and respectfully on Washington during the partial government shutdown to protest federal bullying. They emulated those who marched to DC behind the Rev. Martin Luther King in 1963. It was this kind of action–undertaken by this kind of humanity–that brought Abraham Lincoln to the presidency and galvanized Lyndon Johnson and Richard Nixon after him to bless and support the Civil Rights Revolution to the extent government can make a positive contribution to a grassroots phenomenon. The same equation threw the dictator Marcos out of the Philippines and broke the

Iron Curtain and the Berlin Wall. It is time we demanded a return to a nation of laws and justice rather than politically correct chaos.

There is a catch.

I took the title for this piece from the famous verse in John 8 in which Jesus tells His disciples the truth will set them free. Reality is that–taken out of context–His statement is meaningless. He actually said if we continue as His disciples–if we hang with Him and hang every dimension of our lives on Him–we will then know the truth and the truth will make us free. He is Truth. And no amount of political action will restore our nation to its God given greatness. Only a Great Awakening can do that.

ST. ANSKAR AND THE POWER OF PERSEVERANCE

Anskar was a 9th Century German priest and bishop with a tremendous burden to bring Viking peoples into the Kingdom of God. He was a man who saw visions over his lifetime and a formative one featured an angel telling him God wanted him to evangelize the Scandinavians and return home in glorious martyrdom. Readers wondering how one returns home after being martyred should know the term's meaning is "witness" and does not require death to activate it. Anskar's witness was to the power of perseverance in the Name of his King.

Bishops in that day knew little of the pomp associated with the office in our day. They were simply seen as overseers (literally) facilitating the work of planting and growing churches and Christians in a region by putting their personal backs to the wheel. They got a lot more of the actual work of the Kingdom done and had to attend far fewer meetings, a still common state in remote and third world regions today and all too rare in modernized areas. Anskar entered Scandinavia with a few friends and began introducing this violent and superstitious people to his best Friend – the God of peace which passes understanding. Many thought him crazy to devote his life to going where he and what he represented were clearly not wanted.

Peacekeepers are obsessed with maintaining the status quo – avoiding loss at all costs – but there was no peace to lose in ninth century Denmark and Sweden. Peacemakers are strong yet loving men and women who bring a gift so precious and lifegiving they are willing to risk everything to deliver it. Abraham Lincoln was such a dedicated peacemaker he fought a four-years' war to set the slaves and the nation free. Lyndon Johnson and Richard Nixon were so obsessed with peacekeeping they lost the Vietnam War and 60,000 American lives – not forgetting the million-plus Vietnamese who were sacrificed on the altar of "not losing." Anskar succeeded in planting two churches and a school in two decades of missionary work. He spent much of his time training and sending those who came to Christ in his churches, and as much more negotiating peace between rival warlords and petty kings in the neighborhood. The peace was an end in itself, but also a necessary pre-condition for facilitating the mission work. Anskar was armed with his indomitable spirit and the Spirit of the Living God Who kept him supplied with visions to follow and words to obey. Over the years he ended a civil war and averted a violent pagan reaction to his own work without bloodshed, but still had only a couple of churches and a school to show for it. At the end of his service he returned to Germany, deeply discouraged but still persevering in a God who claims His words never fall to the ground empty.

It took a century for the fruit to come into the bin. Missionaries raised and inspired under the ministries of Anskar and his disciples branched out and brought the Gospel to all of Denmark and Sweden, adding Norway and Finland into the mix. Because of this man's dedication–by choice, and whether circumstances were encouraging or not–Northern Europe came to Christ and the tenth century Euro visitors to America came as servants of Christ rather than of Odin. Granted, some of these converts imagined God's role in their lives was to endorse rather than convert their aggressive ventures, but that is God's problem, not the messenger's. Anskar never knew how effective he was–until he stood before the Throne of Heaven–but he is still today regarded as the patron saint of Scandinavia.

Like Anskar, we live in deepening darkness. War is all around. Men routinely call evil good and good evil, whether it is a dictatorial president forcing us into a healthcare swamp or families calling for retribution against good Samaritans who saved lives by taking out their relatives who were attacking others. Christians are hated over the world simply for being Christians. Unlike Anskar, we live in a time of abundant signs of God's grace–from healing cancers and growing stunted limbs to producing food where none would grow to softening the heart of a hard-nosed judge. Anskar's indomitable spirit is a gift from God and the Holy Spirit is a gift of that same God. We have only to take that God at His word (Is. 62:6-7) that when we call on Him we should give ourselves no rest and Himself no rest until He establishes His Kingdom in our midst. Anskar's legacy of perseverance is ours if we want it.

EASTER–THE GREATEST DAY OF ALL TIME

I preached my first Easter sermon thirty-one years ago. Like any neophyte I wanted to say something about Easter–the most talked about event in history–that had never before been said. I wanted to give people a chance to think about the reality of resurrection–to understand this gift–in a fresh way. My toddler son gave me my big chance.

He had completed potty training days earlier. As we celebrated his approach and graduation to a new level of "big-boy" life I noticed the combination of joy and terror with which he greeted it. And Easter came to mind.

I preached that Resurrection was a lot like potty training. We tend to greet it with the joy that can only be the natural response to the revelation that all of our separation from God and from authentic life itself is just an academic issue if we embrace the most down-to-earth-up-to-heaven Person who ever lived. But we also tend to greet it with the terror of knowing we have no further chance to avoid responsibility for living our life with, for, and toward God–no binding history, no seductive temptation, and no but-I-didn't-know excuse. The Resurrection–the Easter event–has brought us home to stay and given us every means for staying there forever. Any place in the world we go becomes home because we bring the blood, the living water, and the Spirit of the Living God with us. He is in us. Forever and ever; for better or worse.

After the service the senior pastor approached me, eyes wide with horror. "You said 'poop' in church!" Actually I did not use the word, but it was a fine distinction at best. I gave a graphic summary of what resurrection is like for us mortals who experience it–this new life in Christ. Every parent in the room–and most of the congregation was composed of parents and their children–knew exactly what I was trying to say, and commended me for it. Even the senior pastor had to confess I had achieved my goal–to say something new about Easter.

Truth is there is nothing new to say about Easter. It was, is, and will be the greatest day of all time. Anyone familiar with the addiction and recovery process knows the addict chose to self-medicate rather than seek authentic healing for whatever thorn is wounding his flesh. Just as familiar is the fact that there comes a point in the addiction cycle where choice is no longer an option; the addict is enslaved to the choices repeated too many times to be undone by effort–even repeated effort. Along comes the Son of God through Whom all are created. He lives among us, suffers with us, and shows us how to return to God–knowing full well it can only be accomplished through the sacrifice of His life and the gift of His Spirit. In the time ordained by the Father He does exactly that–and rises again on the third day with the promise in His rising that all of us may rise with Him if we only consent to His being the only resurrection game in town.

What is the fruit?

Over the millennia Christians invented social welfare. The Jews began to care for the poor first–their own–and Christians spread this God mandate throughout the world. Christians invented respect for life at all stages; Jewish prophets birthed the concept, but again it was the Christians who addressed mighty empires with the Word of God for life. (Christians–giving their lives in the arena–brought the Roman Empire to its knees over this issue and others.) And it was Christians who began and pursued the process of abolishing slavery all over the world–a process completed only with the destruction of human trafficking and Islamo-fascist groups such as ISIS and Boko Haram. Christians are the only effective–read compassionate–voice against racism today

Christians have fed hundreds of millions via miracles and the hard work of developing new ways to grow and distribute food through the scientific disciplines they invented. Christians have healed–in the power of God–more hundreds of millions through prayers and medical advances that are also fruit of their scientific advances. More than two billion people–alive today–know joy and peace because they accept the Lordship of the Resurrected One. But it is still as scary as it is joyful.

Each time we celebrate our Easter joy we are reminded its cost is the surrender of our authority over our lives. It's the same story of what is still the greatest day of all time.

CHAPTER 9:

ISRAEL

The children of Abraham descended through Isaac are God's chosen people not through biology, but through faith keeping. So the Word says in Romans 9. They are God's children not through circumcision but through covenant. God kept His promise to return and give Abraham and Sarah a child. Abraham fathered Ishmael by his own will; he fathered Isaac through God's will. God kept faith with His adopted son. The Children of Israel are called to reciprocate that faith keeping; they are called to keep faith with Yahweh through His Son, Yeshua, or Jesus, as we Gentiles know Him.

But here is the rub. Jesus often admonished people – Paul reports – to judge not the servant of another. The Jews of Israel are not our servants; we dare not judge them. Whether or not they are keeping faith – or whether any among them are keeping faith – with Yahweh is no particular concern of ours beyond the obligation we have to bear witness to our faith in season and out of season. Our job per the Jews is to love those whom God loves.

In Genesis 12:3 God says to Abram – who is not yet called Abraham – He will bless those who bless the children of the promise and curse those who curse them. By the way, the Hebrew word *barak* – bless – also means God will graft those who bless the Hebrews into His and their family. That is the same language Paul uses in Romans 11:17 and 18. "If some of the branches have been broken off, and you, though a wild olive shoot, have been grafted in among the others now share in the nourishing sap from the olive root, do not boast over those branches. If you do, consider this: You do not support the root but the root supports you."

I will say it again. Our job – and our privilege – toward the Jews and toward Israel is to love those whom God loves and bless those whom God blesses. We are expected to do this publicly and dynamically. How do we do that?

The essays in this chapter begin with an extended view of my three weeks spent in Israel as a volunteer for the Israeli Defense Forces. (No, I was not hunting terrorists; I was repairing radio antennas and hanging out with Israeli soldiers and civilians – and having the time of my life in the land of birth and promise.) Other essays reflect the reality that Israel is the tipping point for the world – and has been – for two millennia. Not only does salvation come from the Jews (John 4) but Israel is the most hated nation among all the nations the enemy of life hates. As that hatred infects nations that are not themselves dedicated to the Lord – that would be most nations and even our own under the present administration – Israel finds herself in the midst of a perfect storm, as the Book of Revelation promises will be the case.

How else than through an endtimes scenario might we explain the fact that so few of so historically beleaguered a nation can be hated to the death by so many?

Other pieces address the truth about the war that has surrounded Israel for all of her history since her resurrection – and the profound reality that only once in history has such a resurrection taken place after so long and so thorough a destruction. God's love and purposes for the Palestinians – possible only through His redemption and their repentance – and the evils of Sharia law for anyone at any location in the world – are laid bare. Finally, it is reiterated once again that Israel is the plumb line by which the world is judged and measured by a just – a merciful – and an almighty God.

If salvation is from the Jews there can be no salvation that abandons them. If we would participate body and soul in the Great Awakening as it unfolds there is no way to separate ourselves from Israel. Our support is no more acceptable in passive mode than is our witness in the public squares of our cities and our neighborhoods.

On the other hand, the opportunity to partner with God as He brings His ultimate purposes to pass – albeit in the role of junior partner – is wonderful beyond our ability to wonder.

THREE WEEKS IN ISRAEL

(Author Note: This piece was first published in 2012.)

I arrived in Israel May 17; there is a lifetime to tell about in the three weeks I spent in the land of God's firstborn. Let me begin it with this: In a land in which every home must have a bomb-proof room the repeated admonition from the people is, "Please do not romanticize us on the one hand or marginalize us on the other. We are not just people of war or people over whom nations bicker and bristle. We are people. We live here. We want to just live here."

I spent two weeks on an Israeli Defense Forces base near Ramla repairing radio antennae that will be re-cycled to service tanks. I spent three weekends with four different Israeli families in the communities of Nes Harim, Be'it Shean, and Jerusalem. I visited a kibbutz outside Caesaria Maritima and the nearby colony city of Zichron Ya'acov. The former is home to Hannah Senesch, who parachuted into Hungary during World War II to gather information for the British and rescue as many Jews as she could. She was caught, tortured, and executed by the Nazis in 1942. The latter was established by Baron Rothschild in the 1880's during the first wave of Jewish settlement. It was one of many locations in which the Jews drained swamps and irrigated deserts to make a living land where only death and disease flourished before. These Jews were urged to go to Eretz Israel and forbidden to enter at the same time over decades because the world hated them and did not know what to do with them. It hates them even more because they have succeeded against all odds. But let me tell you about the people I met, since it is as people they wish to be known.

Daniella and Dashi – eighteen and twenty years old – were my madrichoh – plural for female leaders. Daniella is Sabra – born in Israel – while Dashi came from Argentina less than two years ago. They are soldiers doing two years' compulsory service (three for men) and shouldering more responsibility than most of us do at a decade older. They are observant Jews in this amazingly secular culture – but not too much so. Sergeant Asher is an orthodox Jew who wears his kippah – a small skull cap indicating religious devotion – at all times. He musters out of the army soon to spend more time with his wife and children. He supervises my work and jumps back and forth between clowning with the volunteers and snapping, "I 'ate you," in his frustration at the difficulties in communication, but he always then laughs and spreads his arms to say, "No, No, I love you, Brother." On the last day I clapped him on the back and told him he was a good guy – which he surely is. He looked up with a broad smile and answered, "Of course," as he prepared to play soccer with some of us.

Engel is a twenty-five year-old civil engineer from Holland, on his fourth volunteer trip. He is strong, good-looking; all the girls like to hang with him. He is Christian without Jewish blood, but explains his presence with, "I love Israel." He tells me that if I visit him and wear my IDF baseball cap on the streets I might be killed. Anti-Semitism is running that high in his land, and it is not all from Muslims or immigrants. Aafke and Georgia are young Dutch women–nineteen and twenty-two–making multiple trips to volunteer. Georgia knows she is Jewish but fears she cannot prove it and so claim Israeli citizenship one day. Aafke just wants to live in Israel. They study Hebrew.

Arni and Yonit are American Jews who embrace Yeshua–Jesus–as their Messiah and call themselves Messianic Jews. They emigrated in 1990 and hold dual citizenship. They release worship in Israel and lead international teams to other lands to worship the God of Israel as His representatives. Avital and Shuki are immigrants from Iran and Hungary; their children are Sabras and they are Jews–not Messianics, just Jews–who love Eretz Israel as the only land in the world in which they are the landholders rather than the tenants. They own a Bed-n-Breakfast five miles from the Jordanian border and the Sea of Galilee. When they took me to Nazareth to stand and pray in the church over the site where Mary received word she would bear the Christ it was simply showing hospitality to their Christian houseguest. But when I asked Avital if she felt the peace inside the place as I did she said she did indeed feel it. They are people I love. I do not think of my friends as evangelistic targets, just people for whom I want all that there can be.

These people have been forced into war five times and they stand surrounded today by hundreds of millions whose great ambition is their extermination. These same fanatics hate Americans and the freedom we represent with the same passion; our freedom springs from the same wellspring–the God who "for freedom that Christ has set us free," per Galatians 5:1, and says if we hang with Him we will know both truth and freedom in John 8:32. They are not perfect people, just people who ask us not to romanticize or marginalize them. They are not all about war; they are all about living at home. I am proud to know and serve them as God provides.

That is all very well and good, but why cannot the Israelis return to their pre-1967 borders and everyone live happily ever after?

It seems like a reasonable request. The story goes that all of the disruptions and tensions–and suffering–of the Palestinian people–and hatred of the people of Israel–refers back to the 1967 War. If only we could return to the pre-war boundaries of Israel and start again there would be a hope of real peace. That peace, guaranteed by the United Nations, would leave Israel nothing to fear.

Trouble is, the story is more holed with false suppositions than a swiss cheese. My time in Israel fully convicted me of this beyond anything I believed before going there.

First it pre-supposes a will to compromise on both sides. Yet the history of the region is consistent. Israel has given self-government to the West Bank in exchange for the concession of her right to live, but the Palestinian charter still calls for the destruction of Israel. Israel has conceded full sovereignty in Gaza in exchange for the concession of her right to live, but Palestinian leaders have never made any concession. Israel has gone to the bargaining table after stopping settlements on what the Palestinians call occupied lands in exchange for the mere right to live but–and on it goes. In the meantime rockets are fired from Lebanon, the Gaza Strip, and the West Bank itself. I stood in the shopping street in Jerusalem where terrorists armed with machine guns blocked escape from the narrow way and gunned down scores of shoppers not long ago. While I was there a Palestinian snuck in from Gaza, armed with an AK 47 and hand grenades, for the sole purpose of killing as many civilians as possible. There is a will to compromise–but only on one side.

It pre-supposes well armed and financed Israelis brutalizing the poor and backward refugees of the disputed lands–refugees who want only to worship their God in Jerusalem–a city as holy to Islam as it is to Jews and Christians. This is another myth.

Reality is that Jerusalem is the capital of Israel and has been for three thousand years. It was taken from them by armed conquest and they recovered it through armed conquest in a war they did not start. (They did indeed fire the first shot in '67, but that starts the war only if massing troops on their borders and blockading all their ports is not starting one.) Reality is that all faiths have been welcome to worship as they choose throughout Jerusalem and all Israel since the Israelis re-claimed the whole city–including the temple mount. Prior to that time Jews were prevented from accessing their holy places even though truce accords and UN mandates dating back to 1947 required open access.

It also pre-supposes the grinding poverty of the refugee camps is the sole Arab reality. Though I do not doubt the stories of the camps, I saw plenty of Arabs driving new Mercedes and I saw the satellite TV dishes on their high rise homes. Reality is that the Arabs who live in Israel prefer it to living under Hamas–for good reason–and only those in the disputed zones express the hatred in which they have been steeped all their lives. Meanwhile the Israelis re-cycle everything they use because they are not a wealthy nation–just a nation that mobilizes all of its resources for survival. That is why I spent two weeks repairing radio antennae for military vehicles.

The Israelis are not perfect. They have committed arbitrary acts and sometimes do shoot first and ask questions later. But there is no comparison between a democratically elected government presiding over a culture of freedom and tolerance and a lock-step government dedicated to the destruction of that culture in favor of Sharia Law. There is no ethical touchstone between a culture that has made a thriving economy–and invited non-Jews into it–out of what was once desert and malarial swamp, purchased at exorbitant prices and reclaimed with great labor–and a culture that demands the UN hand it back to them. There is no reasonable way to call the hostilities between them mutually combative when it all began as the British disarmed the Jews and armed the Arabs led by the Grand Mufti Husseini after he returned from years as Hitler's houseguest and apprentice.

The Lord God Himself says, "You, mountains of Israel, will put forth your branches and bear fruit for my people Israel…" in Ezekiel 36:8 regarding the return of the people. The Jews want to live in peace in the only land on earth that is actually home to them. It is not too much to ask.

It is not too much for American Christians to support heart and soul, if we believe what the New Testament says (Romans 9 and 11) about us being grafted onto the original vine that is Israel.

During my stay in Israel I spent two weeks volunteering in what is called the Sar-El program–a voluntary and non-governmental program that recruits people from all over the world to spend from one to three weeks on a military base–as the civilians we are–to live and work alongside Israeli soldiers. We do chores for the soldiers so that they are freed to do more important things. More importantly, we get to know what it means to be an Israeli in today's world. We learn how to know and love Israelis without romanticizing them on the one hand or marginalizing them, on the other. We eat, sleep and shower in their facilities. We play soccer or just visit with them in our off time. My two weeks on the base of three weeks in the country will remain one of the most treasured experiences of my life.

We took one day off work to make a field trip to the town of Zichron Ya'acov. The name means "in memory of Jacob" and the Jacob in question was the father of Baron Edmond DeRothshild. The baron used his family money to found some forty-five settlement colonies in what was then called Palestine, beginning with the first wave of Jewish immigration in 1880. It took fifty years of blood, sweat, and death to make the town what it is today–a garden spot in every sense. But the Jews had their backs so to the wall that there was no alternative. They hung in there.

We visited a kibbutz and learned of the way people lived there once and how they live there today. All the kibbutzim began as experiments in socialism but nearly all are private enterprise today. In the beginning the children were taken from their homes and raised in a collective atmosphere. Eventually it was discovered that this horribly damaged the children and the practice was abandoned decades ago. But all was not lost of the early experiments; the best drug rehab programs and some prisoner rehabs are run like the old style kibbutzim. And the day and its field trip gave rise to the most enjoyable group activity of my time in Sar-El.

Each evening the volunteer group would gather for an educational/entertainment opportunity. Afterward we hung out with each other and any passing soldiers until we drifted off to our bunks. This evening we were divided into two teams and tasked with designing a kibbutz–including rules, areas of emphasis such as what agricultural products we aimed to produce, and a vision for our community. My team knew that strawberries were well suited to the soil and climate of much of Israel. *Tut* is the Hebrew for strawberry and we decided we would form a kibbutz that grew and sold strawberries, strawberry ice cream, strawberry yogurt, and anything else that fit the theme. Our golf carts and bikes for use on the kibbutz would be strawberry red and our logo would be a ripe red strawberry. And the name? You guessed it–we would be the tutti kibbuti!

The greatest honor I received was to be asked to raise the Israeli flag on my first morning on the base. The greatest privilege was celebrating the Lord's Supper on the banks of the Jordan River about a hundred yards from where Jesus Himself was baptized. My greatest surprise was visiting the Old City of Jerusalem and seeing sights like the Citadel of David on a blistering hot Judean day only to find the garden in the middle of the church compound across the street where cool breezes blew no matter how hot it was outside the compound–or perhaps the peace that believers and pre-believers alike feel in the Church in which Mary received word that she would bear the Christ Child. The greatest moment, however, was being overwhelmed and undone by the loving presence of God Himself as I laid my hands on the western wall of the temple of Yahweh. There is no preparing for it.

My first hope was to go to Israel as a volunteer; my next is to return to this God-blessed land and find those who would bully them have been subdued and then–perhaps–healed. I speak of the bullies on their borders, in the United Nations, and even in the United States. But I speak especially of those whose lives are dedicated to bullying Israel into extermination.

The appetite for revenge in a bully is insatiable. This is because bullies have been–by and large–the victims of bullying themselves. Because they are unable to confront their abusers to the point of satisfaction they typically vent their rage at others who become their victims. It is never enough; their original wounds remain unaddressed and so are still bleeding. It was that way with the boy who bullied me.

I discovered only years later–when we became friends–that he had been the victim of an older boy himself. Unable to stand up to his bully he vented on me until the day I fought back. When it was over he promised never again and we eventually became friends. Over the years God literally brought forth from this man the heart of a servant. He brought forth real healing as well, but only over years. It is like that for Arabs and Israelis.

The people we call Palestinians today were bullied for centuries by the Ottoman Empire, a despotic regime that embraced Islam and was centered in modern Turkey. (There has never been a nation called Palestine at any time, although the Romans so named their middle eastern territory.) The empire was a feudal society and the average man had nowhere to go as he suffered under the effendis–the Ottoman aristocracy. When the empire fell in 1918 the system survived under colonial rule. Contemporary Arabs recalled the splendor of the centuries of Islamic expansion when they were the cultural and political rock stars of the world, but it was only a memory. Although persecution broke out periodically, Jews actually fared pretty well compared to their European brethren–so long as they paid the special taxes levied only against Jews and kept out of prominence. But when Jews began returning in numbers to their ancient land–occupied for nearly two millennia by the Arabs who now call themselves Palestinians–and began to make the land bloom and prosper as the Arabs could not–and to favor one another over the other inhabitants–the seeds of resentment were sown. Unable to address those who had and still lorded it over them, locals began to vent on the newest neighbors. Add the power hungry Husseini clan whose head became the Grand Mufti of Jerusalem–and a protégé of Hitler–and you have a volatile cauldron without peer or parallel.

Over the span of two thirds of a century Jews made their traditional homeland bloom. They irrigated deserts, drained swamps, and learned to prosper in the land. They purchased land at exorbitant prices and–admittedly–discriminated against their neighbors when it came to hiring. But the rising tide raised all boats, including Arab/Palestinian boats. Discrimination issues were addressed and the newer settlers could claim–truthfully–that they robbed no one and developed only such lands as had been neglected and abandoned by previous owners. They did this in a time of rising blood lust against them worldwide. Truly resettlement in the land of their fathers was their last and best shot at survival. And yet the colonial authorities did their best to keep the Jews out in significant numbers.

In efforts to win favor from Arab leaders in the fight against the Axis powers the British spurned mercy requests from Jewish leaders to greatly increase Jewish immigration. Arab aggression against Jewish settlements was fanned and ordered by the Mufti and greatly escalated upon his return from Berlin after the war ended. The British literally stripped Jews of whatever arms they had and allowed the Arabs to arm themselves as partition approached and the world waited for the annihilation of the Jews in its wake. Instead, the world watched a miracle unfold as tiny Israel fought off the assault of five nations in 1948. Another miracle unfolded as Israel reclaimed most of her original borders in 1967.

It was in the 1960s that formerly Syrian, Egyptian, and Jordanian citizens began to call themselves the Palestinian People and established the Palestinian Liberation Front for the annihilation of the Jews who claimed citizenship in Israel.

The God who said He would bless those who bless Israel and curse those who curse her apparently heeds His own words. Yet Arab peoples actually stem from the same Abrahamic root as do the Jews if we believe the scriptural accounts of Hagar and her son, Ishmael. God loves these Palestinians and sent His Son to die for them–as He did for the Jews–according to His same Word. As it was with my friend, the first thing to be done with a bully is to stop him in his tracks. But the second and more important thing is to seek healing and reconciliation across the board. The world can help the process by honoring the integrity of both parties to it, addressing the historical wounds the Arabs have suffered but beginning with the Jews' right to the homeland they have reclaimed. All of it. Or we can just watch and ask Israel to shoulder the burden.

ISRAEL IS THE TIPPING POINT

(Author Note: This piece was first published in 2011. Multiple resolutions on Palestinian statehood have been considered by United Nations bodies in the interim. The Security Council did vote on establishing a Palestinian state without reference to Israel or the peace process in December 2014. Eight nations voted to grant Palestinian statehood despite the failure of the Palestinian Authority to demonstrate fulfillment of any of the United Nations criteria for statehood. The vote was eight to two with five members abstaining, including Britain and France. Nine votes were needed for the resolution to be adopted. Only the United States and Australia voted no.)

Four hundred five of four hundred thirty-five Congressional Representatives just adopted a resolution calling on the president to cut off aid to the Palestinians if they force a unilateral state into being through a UN vote in September. To his credit, the president has called on Gaza to withdraw the proposal – one likely to be adopted if advanced. Yet – to his profound discredit – President Obama's state department convened a white house summit on Israel July 11 and excluded Israel from the talks. The Arab League and the European Union were represented; Russia and China were there; only Israel, the subject of the summit, received no invitation.

In other words, in vintage colonialist style, the great powers convened to discuss how to deal with the upstart nation – Israel – that disturbs their peace and their hegemony. Their behavior is beyond rude; it threatens the very concept of Israeli sovereignty. More than that, these so-called great powers ignore that Israel is the sole nuclear armed power in the region, and thus its most potent military player. It might be a good idea for President Obama to include Israel the next time he wants to discuss her future.

Modern Israel came into being in 1948 and was immediately attacked by five Arab nations vowing to destroy her before she could be born; she repulsed those attacks and lived. She repulsed armies again in 1956. She fought for her life once more in 1967, her current borders being determined in that conflict. She is often accused of initiating the '67 war, which is technically correct if we forget that her enemies had been attempting to divert her water supply since 1964, shelling her farmers from the Golan Heights, and vowing in two summits (Algiers, 1964 and Cairo, 1965) to destroy her in 1967. Controlling territory only nine miles wide, Israel did indeed fire first when her neighbors mobilized to carry out their threat. Who can seriously blame her?

There is a myth that the United Nations created Israel and can therefore dictate her shape and her future. In fact the United Nations partitioned the territories mandated to British control and named Palestine following World War I. The British did all in their power to disarm the Jews living in those territories while winking as the so-called Palestinians–who were citizens of Jordan and Syria at the time–armed themselves. Their Arab neighbors received weapons and training from the fugitive Nazis they harbored prior to attacking Israel in 1948. But Israel declared her independence May 15, 1948. Those of us who believe in God contend that God created Israel more than three thousand years ago–and again in 1948. Others may hold that she created herself. The United Nations was at best a bystander to history.

How about the notion that God creates–and protects–Israel then and now? In the Holy Book shared by Jews and Christians–the Old Testament of the Bible, a prophet named Zechariah writes that in the last days there will be such favor on God's favorite people that, "ten men from all languages will take firm hold of one Jew by the hem of his robe and say, 'Let us go with you (Zech. 8:23) because we have heard that God is with you." Paul, writing in the New Testament Book of Romans, says that salvation is so entwined with the Jews that the rest of us should think of ourselves as branches grafted onto their vine. Jesus Himself, in the Gospels, says that salvation–which stands for life and healing as much as it does for redemption–is from the Jews. The Bible is replete with some pretty grandiose rhetoric about God's final reign and how it connects with and emanates from Israel. Can we see it confirmed in our morning newspaper?

Efforts have been made to exterminate the Jews throughout history, from Pharoah's murder of every Jewish baby to the Inquisition to the Holocaust–and a second Holocaust threatened today by Iran and the Palestinians, led by Iran, Hamas and Hezbollah. There are fewer than twenty million Jews worldwide in a world of more than a hundred million who wish them dead. How do they survive and even thrive? I see no explanation for it that leaves out a God who looks like the biblical description of Him. That makes Israel the tipping point–not just for the Middle East but for the world–and she has certainly been the central international issue of all time. I'm thinking we do well to serve God and back the people He calls the winners.

SALVATION IS FROM THE JEWS OF ERETZ ISRAEL

Lynda Prince is a Native American Christian leader of international renown with a special connection to Northern California. Five years ago she prophesied the return of Benjamin Netanyahu to lead the Israeli government. My heart sank when Ehud Olmert became the PM–because I believed the prophetic statement Lynda had released in my hearing, and because I knew Olmert's commitment to Israeli security did not include commitment to God's covenant with Israel. The covenant with Israel includes the Land of Israel–known to Jews as Eretz Israel.

My heart sank again when Netanyahu failed to gain a majority vote in the most recent Israeli elections–he was not even the top vote getter–because I forgot again that God does what He plans in His way rather than in my way. I was reminded of the truth when the prophesied leader emerged as the only candidate capable of forming a government–and he has done just that by the grace of his God and mine.

The United States fought a major war in the sixties, sustained a civil rights revolution, and undertook the incredibly expensive War on Poverty. Whatever we may think of any of these phenomena, history shows that we endured such upheavals during the Kennedy and Johnson Administrations without harm to the economy. Israel fought her six day war during this period and had an unwavering ally in the United States. She fought the Yom Kippur War in 1973 with major league support from the Nixon Administration and much less from the Ford and Carter White Houses. The economy tanked during Ford and Carter years while inflation shot into space. The Reagan years marked a return to support for Israel and prosperity at home. Lyndon Johnson was a political liberal, Ronald Reagan a conservative. The only common denominator between them is Israel.

George W. Bush has been one of the most supportive-of-Israel presidents we have ever known. Yet the current recession, marked as it has been with the housing market meltdown beginning in 2007, bears a remarkable chronological correspondence to President Bush's push for Palestinian statehood at the expense of lands God dedicated to Israel four thousand years ago. (To Bush's credit, he consistently demanded performance rather than promises from Palestinian leaders and suspended the process when performance was not forthcoming.) The Obama administration is on record as favoring the division of Jerusalem along with the division of Eretz Israel, and the economic chaos in which we find ourselves deepens.

Is there a simple one-to-one correspondence between the way we treat Israel and the goodness of life we experience? Certainly not. We were not spared the street riots and lynchings of the sixties; divorce rates shot through the roof; sixty thousand American dead and hundreds of thousands maimed in multiple ways paid for a war our leaders never intended to win. But there is the Word of God (Genesis

12:3) that says–in its context–that those who bless Israel will be blessed and those who esteem her lightly will be cursed. The Word of God cannot be broken; attitudes toward Israel count–and they count for a lot. We blessed Israel in the sixties; the early seventies, and again in the eighties; our people had jobs like never before; the standard of living increased for all. (The Arab oil embargo shocked us but did no serious damage to the economy.) We emerged from that time ready to write new chapters of the national adventure. And there were the twin revivals of the Charismatic renewal and the Jesus People in which millions (including me) came to know Jesus personally.

Jesus tells the Samaritan woman at the well (John 4) that salvation comes from the Jews. He also tells her that He is the promised Jewish Messiah, but He does not leave it at something like, "Salvation comes from me," although this would be a perfectly true statement. He says, "We worship what we know," while others worship in ignorance. He implies something special about the people of Israel that transcends the Messianic gene pool, and Paul is a good deal more explicit in Romans 9-11. He declares we Gentile Christians are grafted onto a vine without which we have no root; that root is the Jews.

The bottom line is that we Christians have a mandate to guard the flanks of our elder brother until he too comes in from the cold and confesses that he is a prodigal who wants to come home. Paul goes on to say in Romans 9-11 that the Gentiles received the fullness of grace in order to provoke jealousy in the Jews–that they too might receive the abundant life that is the fruit of their covenant. The Jews are in crisis as never before–between Palestinians shooting rockets at random, a soon-to-be nuclear armed Iran, and the resurgence of anti Semitism around the world. All of this comes in the face of increasing pressure from their so-called friends to place themselves at the mercy of people who seek their extermination through land for peace schemes that never seem to change. (The Saudi plan is scarcely different from that of the Nazi sympathizing Grand Mufti of Jerusalem of sixty years ago.) The time to pray for the peace of Jerusalem and the blessing of Israel–as though everything depended on it–is now.

My friend, Ray Shelton, is a NorthState pastor with a heart for Israel. He tells of the walnut industry in Butte County–of how the trees grow English walnuts because their flavor is so much sweeter than that of the black walnuts that are native to the area. But in order to get a crop it is necessary to graft the English walnuts onto the stump of black walnut trees. The hardier black walnut will flourish in our soil as the English walnut will not. We need each other–cannot thrive without each other–and once again God does it His way rather than mine. Who knew?

PERFECT STORM FOR ISRAEL–OR TIME TO STAND WITH HER?

Media reports Hamas and the Palestinian Authority merging interests and assets into a unity government. It is good for no one when a terrorist organization merges with a so-called former terror group. It is especially ominous for modern Israel–a nation that has spent its sixty-seven years of life under constant threat of annihilation and at least five credible attempts to destroy it by enemies more than twenty times more numerous.

BTW–the United States gives hundreds of millions of dollars to the Palestinian Authority each year–tax dollars. In light of this merger we are now funneling that money to Hamas, the most notorious terrorist group in the world after Al Qaida.

The Palestinian Authority theoretically recognizes Israel's right to exist but only if she gives up so much of her land over nearly four thousand years to a group of refugees who claim it without ever having owned it. Hamas won't even go as far as recognition. And now the United States–under Barack Obama and John Kerry–have telegraphed our intention to bring Israel to heel by any means necessary. Kerry recently claimed an Israel that does not return to her pre 1967 borders is ripe to be labeled an apartheid society. (He hinted at sanctions should Palestinians resume attacks on Israel. My question would be when did those attacks ever cease?) There is no more serious anathema to be hurled by one nation at another in our politically correct-on-steroids world. We have thrown our closest ally under the bus–or at least promised to do so if they continue to displease us. This is a perfect storm for an isolated Israel. But what is it for the American People–the vast majority of whom believe Israel is God's chosen nation, an underdog worthy of support, defense, or both?

Some will point out Kerry has already pulled back from the apartheid label, that he didn't really mean that. Experience shows people speak the truth they truly believe when agitated. In any case, Kerry and Obama have demonstrated their hatred of Israel since the beginning of their respective tenures in office, as did Hilary Clinton when she helmed the State Department. My question for the American people remains.

Israel is the only democracy in the Middle East–as Democrat Barbara Boxer points out in her denunciation of Kerry's apartheid statement. She is our closest and most consistent ally, and a light to her region–the most volatile on earth–if they will have her. After the US she is the first nation to aid others in time of disaster. We owe many of our medical and computer advances to her tradition of innovation, not to mention her agricultural advances making deserts bloom. We owe her better treatment than this.

The people of Israel have suffered more tyranny, butchery, and persecution than any on earth. In each of the five full scale wars in which she has fought in less than a century the other side has been the aggressor–including the 1967 war in which she won back so much of her ancient territory and made of Jerusalem a holy city in which all faiths are welcomed and honored. (Palestinian Arabs had turned Temple Square into a slum; Israeli forces restored it.) The so-called Intifada came about because an Israeli leader had the temerity to seek to worship God on the Temple Mount, which was then and is Israel's property and holiest site. Justice demands better treatment than this.

Finally, the Word of God calls the Jews God's chosen ones, His firstborn whom He will never abandon. Christians and Jews, comprising more than a third of the world's population, believe the prophecies about Israel rising from the ashes–a unique achievement in world history–because they have all come true. Jesus was born and remains a Jew of Israel. He says if we expect to be acknowledged by His Father we had best acknowledge Him. Where I come from if you want to acknowledge me you acknowledge those I love. The Holy Scriptures–and I refer to materials that have proven accurate in the crush of world events–demand better treatment than this for Israel.

I asked what this means for the American people. The great majority of us know the truth–and the justice–of what is written here. It means we must rise up as a people and demand our government act with justice, mercy, and a newfound humility toward people who deserve our support. It means we must stay in the game until truth prevails. The Israelis have suffered enough and we have waffled enough.

EYELESS IN GAZA: LET THE SCALES FALL

Enroute to Israel in 2012 I flew with a young Israeli couple. They said Israelis are ordinary people trying to live well. "Millions hate us just because we live, and so we live in constant danger. But all we have ever wanted is as normal a life as possible. Please do not romanticize us, nor expect us to accept death passively."

As I write in late 2014 the guns have fallen silent three days before Hamas resumed rocket fire and Israel responded with air strikes. Israel, in a fight for her life but humanitarian to the end, withdrew all her troops a week ago. It is the same fight for life that began with her founding in 1948. And the aggressors are the same neo Nazis whose forefathers cut their teeth in Berlin when the Grand Mufti of Jerusalem was the guest of Adolph Hitler throughout the war. Let any who doubt read any history of the Middle East during the war years not written in Iran. And let them wonder why so many Palestinian and Arab agitators deny the Holocaust as an isolated fringe group among the leaders of the world. Their Nazi mentors taught them well.

But let's review the events of the past month. They began with the brutal kidnapping and murder of three Israeli teens, one of them an American citizen. They did not begin with the rain of thousands of unprovoked rockets each year on Israeli civilian areas, although that would be provocation enough. They did not begin when Israel withdrew from Gaza in 2005, even though the rocket fire increased by about 500%. But the kidnapping and execution of three of their children was the straw that broke the camel's back. Israel determined to destroy the tunnels that made these crimes possible.

Israel stands accused of targeting civilians. Yet they are the only nation on earth–besides the United States–who warns civilians to evacuate the area of their operations, giving away any hope of surprising their enemies. They warn Palestinian civilians placed at risk–sometimes days in advance–while Israeli sirens are able to give about fifteen seconds' warning before an incoming Hamas rocket detonates. I find it remarkable that we see nightly coverage of Palestinians left dead, injured, and homeless by Israeli air and artillery strikes while seeing no pictorial coverage of the destruction in Israel wrought by thirty-five hundred rocket strikes in this month alone. Truth is exactly what Prime Minister Netanyahu has said, "There is a difference between us. We are using our missiles to protect our children. They are using their children to protect their missiles."

Truth is Hamas deliberately stores and launches its rockets from beneath schools, hospitals, and even private homes. Truth is Hamas has been a complete bust at governing Gaza even after they were democratically elected by the very people the commentators call innocent. (Don't get me wrong; all children are innocent; the question is who puts them at risk.) The Gaza government was bankrupt after losing the support of Syria, Iran and Egypt; they had no way to pay their forty thousand employees and unemployment was 50% — way up from when Israel pulled out in 2005. Their attitude was, "Why not attack Israel? Our charter demands their obliteration. What is to lose?" And they have proven right. Our president gifted them with forty seven million dollars in so-called humanitarian aid; does anyone believe it will be used for aid? The very tunnels the Israelis blow up are made from concrete they donated for building houses, schools and hospitals. But that means nothing when a government views its citizens as weapons of warfare.

It is incredibly rare when war is so clearly a contest between right and wrong; yet this conflict is just that. But what–some say–about the United Nations?

Since 1948 Israel has asked only to live in peace. Her enemies have demanded war and extermination, per the charters of both Hamas and the Palestine Liberation Organization. So why do the United Nations repeatedly condemn Israel as the aggressor, and especially in the current conflict? Can it be this objective organization, dedicated to world peace, is not as objective as its press releases declare?

According to the New York Times the United Nations Relief and Works Agency–UNRWA–is the second largest employer in Gaza. Known locally as "the agency," it runs hundreds of schools and medical centers for Gazans. These are the same schools in which students drill daily in hatred for Israel. They are the same schools and hospitals in which Hamas rockets are stored and tunnels are buried. When Israel found caches of rockets in three UNRWA run schools the rockets were turned over to UN personnel who promptly returned them to Hamas.

Israel warned the first school it is accused of attacking days before the attack came. The UN evacuated its personnel but waited several days before promising to evacuate the civilians. As the busses approached the school was rocked by three to five explosions; sixteen were killed and dozens wounded. Israel denies firing on the school and even the UN has published no conclusion to its investigation of the cause. But no matter, Israel has already been blamed for a crime it has no reason to commit. Hamas, on the other hand, has a track record and an interest in maximizing civilian casualties on both sides–from sheer hatred on the one and political expediency on the other. Granted, the explosions could be the result of ordinance malfunctions from one side or the other, shots falling short or long, and the like. But there is no reason to believe Israel maliciously attacked a civilian enclave; they have never done it before and it defies their policies and history.

Detractors of Israel love to point to firing the first shots of the 1967 War as proof of Israeli aggression, and it is true the opening salvo was from Tel Aviv. I ask myself, and recommend readers ask themselves, "What would I do if I saw an armed mob walking up my driveway shouting threats of murder on my children? Would I wait until they were in my living room straddling my children before I opened fire, or would I shoot the moment I could and hope to take as many down as possible before they breach my front door?" Critics will say I over simplify the issue, but the issue actually is just that simple. Israel was surrounded in 1967 by armies poised and promising to strike. She had been under fire from strategically placed artillery more than two years. She had been denied passage through the Suez Canal and international waters. The war was long since underway when Moshe Dayan and Levi Eshkol sent their divisions hurtling into what became the miracle of the Six Day War.

Israel is the only Middle Eastern power to exercise restraint in the conduct of war. When an Israeli paratroop brigade took the Temple Mount and raised the Israeli flag over the Dome of the Rock, Dayan immediately ordered the flag taken down and the mosque returned to Muslim authorities. Israel practices authentic freedom of faith and equally authentic respect for all faiths within her borders. When Jordan controlled the Temple area the Western Wall of the Temple was an Arab slum.

Israel has greatly improved the lives of all who call her home. There is terrible poverty in the refugee camps, but none of those camps are Israeli controlled. I saw many Arabs driving late model Mercedes and living in very classy high rise apartments. They are able to vote, hold office, and do anything they want other than attack and kill. There is no comparison between the lives led by Arabs in Israel and those in the Palestinian controlled areas and certainly no moral equivalency between the aspirations of Palestinians to deal death and the hope of Israelis for life and peace in the region.

Aldous Huxley earned fame in 1936 writing his novel, *Eyeless in Gaza*. The title refers to Samson, the Jew who put out the eyes of his own heart before his enemies burned out the eyes in his head. Before death Samson replaced his heart eyes and returned to serving God. He redeemed himself, albeit too late to save his physical sight. The American government and many peoples of the world have blinded themselves to the simple choice between the God of life and the god of death in Gaza, but the blinding need be neither physical nor permanent. Let us follow the God who says (Genesis 12:3) we are blessed when we bless Israel and cursed when we reject or ignore her.

Will we Americans replace our heart eyes, or will we remain eyeless in Gaza? The issue of justice is clear. For us who believe the Christian Scriptures the issue is clearer still. Israel does not need us; God has her back. But we need to back Israel if we would stand before God–or even walk in integrity apart from the claims of faith. The soul of our nation is on the line; it is time to speak up and speak loudly enough that our leaders hear and tremble.

REBUILDING GAZA? HOW ABOUT AIDING THE INNOCENT?

Even today the cultural tendency for people in authority is to ignore bullying until the victim protests. After that the default is to blame the victim; everything was fine until he began to make others uncomfortable. This is especially so if the victim has fought fire with fire. Sometimes–if the victim perseveres–the bullies are confronted. In any case, it should surprise no one that this dodging of responsibility by authorities translates readily into relations among nations. The policy makers at the macro level are the spiritual and cultural siblings of those who make the rules in family and school communities. And the first rule is the victim is not allowed to take matters into his own hands and just fight back against the bullies. Said victim is to wait upon the goodwill of the very authorities whose inaction permits the bullies to flourish.

That said, why–in the name of all that is good–are the United States, Western Europe, and the United Nations rebuilding the Gaza Strip without so much as a dollar going to rebuild Israel?

The destruction in Gaza is a tragedy. This is especially so when we consider the vast majority of casualties are civilians and the destruction of homes and schools is a mutilation to the survivors. But the civilians of Gaza elected Hamas to be their government; they are not innocent. Truth is the present tragedy began when Hamas kidnapped and murdered three Israeli teens. Fact is Hamas fires about three thousand rockets into Israel each year with the sole intent of killing Israeli civilians; about that number has been fired this summer alone, and the tunnels destroyed were equipped with handcuffs and tranquilizers meant to facilitate the murder of many more–after being taken alive. Reality is Hamas–the legitimate authority in Gaza–places civilians between its weapons and the Israelis in hopes that many will die and world opinion roast the "ruthless" Israelis for defending herself. So far the strategy is working well. The UN investigates war crimes allegations against Israel without a word about Hamas targeting their own civilians by using them as human shields. American journalists report ceasefire after ceasefire shattered without mentioning who did the shattering. Apparently our media is too delicate to tell it like it is.

We give half a billion dollars to the bullies to repair damage done when the victim struck back. We give nothing to restore the innocent party. Of course some will say–and it's true–there is much less damage done in Israel. But since when does the fact Israel is so much better at defending herself than the Palestinians are at attacking her a moral failing? Since when is the sixty-six year absence of Jewish aggression in the Middle East compared to five wars of extermination and God knows how many murders evidence the Israelis deserve anything but sympathy and support?

The predecessors and founders of every Muslim/Terrorist organization were mentored, supplied and suckled by the remnants of Nazi Germany after the Grand Mufti of Jerusalem spent the war as Hitler's guest. They have proven worthy heirs, and their movement is resurgent in the Europe from which so many Jews fled after World War II. My Dutch friends told me when we volunteered together in Israel that if I wore my IDF baseball cap on the streets of Rotterdam at night I would likely not survive the night.

Yet the Father God who creates the world and redeems it through His Son in the Power of His Spirit is sovereign–whether we acknowledge Him or not. This God said it in the Old Testament before He paid for it on the Cross in the New; justice is to roll like a river and He will save His people. Israel does not need our help to prevail. We need to help Israel and so align with Israel's God if we want His blessing. Yet it remains a matter of simple justice any intelligent person can comprehend.

People on the fence over this ought to check out the 1960 film, *Exodus*. It illustrates the story textbooks only tell, complete with the Nazi forebears of the Islamo-fascists of today and the merciless brutality of the so-called Palestinians when one of their own tries to walk in truth. Some will opine that this movie is fiction, but the real fiction is the absurd notion that Hamas–or any of the other Islamo terrorist outfits–have even the remotest claim to any moral high ground. Or that their goal is anything but genocide–beginning with the Israelis and moving on to the people of our land.

FREEDOM FOR PALESTINIANS–TRADING TRUTH FOR LIES

The well known promise of God for Israel is expressed in Genesis 12:3. The Father of Father Abraham says his children will be numbered as the grains of sand and the stars in the sky. He says any who bless Israel will themselves be blessed beyond imagining and any who curse Israel will be cursed beyond thought. Cursing is as much to reject or abandon as it is to attack. In other words, those who ignore Israel's status as the firstborn of God are in for some serious ignoring by God when the chips are down. Jesus Himself declares of those who say they know Him but have ignored His will, "Go away from me; I never knew you."

I noticed a photo on the internet the other day of Pope Francis stopped before a wall in Bethlehem. The wall held scrawled graffiti calling for the liberation of Palestine. I cannot know the heart of this Catholic Pope and so I cannot know whether he favors Palestinians or Israelis, or whether he naively believes peace is possible in the Middle East if both sides just agree to live in peace. I do know that I too long for the liberation of the Palestinian people, and I know there is no authentic liberation possible while so many believe the hate soaked lies Palestinians are fed by their leaders.

Israel herself bought the lie in 2005 – under pressure from a gullible George Bush – that if the Palestinians were permitted to govern themselves peace would come. Has life improved for Palestinians in Gaza since Israel handed over the land in 2005; has even one refugee camp closed? How about the limited self-government Israel permits in the West Bank? Any new status quo, or just more places for rocket launchers and riots?

I know a few other things as well. I know the Israelis have never launched terrorist attacks on their neighbors – civilian or military. Palestinians are as free as Americans to shop in their bazaars and take their children to school or to play dates. That all too many of their schools are filled with munitions and their homes rubble is due to deliberate choices of the Hamas government they elected. Hamas used the concrete donated by Israel for housing and infrastructure to build tunnels for infiltration and murder. Even so the Israelis give warnings by text, phone and leaflet before attacking these militarized neighborhoods. It is Hamas who forbids families to flee under penalty of death, and Hamas that uses Palestinian children as shields for their soldiers.

Israel begged the Jordanian and Syrian citizens of her Arab population to stay and build with the Jews in 1947. Some did, and they live well under Israel as full participants in government and culture; I have seen their high rise dwellings and their Mercedes and Audis. Others answered the call of Jerusalem's nazified Grand Mufti and his armed thugs to leave, returning only to attack the civilian settlements of the Jews. Hitler is dead, but his hatred lives in the heart of his satanic master and those who serve that master. In five wars and multiple smaller military actions the Jews have bought space for their children to go to school and to play with their friends. In 1967 they re-captured their ancient capital and much of their plundered lands while defending themselves against overwhelming aggression from five nations attempting their annihilation. Even today Jews are stoned by Palestinians from above while they seek only to pray.

In recent days Israelis are dragged from their cars and beaten to near death while the world press moans about the "innocent" Palestinians who are hurt or killed when Israel protects her own from their fanatical incursions. A mother of five was attacked in her car with Molotov cocktails and rocks; light rail trains have been attacked and bombs hidden on highways. Palestinians and Arabs are rioting in multiple towns and cities. At least eleven Israelis are dead at Palestinian hands – five of them hacked to death while worshipping in their own Jerusalem synagogue. Are Israelis attacking Palestinian and Arab civilians anywhere? No; the provocation of "grave concern" – per America's government – is that the Israelis dare to build housing projects in their own capitol city.

The good news is there are decent Arabs – appreciative of what they have in Israel and of the standards of common decency – who saved at least one assault victim by protecting him from the mob until police arrived. They would fear for their lives if they intervened in such an incident in Gaza or the West Bank. Even in Jerusalem a number of Arabs have died in the recent violence, some killed by their own people when they intervened; others just caught in the crush.

The better news is there is one – only one, and it is ultimately inexorable – prospect for both peace and liberation. "For He Himself is our peace, who has made the two one and has destroyed the barrier, the dividing wall of hostility, by abolishing in His flesh the law...to create in Himself one new man out of the two...and in this one body to reconcile both of them to God through the Cross," is how it comes across in Ephesians 2.

I cannot forget the images – broadcast via television news nightly during the summer's fighting in Gaza – of Palestinian children victimized as pawns by their own government while the world condemns Israel for defending her children. I saw no photos of Israeli children made homeless by Hamas rockets – the media suppressed them – but I have names. Avi and Leah; Shuki, Avital and Adi; Yoel and Laura; Arni and Yonit; Asher and Daniella – these are my friends who live in Israel showing grace and mercy wherever they can to people dedicated to their destruction. Make no mistake; Israelis show up as fast as Americans to reconstruct and rescue the victims of disaster worldwide, even when the victims are their own sworn enemies. I say to Pope Francis–and anyone else who is listening–I stand with you for the liberation of the Palestinians.

But it must be authentic liberation. It must be liberation through truth and a commitment to authentic justice for the people who remain the only bright spot of civilization in the Middle East. And it must begin with the blessing of the children of Abraham through Isaac–if not for the sake of Genesis 12:3 then simply because it is the right thing to do. Only then can we truly bless the children of Abraham through Ishmael.

LET US IMAGINE FOR A MOMENT

Let us imagine for a moment. Imagine my own state of California.

Imagine California surrounded by Arizona, Nevada, and Oregon – as she is. Imagine Texas and Colorado pushing their way in to border California as well. Conjure up seething hatred for California and an armada of tanks, artillery and aircraft dedicated to her destruction once ordered. Visualize a state-within-a-state the size of California's Central Valley running from the Bakersfield oil farms to well north of the state's capitol – more than half the length of the state; imagine the death of California enshrined in its charter. Finally, imagine California reduced in size by seven eighths, and her population of forty million shrunk by the same proportion. What you have is Israel.

Some will say analogy is dangerous; the parallels fall apart after awhile and no longer apply. This is no analogy. It is simply a description of Israel and her neighbors today with the names changed to reflect American realities. Expand the vision to take in the majority of the other United States and imagine they are blaming California for the implacable hostility surrounding her and threatening to grant independence to that state-within-a-state, even threatening to support all-out war against California if she does not withdraw behind borders determined by her enemies. This too is Israel today.

Many people say Israel is aggressive; she shoots first and asks questions later – if at all. Sometimes she does – shoot first, that is. In 1967 she was surrounded by five enemies bent on her extermination, just like our imagined California. Unlike our fantasy state, they had twenty times her population and an even greater disparity in military resources. They blockaded her ports and announced imminent war. They had already fired on her people but had not yet crossed her borders. Israel struck first – with devastating impact. She drove these homicidal bullies from her ancient territories and reclaimed her stolen capitol city. This is Israeli aggression?

Israel has never fought a war of aggression in her sixty-seven year history. It was the same in the recent Gaza conflict, except this time she was attacked with thousands of missiles instead of artillery and kidnap/murder squads instead of aircraft. She now faces the same militant Islamo fascists – spiritual descendants of the Nazis who harbored and mentored them seventy years ago – augmented by a host of new ones. To their strength is added the one hundred thirty-five nations now clamoring for them to cede to their enemies the land and security they won nearly half a century ago. Is it strange that they resist? Imagine California fighting for her existence as Israel now does.

Many American voices declare Islamic militants to be a lunatic fringe of an otherwise peaceful religion. They point to the millions–perhaps hundreds of millions–of Muslims who are law abiding citizens, content to care for their families and worship God as they understand Him. Indeed there are many such, and many of them live right here in the United States–even in California But where in the world has Islam become the ruling power and repression of non-Muslims does not follow in its wake?

Deal with it. Every nation in which Islam rules imposes restrictions of some type or another on the freedom of faith and speech of their inhabitants. Some are as brutal as Saudi Arabia–in which a man has just been sentenced to ten years in prison and one thousand lashes for setting up a web site demanding freedom of speech. Many are much less so–thanks be to God–but none understand freedom as we do. Where Muslims are a minority they move as quickly as possible to establish enclaves in which they can rule by some form of Sharia Law. In France–prior to the attacks on a French newspaper and a Kosher market–there were more than seven hundred zones into which French police refused to go for fear of attack; non Muslims are forbidden to enter. Efforts are underway in our nation to establish such zones.

Don't get me wrong. Jesus Christ gave His life for every Muslim as well as for every other human being. All who confess Him on their lips and believe Him in their hearts (Romans 10:9) are destined for eternal and abundant life. He is determined to love even those who do not. But He does not love a religion of brutality against non-adherents. He–Word of His Father–sent the armies of Israel against those who threatened her yesterday and today. He expects the rest of us to accept truth and seek justice for all–especially His chosen ones, Israel

THE ARAB SPRING AND SHARIA LAW

When is democracy not a good thing? When it becomes the French Revolution, the Russian Revolution, or Nazi Germany. Many people forget that Hitler was first elected to office, Robespierre and the Reign of Terror were the fruit of a popular uprising, and–although Lenin overthrew the elected government in 1917–it was the democratic chaos following the Czar's ouster that made the communist revolution possible. Democracy is only a good thing when the popular will is restrained by an enforceable constitution with built in checks and balances. Majorities are every bit as capable of tyranny as minorities when they are in absolute power. The difference between mob rule and a community in covenant is constitutional restraint. So what about the Arab Spring?

First let's be clear that there is plenty of provocation for the uprisings that swept the Middle East in 2011, just as there was for those earlier revolutions that resulted in tyranny. The kings of France were as corrupt as they were decadent, Nicholas II dragged Russia into a war that killed millions of Russians because he liked French culture and had a cousin on the British throne, and the Weimar Republic made fertile soil for Hitler with its hyper inflation and the complete collapse of morality on its watch. Likewise dictators like Mubarak and Quaddafi butchered their own people and–in the latter case–terrorized other nations. The same goes for Tunisia, and the Iranian people certainly made clear their preference for the mullahs over the despised and despicable shah.

Although I make no excuses for the deposed autocrats, it is just as clear that things have gotten–and are getting–worse rather than better. The Iranian shah was a threat to his people; the mullahs have a well worn track record for being a threat to all of us–and their admiration of Hitler is as well documented as their longing for a worldwide caliphate under Sharia Law. This will guarantee that petty thieves have their hands cut off, women raped can be themselves executed by relatives, and any who leave Islam are subject to death from the state. Tunisia, Egypt, and Libya have gone the same route–although the Muslim Brotherhood has been deposed in Egypt for now–imposing Sharia by popular vote and joining the coalition determined to first annihilate Israel and then to complete the work of world domination begun and halted centuries ago.

Once the Muslim Brotherhood emerged as the money player in Egypt; they began partnering with the revolutionary government of Libya, and their allied party won big in the Tunisian elections. In all three nations a populist agenda calls for the destruction of Israel and imposition of Sharia as soon as possible. Surging mobs in Cairo chanted that they are building gas chambers for Jews, and hold up signs to that effect. Christians have being murdered and persecuted in all three nations–as they are in Iran. Yemen is the latest state to join the march into hell. The writing is clearly on the wall, while the American Government courts these nascent regimes–and our president claims credit for their victories. What should we do?

The first thing is to stand up to them. That begins with not a penny of aid to these revolutionary regimes and nascent insurgencies, and a renewed pledge that any attack on Israel is an attack on us. It continues with holding the remaining dictators in the Arab world accountable; I don't mean we invade Bahrain, but we stop propping them up. We let them know if they want to be safe they treat their people with common humanity. We remember that we didn't go to Afghanistan to help them, but to respond to an act of war; we stayed out of our humanity, and we can leave if they cannot demonstrate a reciprocal humanity. (Declaring they would side with Pakistan in a war with us is not a good beginning; neither is imprisoning Afghans who change religions.) We let it be known that people who trash our own cities while calling for the overthrow of our culture and assaulting our police will be treated like the mobs they are. And finally we pray for those who hate–whether they hate for political or religious reasons–that God would bless them with His peace–rather than replacing hate with hate. The Christian scriptures say that in the last days men will call evil good and good evil. They also say that when these things happen the Lord Christ of real peace is not far behind. I haven't got a clue how long that process might take, but I take the declaration to the bank.

It promises a real Spring after a long and bloody winter.

ISRAEL: THE PLUMB LINE OF THE WORLD

Israel is the only nation in history to be restored after two millennia of exile and obliteration. She is the only nation to have lost half her population in a massive act of genocide only to become the most powerful nation in her region and a world leader in multiple technologies. She is the only nation in her region to respond to international disasters on a scale proportional to what we Americans do, and she is unique to her region as an exporter of the fruits of both agriculture and high technology.

Israel is the sole nuclear power in the Middle East – so far – and the only nation to live under the constant threat of annihilation at the hands of nations with twenty times her population. She has beaten back wars of extermination five times in her sixty-seven years of life. And she is the only nation with a vital interest in the recent peace talks with Iran to be excluded by our secretary of state from those talks. The United States and multiple allies now seek to dictate peace to her if she gives up more than half her territory – including the portions that make possible the defense of the rest – portions won in battle when she was attacked simultaneously by five nations. And we wonder why she views her most dependable ally – us, at least in the past – with suspicion.

According to the Associated Press piece dated January 2, "Kerry would not impose ideas...Instead he is allowing time for debate," but even the AP admits the US expects a final agreement by May that includes Israel giving up most of her capitol city and the site of the Temple of Yahweh along with much of Judea and Samaria. The Palestinians would be asked to recognize Israel as a Jewish state, which in their minds compromises the right of return for their refugees and the rights of nearly two million Arabs who are Israeli citizens living in Israel. The AP goes on to refer to Palestinians who "fled or were expelled in the war over Israel's creation in 1948."

This nonsense masquerades as journalism. Reality is the Arab-Israelis are not and have never been Palestinian in any sense; they are Israelis who live a lot better, and a lot freer, than any Palestinians in Gaza or the West Bank. Many of them drive Mercedes autos and live in high rise buildings, unlike their poverty-stricken brethren who are so frequently photographed. I have seen this with my own eyes. No Arabs were expelled from Israel in 1948; many left despite Israeli pleas that they remain, although it is true they have not been allowed to return after turning their backs on their neighbors who were attacked by multiple armies trained and encouraged by the escaping Nazis of a defeated Germany. Fact is that Israel withdrew from Gaza in 2005 and their thanks has been a rain of rockets and bombers. I have stood in a marketplace with only one exit in which Palestinians with AK47s mowed down shoppers just a few years back. Truth is there has never been a nation called Palestine until Yasser Arafat invented it less than half a century ago. The Arab people who left Israel were citizens of Jordan, Syria, and Egypt; their own nations refused to receive them after the 1948 war and so they became refugees.

A required–by John Kerry–goodwill gesture before talks begin was the release of twenty-six terrorists held in Israeli jails. No corresponding gesture was required of the Palestinian Authority. Those released include school bus bombers; they returned home to a heroes' welcome. How intelligent people can believe the Palestinians are serious about anything but destroying Israel is beyond imagination. American citizens need to demand this mirage of a peace process be halted until the Palestinians prove they are serious about it–at a minimum. Our decision is a plumb line of our national character.

If you are a Christian in love with the God who became flesh in Christ–and the one does not necessarily imply the other–the fact that God promised to restore and protect Israel while destroying those who curse her in Ezekiel 16, Zechariah 12-14, Isaiah 49-54, and other places beyond count–should be enough to clarify His will in the matter. That we Christians are grafted onto the Jewish people, and so bound to their fate and the favor God shows them, is stated simply and directly in Romans 11 and in other places. Our responsibilities are as clear as our rights. And if you are not a Christian it is a matter of simple justice.

CHAPTER 10:

ACKNOWLEDGING HIM BEFORE MEN

Jesus imprints His word from Matthew 10:32-33 on my heart–seemingly–on a daily basis. If we acknowledge Him before men–He says–He will acknowledge us before His Father. If we fail to do this He will decline to acknowledge us before the Abba we so desperately need. He speaks these words, of course, in the context of when the chips are down and we are commanded by those with power to kill the body to deny we are part of His Body. But acknowledgement has many forms in scripture and in life.

Every time I have a chance to pray for my server when I am out to eat is a chance to acknowledge Him. Whenever I blog it is a question He asks, "Will you reference me explicitly or expect people to listen only to what you call wisdom?" When I see someone sick or injured in a public place–or even where only they will know–do I ask if I might ask the Lord to intervene? And certainly any time I meet someone and it comes organically into the conversation I have an opportunity to share the history–my personal history–of life with my best Friend and how we came to know one another. If it is true that every act God commits in scripture or in the world we see is for the primary purpose of His revelation–and it is–then every act committed by one made in His image must be properly understood as an opportunity to reveal Him in ourselves.

The longest piece in this chapter is a summary of an amazing journey to which God has called me and which is far from complete as I write. Last summer I responded to a five-year-old vision from the Lord to begin the building of a bridge of prayer across the United States through state capitols. I visited nine western states and prayed in their capitols with local leaders. I went as guest–for this is how we learn to be heirs; as servant–for this is how we learn to be leaders; and catalyst–for this is how we give God glory through the fruit of others giving Him glory. It was my privilege to encourage leaders in renewing their faith, to honor praying people to whom God had revealed a revealing name for them and to participate in healings of bodies and hearts.

When I prayed for a restaurant server after asking her if she knew how much God loved her I saw tears well up; she realized God loved her enough to send someone to pray. When I discussed global warming with a graduate student in Physics I remembered to point out that–although it is not a science text–the Bible has never been wrong on a scientific statement it makes from time to time (He did not believe me when I told him cyclonic wind patterns were discovered by science in the nineteenth century and by the people of the Old Testament three thousand years ago in the pages of the Old Testament. But the acknowledgement was there.) And when all my plans fell apart in one of the states God led me to minister to a staffer in the governor's office and she acknowledged–with me–that God orchestrated the whole thing so I could get staff input before prayer. It is all–and always–about new chances to acknowledge Him before men. Or not.

The essays in this chapter begin with the new perspective we receive when we allow Him to turn our hearts to the children because He has called all of us in this season to function as fathers–mothers are the other side of the coin and just as important–of course. The Capitol Prayer Bridge is chronicled–and encouraged–in whatever form readers may be called to honor Him in ways both public and unexpected. The connection between praying and actually doing something about God's response is explored, along with the concept–and the command–to live our lives drunk in His Spirit. The imperative to seek racial reconciliation rather than one-up-manship in the grievance department is shared The triune topics of prophetic authenticity, pragmatic application, and purposeful parenthood are explored in successive essays, and the chapter closes with another look at the Eucharistic–thanksgiving based–heart as the pathway to living in the Prophetic–or Kingdom or Consecrated or Covenental–Community (choose the term that feels right) God is forging in the New Testament realization of His unchanging but ever expanding revelation of Himself.

This book intends to be an extended exercise in the unlimited varieties of acknowledging Him before men and women. But if we take Him seriously when He calls us to (Luke 10:1-9) bless, hang out with, minister to, and share our faith with everyone we meet we can be making breakfast, filling our car with gasoline, or going to work or play with family, friends, colleagues, and neighbors. It is all part of the grand opportunity and obligation to acknowledge Him before men.

TURNING THE FATHERS' HEARTS

The Genesis Generation – born after 1983 – has been called a fatherless generation, as has my own Boomer Generation. In 2008 God called out a new season based on Luke 1:17. The verse – in its prophetic context – proclaims a John the Baptist generation of fathers (and mothers) turning their hearts to the children...all children. Fast forward to 2014 and I happened to watch two movies about fathering on a flight from Malaysia home to the States.

The first was the critically acclaimed *Nebraska*, a film I cannot acclaim. It depicts an alcoholic, thoroughly self-absorbed, and utterly disengaged father played – superbly – by Bruce Dern. He imagines he has won a million dollar prize and is obsessed with traveling from Billings, Montana, to Lincoln, Nebraska, to claim it. His sons and his wife move heaven and earth to get him there, in the vain hope he might actually notice the sacrifices they make for him. He stops in his home town – in Nebraska – and interacts with old friends and relatives just as useless as he is; their reason for living is to con or coerce him out of money he has not won. The few people he knows who have lived decent lives and want nothing from him are given a few meaningless moments of screen time. It is all about this loser who never gets it and does nothing to justify his existence, relieve the suffering he has caused, or bless his children.

The second was the un-acclaimed *Delivery Man*. Vince Vaughn plays David Wozniak, another loser, but with the difference that he wants to be different. David donates sperm twenty years back and takes his whole family to Europe on the proceeds from his donation. He discovers the clinic used his sperm to sire more than five hundred children with nearly one hundred fifty demanding to know him despite the confidentiality agreement he signed. Although his lawyer assures him he can win a lawsuit against the clinic if his name is leaked – he does win the suit – he comes gradually and freely to accept responsibility for fathering these kids. Beginning with reluctance, and without revealing his identity, he helps one secure a job, another kick a heroin addiction, and gifts his time to still another. Turning his heart to his children moves him to get rid of the marijuana grow in his apartment and, ultimately, to reveal himself. In other words, turning his heart to his children changes him and creates authentic adult humanity in him.

David freezes when he meets his son with cerebral palsy, but – haltingly – steps up to the plate for this challenge as well. He makes the necessary commitment to really father his newborn son with his girlfriend, and commits to marry her. This is a film I do acclaim for presenting a man donning authentic humanity by taking up the challenge to turn his heart to the children – any children – because that is God-in-Christ's heart in this season.

There is plenty of good teaching about the Father Heart of God. There are plenty of opportunities for fatherless ones to experience that love from Him, mediated through men and women willing to parent in His image. But there is precious little on the reality that the act of fathering is what makes us good sons and daughters as well as good fathers and mothers. It works a lot like the centurion's faith in Matthew 8:5-13. The centurion understands that Jesus need only order it and his paralyzed servant is healed. He understands Jesus' authority because he operates both in and under authority as a Roman officer. Jesus applauds his faith as unparalleled in Israel. And the best news is that we need not know how to parent to begin. It is on-the-job training, just as it was for David Wozniak.

My own father had no patriarchal role model growing up. He made plenty of mistakes raising me–hurtful mistakes. But when the chips were down he stepped up to the plate. He pushed when I needed pushing and had my back when I needed him behind me. He blessed me on my wedding day like one of the biblical patriarchs although he could not have understood–in biblical terms–what he did. I hope my children–those I raised and those I spiritually father–see my father and my God in me.

Our alternatives are simple. We can be as self-centered as the Bruce Dern character and kid ourselves that he is interesting, or we can be as Christ-centered as David Wozniak turns out to be–whether or not he knows it. The choice is very simple.

A CAPITOL PRAYER BRIDGE–ALL THINGS WORKED TOGETHER

I spent July 7 through August 3, 2014, traveling through the capitols of nine western states. I met with local teams, praying and worshipping inside the capitol buildings. I preached and taught in various venues along the way. We asked the Lord to intervene in areas of concern to the whole state; in California and Oregon we prayed about the drought; in Idaho it was about illegal immigration and a spirit of rejection; in Montana and Wyoming a militant spirit of independence that leaves little room for God or human cooperation. The journey became an extended demonstration of Romans 8:28, in which God promises to work all things together for good in those who love Him and are called according to His purposes. He does not promise immediate or even uninterrupted bliss, just that sooner or later–one way or another–He will bless His people across the board. He never lies.

Lots of people think vision is just a really spiritual sounding word for an imaginative plan. But a vision is actually...well...a vision. Anybody who thinks the Lord God cannot communicate with His people in literal visions does not get what it means to say He is the first and authentic source of every great painting, sculpture, and motion picture. And what the Lord showed me–in the interior of imagination He creates–was a suspension bridge spanning the United States. It was composed of local people praying and worshipping inside their selected state capitols. I saw myself called to join them as guest, servant, and catalyst.

When we begin–anything from new ministry to new business to new art–with a vision we are next called to use our God-given brains to posit a rational route to realization of the vision. In the capitol prayer bridge I identified nine western states more or less surrounding California as the west coast anchor. I spent six months networking one contact person at a time, beginning with friends and relatives I knew in some of the states and later asking ministry colleagues to connect me with others.

I met people who have transformed a nightclub–once a center for drug dealing and human trafficking–into a place of gathering for Downtown Salem, Oregon, where good food and music are served along with uplifting programs and some of the trafficking victims have returned to receive healing for horrific wounds in body and spirit. We prayed with representatives of the state government, finding bookmarks randomly placed on the same scriptures God planted in other people's minds to shape the prayers. We spoke of a budding partnership between Salem, Oregon; Sacramento, California; and Olympia, Washington; of praying and having each others' backs. We saw miraculous healings–medically verified–from a heart condition to chronic skeletal issues and conditions of the heart.

Even things that apparently went wrong became things that went righter than we could imagine. In one state I was forced to visit the capitol alone–a one-eighty from my intention and what I thought to be God's plan–because the organizer for that state was hospitalized and there was no team awaiting my arrival. Yet separate (apparently) chance meetings with a tour guide and a member of the governor's staff netted me as good information about topics for prayer as any team could provide. And when I opened my Bible–seemingly at random–to see what God might reveal from His Word to shape my prayers it quickly became evident He was downloading information I would never have received listening to a team instead of opening my heart to Him. I love to teach that we put our faith not in our ability to hear, but in His ability to speak. It is true.

The most dramatic convergence of God' graceful pro-vision and pragmatic reasoning came when I committed to visiting the site of a nineteenth century massacre of peaceful Cheyenne and Arapahoe by white American militia. Two days before my planned visit to Sand Creek I got a call from an Arapahoe Elder who had welcomed me onto the land of Wyoming in that state's capitol. She had just learned through another (seemingly) chance encounter of my plan to pray at Sand Creek. When I told her I did not yet have the requisite blessing of tribal elders to enter the land–nor any idea how to obtain it–she identified herself as a direct descendant of Chief White Antelope, murdered at Sand Creek. She agreed to accompany me and welcome me onto that land as well. God gets the glory for the healing and reconciliation that are well underway.

It begins like this.

On November 29, 1864, a body of cavalry attacked a sleeping camp of Cheyenne and Arapahoe people at Sand Creek, Colorado. Commanded by Colonel John Chivington, they rode down and massacred nearly two hundred as they lay clustered in family teepees. The Indians, roused from sleep, fought back as well as they could but were outnumbered, outgunned, and taken by surprise. Women and children were slaughtered and mutilated along with the men; babies were literally snatched from their mothers' breasts and their heads crushed. The soldiers were initially hailed as heroes on their return to Denver; the true and horrific story of the massacre only began to come out as they days went by. This peaceful band flew an American flag and a white flag of surrender over their camp as tokens of their covenant relationship.

Captain Silas Soule forbade his men to fire on the camp. Upon his return he denounced his commander, becoming one of nineteen witnesses who testified against Chivington during the subsequent investigation leading to three different hearings. Days later Soule was gunned down on a Denver street. His killers were known but no charges were brought. Although Chivington lost his commission and his life became a trainwreck of failed businesses, incestuous marriage, and a painful death from cancer, no charges were brought against him. The stain on American history remains.

Even the land bears the marks of the slaughter. Believers of the Bible know when land is defiled by the gross shedding of innocent blood, idolatry, covenant breaking, or sexual sin the very rocks cry out per the Genesis story of Cain and Abel; other Biblical examples abound. Sand Creek–once a place of flowing water and access to game–has been bone dry and utterly desolate since before anyone living can recall. Land and people cry out for healing and reconciliation, graces that can only occur in the face of repentance before God and the people so horribly wronged.

When I accepted God's call to visit and pray with local teams in the capitols of nine western states I knew of the coming one hundred fiftieth anniversary of Sand Creek. I felt called to go there and pray during my few days in Colorado, although I had no idea of the site's location, nor of how to obtain permission from the appropriate Cheyenne or Arapahoe elders to visit. Permission is obtained through relationship and I knew no one in the area. Permission is a necessary act of respect, just as it would be for members of my own people if someone wanted to do something on the gravesite of our ancestors. I knew it was a matter of common courtesy no matter whose name might currently be on the title deed.

The first thing needed was to locate the site. After initially telling me the site was too distant for a day trip, Kelly, my Denver hostess, e-mailed next morning to say her husband, John, awakened practically shouting his conviction that he and I were to visit Sand Creek and he would drive. Fully confirmed now that I was called as John was, I consigned the matter of permission to my God. It would not be the first time I had known I was to visit a site at an assigned time and depend on God Himself to connect me with the right people to bless the visit. And then the phone rang.

Rhoda is a Native American woman I have known the past decade. We re-connected after a long absence during a conference call in preparation for the capitol prayer bridge trip and she promised to be at the Wyoming Capitol when I arrived. She met Gina, National Day of Prayer coordinator for the mountain states region, for the first time at that meeting, and they decided to have dinner together. When Gina mentioned my plan to visit Sand Creek Rhoda called me the next morning. After I confessed I was called to go at this time but had not made the requisite elder connections and was depending on God to close that gap, she revealed herself as a direct descendant of one of the chiefs murdered at Sand Creek. She drove five hours to meet me in Denver and another five to Sand Creek so we could wash her feet and make our act of repentance to her. She forgave and welcomed us onto the sacred land; we worshipped the Lord together through our tears and prayed healing over the people–red and white–and full reconciliation–even for the land itself.

It is a beginning. And Romans 8:28 is fulfilled again.

Miracles are nothing more–and nothing less–than incidents of God's intervention in our lives. The reality that our hearts continue to beat is no less miraculous than a limb growing out or a cancer being cancelled–unless we really believe a heartbeat is an involuntary muscular activity. Somebody volunteers.

The message of Romans 8:28 that God works all things together for good in those who love Him and are called according to His purposes is simply His declaration that He is a chronic interventionist. The miracles in this narrative of the capitol prayer bridge journey are not primarily for my benefit, although I praise Him for taking care of me in the way that He has. Has He repaired a heart in which the bypasses were detaching sans medical care through my prayers? Did He restore the ligaments in a knee in one person and realign a spinal column in another as I worshipped with others? Did a woman discover her ancient sins really are forgiven as I laid hands on and blessed her? God does not love me any more passionately than He loves every human being He has created and to whom He is calling in this season of His special favor. These stories are told and these incidents are occurring to waken everyone reading them to the authority God placed in us through baptism and commitment to the Lordship of Jesus. We are the people who love God and are called according to His purposes. He doesn't care whether we are charismatic, evangelical, or mainline; He cares passionately that we confess with our lips, believe in our hearts, and struggle to match behavior to belief.

And to any reader who has not yet made such a commitment, what are you waiting for? To any who has talked the talk but is not walking the walk in its fullness...rise, take up your pallet and walk. The time of paralysis is past.

Washington was the last state I visited. There I had the opportunity to teach in some depth on the theme, "For Such a Time as This." I shared the reality of the Wild Horse Nebula, a cluster of stars and dark matter thirty million light years from earth. This nebula is so distant it was undiscovered until the Hubble Telescope was placed in orbit. In the heart of this celestial body is a black hole several million miles across. That hole is shaped like a cross–the Cross–and we become aware of it only in this century. Does not the Scripture (Psalms 19:1) say, "The heavens declare the glory of God."

Laminim is a protein molecule so tiny it can only be seen beneath an electron microscope–an invention of the past half century. It is what is known as an adhesion protein; its function is literally to hold the human body together, joining bone to muscle, skin to flesh, enzymes to organs. It too is shaped like a cross–the Cross–and we discover it only now. Does not the Scripture (Col. 1:17) say, "In Him all things hold together."

Had the Hubble been invented a few thousand years earlier we would not know of the Wild Horse–the universe would not have expanded enough to provide sufficient contrast between light and dark materials for viewing. A few millennia later and the nebula would be too distant even for the Hubble to pick it out of the cosmos. Reality is we were born for such a time as this–a time of unprecedented opportunity and equally unprecedented challenge.

The last half century has featured more documented miracles and decisions to live for Jesus Christ than all previous seasons combined–including the explosion of faith we call the First Century; the Lord has put it on steroids in the last half decade. We live in a time of darkness not seen since the world began, a time of wars and rumors of war; men calling evil good and good evil; a time of Christians being hated for the name of Christ we bear. And we are nowhere–in scripture or the template of history–promised anything but a shortening of the suffering that accompanies the birth pangs of the Kingdom. Yet when we undertake a journey in obedience–as I did–even a lost cell phone charger is replaced by way of gift (Wyoming) and the tires my mechanic said would need rotating and replacement when I left were found to be without defect when I returned–fifty-two hundred miles later. He really does work it all together for good before the fat lady sings.

PRAYING AND DOING AT THE HEART OF HUMAN ACTIVITY

A quarter century ago my friend was indicted for allegedly molesting a boy. The accusers were a man-hating single mother and her easily manipulated son; they looked for an adult to victimize and found my friend. He was naïve enough to allow them to place him in a compromising position and then they simply lied about what supposedly happened. His first attorney disbelieved him and had convinced him to plead out when I became aware of the situation. Knowing all the parties fairly well–she even tried to set me up but I smelled a rat–I first referred him to an attorney who believed him and next flew out to California to arrange a prayer team for duty during the trial. I offered myself as a witness for the defense, as I had knowledge of the accusers' chronic and malicious dishonesty over the years.

The prayer team engaged in silent daily prayer inside the courtroom. They prayed not for acquittal, but for justice and truth. We faced a prosecutor who added a charge during the trial, a judge so biased he refused to drop it even when the prosecutor agreed, and damning statements the defendant admitted making to the boy. When the jury voted not-guilty they were just as unanimous that the defendant had been set up. Truth and justice prevailed.

It wasn't all about prayer. Although my testimony was ruled inadmissible my highest use was leading prayer and responding to tactical revelations God provided. One of the most damaging statements of the defendant–a former fighter pilot–was that certain military airplanes gave him a "hard-on" while showing the boy photos of those planes. When God reminded me of lines from the famous film, *Top Gun*, the defense attorney called the pilot's former CO to the stand and he confirmed a common phrase in fighter-jock-talk that has no sexual connotation whatever. When the defense attorney tried to hypnotize the defendant, so as to curb his angry responses under questioning, there was no joy. Yet when I prayed God's peace over him he was able to be a calm and credible witness. Couching the events in prayer from the get-go lays the proper foundation for God to move in each of us–from giving strategy and tactics to building courage and peace to creating favor with a jury in an atmosphere of extreme prejudice. But it is still incumbent on each of us to act as God gives inspiration and instruction.

As important as prayer itself, is prayer for what God wants. We wanted our friend acquitted; God wanted justice and truth. "Thy will, not mine, be done," are words uttered from the Cross, but likewise from the empty tomb and every location in between.

Sometimes one group prays dynamically while another group acts diligently–though all should pray all the time per Mark 11:17 and 1 Thessalonians 5:17. When California's Proposition 8 was fatally behind in polls, political and church leaders campaigning over the state were unable to halt the slide, let alone turn the tide. A determined prayer campaign was undertaken and the prayers were shaped by God for blessing, forgiveness, and healing for all. The proposition passed by a large majority.

"Well, yeah, but the courts just threw it out. The prayers didn't work." Again, prayer is not something that works; it is something submitted. But the obvious conclusion is we need to pray–and work–more–and let God–not us–win.

A federal judge closed the pumps in the Sacramento Delta and threw thousands out of work based on dubious science. One solid presentation after another failed to sway him. An eighteen month prayer campaign–for his blessing–saw his eyes opened and when he reversed his decision he told the environmentalists who howled that he was just not impressed by their version of science. Scientific and legal presentations were necessary, but prayer sowed the ground for opening his mind.

My favorite personal witness is Anderson Middle School, where faculty and staff worked for years to create the atmosphere of peace and curiosity that fosters learning only to see their school spiraling into violence and hopelessness. After a summer day of concerted on-campus prayer the violence disappeared, the new reading program took off, and the faculty returned for Fall with renewed hope. The school became a California distinguished school. It was their efforts that determined and shaped the renewal, but it was prayer that sowed the ground for it. When we submit to God in prayer it is more natural to submit to Him in action and only great good can come from it.

DRUNK IN THE SPIRIT

I write in Chapter 5 of the evils that issue from big players and small when they are drunk with power. As Tolkien wrote so well in *The Lord of the Rings*, power manifests in a size and scope consistent with the grasp of the bearer, but it always devours the bearer as surely as it seeks to devour its victims. The only alternative to eventual death for all concerned is to surrender the power to destruction–as Frodo did with the help of Sam and even Gollum. It is actually true that–once we decide to obey rather than defy God–He works all things together for good as He promises in Romans 8:28. Not always right away, but one way or another.

Think of Israel. How drunk with power must Secretary of State John Kerry be to convene talks on Iran's nuclear weapons program, conclude an agreement, and exclude Israel? The avowed purpose of Iranian foreign policy is the destruction of Israel first and the US thereafter. Does Kerry actually believe Israel is going to say "Please and thank-you," to the gathered might of the nations in these talks designed to seal her fate without so much as a howdy-do? But, some would say, what can a nation of seven million do if we throw them under the bus? The question should be, rather, how we will fare if we let Kerry lead us in his ignorance and his arrogance. Israel is the only nation in the region already having a nuclear arsenal, and the only nation standing to have never lost a war. She is the only nation banking on a promise from God Himself that He will never again tolerate injury to His first-born. How drunk must we be to not get that?

Of course many will say it is blue-sky thinking to claim God has made–or will keep–such a promise. But it is a fact of history that no nation on earth has ever been resurrected after total destruction like that of Israel in the first century. They have fought to victory in five wars against overwhelming odds. They have made the desert bloom despite the poverty in which they arrived after World War II. If there is a better explanation than God having their backs let someone share it. Or we could decide God actually spoke the Bible–and the world–into existence with a particular plan and He is going to have His way. We could become drunk in His Spirit.

When we are drunk–on anything–we tend to discard our inhibitions, our judgment, and our ability to carry out our plans. But when the intoxicant is power we tend to become full of conceit and when it is God's Spirit we tend to fill ourselves with humility. In His Spirit we tend to behave like He does. That could mean engaging with Israelis as well as Iranians instead of deciding Israel's fate and breaking it to them. It could mean reforming healthcare along the lines of the Price Plan – advanced by Rep. Tom Price of Georgia – which provides all of the relief and none of the coercion of Obamacare. It could even mean little things like observing the half century passed since the Kennedy assassination with all living former presidents attending, not just the Democrat ones. (This is one of the crassest examples of official pettiness, rudeness, and vindictiveness I have ever seen.) Being filled with God's Spirit ultimately leads us to do right instead of what we want. The fruit is better and a whole lot longer lived.

Now in my own city of Redding the local government has engaged in talks with the McConnell Foundation – who leases land on the Sacramento Riverfront, which is owned by the Kutros family – on the future development of that land. The owners have been excluded from the talks. God has a few choice things to say about people who disregard the rights of landowners. In Florence, Colorado, a school district is persecuting a group of high school girls because they and their parents object to a boy showering with them after the school board has made a policy permitting it. God has something to say about arrogant authorities harming His little ones. Officials in both cities appear drunk with power. It might be Redding needs a better plan for these talks. It might be Florence needs to come alongside its families instead of its social engineers. It could even be we all need a whole new attitude about intoxication – are we after power or seeking the Spirit of the living God?

Make no mistake; God does not insist on sobriety. He actively wants and is campaigning for His people to be intoxicated at all times. But He is very picky about the substance of our intoxication. In John 2 – at the Wedding in Cana – the onlookers are astounded to see the steward of the feast, as they suppose, has held the very best wine until the end of the feast. Those who have indulged to the point of being drunk are by this point fast asleep and utterly oblivious to the climactic moment of the wedding feast. We Christians identify new wine with the blood of our Christ. Settling for the lesser vintage is an astronomical tragedy with very practical results. The alternatives are stark but simple – the world as we have made it and from which we have drunk freely until we pass out and miss out – or the world has He has created and resurrected it and from which we who reject the good in favor of the best will drink freely forever.

In Ephesians 5:18 Paul warns his listeners to avoid becoming drunk on spirits and to prefer being drunk on the Holy Spirit. That kind of intoxication begins with a commitment to walk with Jesus. But that commitment is paved with one decision after another to stand with the people Jesus has sent to us for backing. This is so whether it is Israel with whom we stand or the rightful owners of riverfront property. This is true whether it is faithfulness to our families or faithfulness to the God-breathed ideals on which our nation was founded. Surely it is true in our standing on the Great Commission and the Great Commandment.

We speak here of a spiritual condition that is thoroughly grounded in this world–as it is in heaven. All things done in the Name–read in the Will–of Jesus–will lead us into this kind of intoxication for which we are created.

LIVING BETWEEN NAZARETH AND JERUSALEM

When Jesus came into His hometown of Nazareth–where He could do virtually no miracles because the people would not receive Him–He spoke from Isaiah 61 that the Spirit of God was on Him and He was specially appointed to preach good news to the poor, restore the broken, and set captives free. Part of living in the tension of now and not now–of knowing He always speaks the truth and yet wondering why we sometimes have little evidence of it–is wondering why He set no one free in Nazareth.

It is not because He failed of His identity as the fully God Son of the God Abba that he achieved little in the town where He grew from toddler to manhood. It is entangled in the gift of human freedom, the reason Christ entered the world. It is the issue we need to engage, and there is no better context for engagement than the phenomenon of addiction and release. The people of Nazareth failed to see God in their own homey not because they could not, but because they would not.

Something like one third of Americans–Christian or no–are caught in the bondage of addiction to one substance or another. There is no way to break that cycle through individual human effort; indeed, one of its principle components is the silly little fantasy that we can self-medicate our way to health and then "quit any time I really want to,"–as though it being all about me were somehow the solution rather than the problem.

What can break the cycle is the overwhelming love of God and the people He sends to stand with the addict. It is rare for God to dramatically and instantaneously release an addict from addiction. Far more typical is the scenario in which the addict comes to a place of such desperate impotency before the bondage that he surrenders–not to the bondage but to God and those who love him enough to neither make nor accept excuses. That desperation is accelerated when his loved ones intervene with God's love and unblinking rejection of his effort to destroy himself. Intervention is an act of faithful community, not individual machismo; subsequent treatment works through the same process, but with different players. The issue is whether we seek Kingdom community in Christ or hell with no one to turn to but ourselves.

The process is described in Matthew 18:15-20. Most people think it a formula for ridding ourselves of troublemakers, but it is really a model for progressive redemption. It is about stepping into disease processes that are the creation of ungodly choices–whether or not the chooser recognizes his dysfunction. The model is effective for any idolatry, whether it is of alcohol as pain reliever or the justification of self-righteous behavior on the grounds that nice guys finish last and if I don't do for myself no one else will do for me either. Jesus says the one who would live should sacrifice his life in favor of eternal and abundant life.

This is not a recommendation to commit suicide, but a reminder that our lives are derived and dependent on the Life of Another. As long as we forget that we slip further and further into bondage–whether to chemicals or abusive behavior or the wasted life of narcissism. As long as we remember and bow to the reality that it is all about Him and not about us, the closer we come to the life for which we were born. And if we seem to make only baby steps each day–if we keep having to go to meetings or turn away from the same sins or submit ourselves to the same Redeemer every day–that is simply the evidence we live in the tension of now and not yet.

The created world was organized around sacrifice. Every species of animal features the sacrifice of parental lives to launch the next generation. Everyone reading this is the product of a sperm and egg that sacrificed its life to begin a new and human one. Jesus sacrificed Himself not to change but to restore that order. We are invited to join Him not in death but in life lived for others that releases real freedom from addiction to self–or anything else.

The good news? Just as the Son ordered the formerly paralyzed man to rise and walk in Mark 2, so He speaks to us–that we can rise and walk in His grace. Of course, He's not in Nazareth when He speaks. We need to choose reception.

CHOOSING RACIAL RECONCILIATION OR PLAYING CARDS

I didn't know Susan Rice was a black woman until her supporters accused anyone opposing her nomination to a cabinet level post of racism. (I had never seen her photo.) I did know she was a woman who lied to Americans about the Benghazi massacre. That–and not her ethnic heritage–is what disqualifies her for office. But the assumption of racism–playing the so-called race card–when that is so clearly irrelevant to the issues at hand is itself the act of a racist personality. It takes a deficient character to imagine no other identifier in Rice than her ethnic origin. (Likewise anyone's sexuality.) It is the same character sickness that contends failure to vote for Barack Obama in the last election is motivated by bigotry. It is the bigotry of the accusers that is on display.

Think about it. The Revs. Jesse Jackson, Jeremiah Wright, and Al Sharpton are nationally known black men who regularly claim no black person can get a fair shake in racist America. Congressman Allen West, Supreme Court Justice Clarence Thomas, and Syndicated Columnist Thomas Sowell are nationally known black men who refuse to be defined by that rhetoric. The political left–white and black–considers the former group authentic African Americans while the latter are subject to such racial slurs as "Uncle Tom" and "Oreo" on a regular basis. Washington Redskins Quarterback Robert Griffin III recently said, "I am an African American in America. That will never change. But I don't have to be defined by that." ESPN spokesperson Rob Parker quickly denied Griffin's authenticity as a black, calling him a "cornball brother" for declining to play the victim. (Parker sort of apologized.) Who are the real racists here?

The answer is obvious and it is past time for denials. It is way past time to 'fess up to the truth that anyone who believes black people–or any other minorities–can only make it in our culture with government protection, coddling, and subsidies is the real villain in the distribution of racial stereotypes. This racism–or any other kind–is way beneath Christians, and we mostly know it.

There was a time when we as a nation needed desperately to repent of our racist inclinations. California adopted Proposition 14 as recently as 1964–it okayed racial profiling in real estate transactions. Emmett Till, Medgar Evers, and Dr. Martin Luther King are among the many who died for the supposed crime of being black and wanting equality with whites. There are still pockets of racism in the land; there will be, even in the Church. But when more than ninety per cent of an ethnic group vote for one of their own simply because he is one of their own while some of their leaders cry racist because I–as a white man–did not go along with that black man who is bankrupting my country and stonewalling after his own ambassador is brutally murdered, I say "Get a life."

When people of my ethnic group vote for that same man only because they fear appearing racist if they don't, I say again, "Get a life." But I say it with the genuine hope that we will all do just that–get the real life God intends.

There is nothing more desperately needed in our world than authentic reconciliation between our separated constituencies. For that to occur requires not just education but respectful encounter. (Encounter, by the way, is incredibly educational.) Jesus Christ came into the world to secure that reconciliation–first with His Father for us and just as importantly with His brothers and sisters after the flesh, as the Bible states in 2 Corinthians 5:16-20 when God calls His people to be ambassadors of His reconciliation. We Christians–even from within our own desperate need for repentance–are about half as likely as non-Christians to express racism. Serving our Savior has that impact just from the proximity to His love.

As a Christian who knows himself to be a work in progress I am going to keep asking my Savior to examine my heart and show me any latent tendencies to do anything other than love those for whom He gave His life. That includes all colors and classes. But I am going to encourage all of us–Christian or no–to drop the name-calling and refuse to be intimidated by those who shriek, "Racist!" and "Bigot!" whenever they are losing an argument on its merits. The hypocrisy of the shriekers stinks to high heaven. But the fragrance of authentic and respectful encounter feels like a new lease on life.

PROPHECY AND PROPHETIC AUTHENTICITY

I sometimes receive e-mails objecting to my addressing public issues in spiritual and even prophetic terms. Critiques range from spiritualizing complex issues to being judgmental to playing the God card. Such people have no idea what prophetic authenticity is about. Neither do Christians who think God always in such a good mood He would speak only sunshine, or folks who think prophecy is some sort of Christian clairvoyance–all about predicting the future.

There are prophecies that predict–whether a man telling Saul of Tarsus he will be visited by another man through whom his sight will be restored or the amazing predictions found in the Book of Daniel. Daniel alone has proven so accurate scholars used to think it written after the fact; that fantasy has been thoroughly debunked by recent scholarship. I predicted the end of California's last drought in early 2010–people thought me crazy because the meteorologists disagreed; I simply spoke what I heard the Lord saying. (I predict no time table for the current drought until the Lord speaks to me.) But the majority of prophecy–whether in the Bible or in our contemporary lives–is interpretive of past and present events through the lens of God's own perspective. Prophecy is simply repeating or accurately paraphrasing things God says. A pre-supposition, if we are to comprehend any of it, is that God actually knows more about us–and about our well being–than we do.

When the Prophet Nathan confronts King David it is not because of future events but because David puts the Kingdom in jeopardy by undermining the military when he orders death for Uriah the Hittite to cover up his adultery with Bathsheba. When Elijah accuses King Ahab it is because his idolatries jeopardize the future of Israel; Jeremiah continues that tradition under multiple kings. Truthfully, the whole prophetic tradition throughout the Old Testament is one prophet after another confronting one government after another with the gap between what God expects of rulers and their actual behavior.

If secular commentators had written the Bible Kings Ahab and Herod would have come down as the greatest kings Israel ever had. They brought prosperity and security during times of internal unrest and external threat and that was enough to earn them approval from a secular standpoint. But their uncaring attitude toward God and men earned them harsh criticism from authentic prophetic voices. John the Baptist continued the tradition into New Testament territory and Jesus Himself urged His followers to confront abusive authority in Matt.10, Mark 13, and Luke 21. He told the Roman governor he had no authority over Him that was not given by God.

Does the Word of God tell us to bless, pray for, and respect secular authorities? It does indeed, and authentic prophets–then and now–do just that. But it also tells all God's people to remind those same authorities they are servants rather than masters. And the Word is not shy about warning rulers they can be replaced if they mess up. In Ezekiel alone God calls on all Israel in Chapter 3–beginning with her leaders–to repent before the inevitable consequences of disobedience overwhelm them. In Chapter 37–the famous one promising resurrection to the valley of dry bones–He reminds the prophet to tell the whole story of what God does, has done, and will do–in that order. And–lest we forget how much God loves us even when we bitterly disappoint Him–in Chapter 39 He declares He will pour out His own Spirit on the whole land and people in the end. Prophecy may not be all blue skies but it always contains a blessing because it comes from One who cannot help blessing those He loves.

Likewise, when a prophetic voice like Jim Garlow speaks out about judicial interference in God-given marriage (Proposition 8) or Michael Farris speaks of government restrictions on parents' rights to raise and educate their children–absent abuse of children–without fear that a Boston hospital will kidnap a child or an immigrant couple seeking asylum will be deported–they need to be sure they are accurately reflecting what God says in Scripture. That done, they speak with the same authority as God Himself when they repeat or accurately paraphrase what He says.

I understand that some reading these words are grinding their teeth at what they think my arrogance. They are perfectly free to reject this message. But for the rest of us, it is high time we took our rights and our responsibilities under God a whole lot more seriously than we have in the past.

IF IT'S PROPHETIC IT'S PRAGMATIC

It was 1984 when outlaw biker Roger Ralston had a prophetic dream. God told Roger to found a ministry of compassion for pregnant women in crisis. A new Christian, he knew only to obey the voice of God; obedience was a new concept to him. God said more. If Roger and others would be faithful the ministry would become a full service medical facility, operate in three counties simultaneously, and one day take over the facilities of a local abortion referral service.

Roger retired after a few years as the first director of Crisis Pregnancy Center in Shasta County. Those who knew of his dream continued to pray it, and countless volunteers worked it whether they knew or not. By 2006 the name had changed to Carenet Pregnancy Center, they were operating a medical facility with volunteer doctors and nurses, had expanded into Trinity and Tehama Counties, and taken over the facilities of the abortion service at the provider's invitation. The dream was as pragmatic as it was prophetic, and this is one of the principle reality checks to be passed by any legitimate prophecy. If it is prophetic it is pragmatic.

Carenet is now part of a national network. Just as nationally well known is LifeLight; both have chapters in my city of Redding. Their donor bases tend to cross-pollinate. In 2005 they inadvertently scheduled their primary fundraisers for the same night. Aghast at what seemed a disaster for both ministries in the making, they listened to my prophecy to leave the double scheduling intact and bless each other that the Lord might bless them both. Each sent people to assist the other ministry that night and both ministries broke all previous records for fundraising. Again, if it is prophetic it is pragmatic.

The contemporary prophetic movement is an authentic move of God. He has been speaking to and through His people from the beginning. He speaks because He is a God of speech; He spoke the world and its creatures into being. What changes with the incarnation of His Son is the disbursement of His words through the whole community of His Body and His Blood–with many voices contributing a panel to the tapestry–just as He promised in Isaiah 59, Jeremiah 31, Ezekiel 39, and Joel 2.

The role of the prophets in this fulfilled divine economy is to release and pastor the prophetic voice He has released over the prophetic community. But the Old Testament prophets were ever focused on what was happening at ground level–whether they spoke of past, present, or future events. No authentic prophet of Israel would have been content to speak in a rapturous tone of voice about some mystical and non-specific "shift" in the heavenlies, or to predict year after year that this was the year the Lord transfers all the wealth of the world to the saints and all our dreams come true. The people tested the prophetic utterances then and we need to test the spirits now–as Paul insists in 1 Thessalonians 5:21.

Proper testing of prophecy is not rocket science. It must be consistent with the scriptures; God does not contradict Himself. It addresses present, past or future events through the lens of God's perspective. And it includes a practical directive toward a pragmatic outcome. That said, some prophecies deal with the apparently mundane while others deal in what can only be called grandiose. The Alamo prophecy is downright grandiose and the jury is out on its fulfillment.

On a 2009 visit to the Alamo God called me to pray fulfillment of His purposes for that 1836 battle in our nation today. He said those purposes were fulfilled then in the crucible of encirclement, assault, and massacre. He identified them as the garrison becoming one race–as Indians, Americans, Europeans and Hispanics came together in the common cause of freedom–and one faith–as a garrison co-commanded by a Baptist and a Catholic and representing every known Christian background learned to pray together as they fought and gave their lives. The third purpose was personified in the thirty-two from Gonzales who rode in on the ninth day–they rode toward rather than away from the place of danger. He says our nation struggles in that same crucible today; it is a spiritual, political, and physical assault, and in that order. He says that what cost the Alamo defenders their earthly lives and brought them to eternal life is on the table for our nation today. It passes prophetic muster; the question is whether it passes from our ears through our minds and into our hearts.

Authentic prophecy is ever thus.

THE PURPOSE OF PARENTHOOD

Famed pitcher and San Francisco Giants manager Roger Craig tells how his father did authentic parenting. The dad left for work one summer's day after instructing 12-year-old Roger to clean the garage before fishing or swimming. Roger procrastinated until his father's return was imminent, realized he had neither done his assigned task nor had any fun, and leapt to give that garage a lick and a promise before disaster struck. He knew his dad always headed straight for the house on arrival, and he hoped for luck. But Dad made straight for the garage, took a good look, and emerged into the driveway coatless and in the process of rolling up his sleeves. He said, "Son, I am going to teach you how to clean a garage." Roger saw a trip to the woodshed in his immediate future.

That's not what happened. Instead, the elder Craig spent two hours cleaning the garage while Roger watched. As he headed for the house and a very late dinner he said, "Don't ever betray my trust again." The son never did.

Craig was perceptive enough to have seen the gift of leadership in his son and to mentor leadership by example. But leadership's other side is rebellion. Dad was wise enough to understand that the best way – the Godly way – to discipline is by playing to our kids' strengths instead of trying to break them of the dark side of those strengths. I don't say the rod has no place, but I do say discipline – as opposed to punishment – is a gift we can give our children.

The Fifth Commandment – honoring fathers and mothers – is the first to include a promise – long life and prosperity. (Some say the Third Commandment has a promise – the one about honoring Father God by not misusing His Name.) But the fifth is about respecting the primary responsibility of parents to teach and impart relationship to God, including drawing forth the special gifting God places in each of His kids. The injunction to respect parents is inseparable from the parents' calling to teach and impart – it actually transcends obedience to the persons themselves when they fail or resist their role. Our job is always to become the particular persons God created. We are given parents to help us, but children are called to become people of God in spite of – even in opposition to – their particular parents if that becomes necessary in order to walk with God. In other words, the onus is on us more than on our children.

My own parents did not raise me to respect God; I was expected only to respect them. When I became a Christian I dedicated my life to becoming the kind of man my parents should have taught me to be – with the usual mixed bag in the results department. My father – who never mentioned his own faith in Jesus until just prior to his death – had deferred to my mother's militant atheism and remained silent about many things I needed to hear from him; yet he was proud of my efforts and said as much in the wonderful relationship God gave us as I strove to be closer to my Heavenly Father and it rubbed off with my human dad. My mother–who was a drug addict and afflicted with mental illness–escalated her abusive attitude toward me. Yet God intervened in her life just before her death–I was the instrument He chose–and all was forgiven; the Fifth Commandment was fulfilled and the fruit was good. Of course it could have been better had my parents chosen to walk as God intended parents to do from the beginning.

God ends the Old Testament declaring He will turn the hearts of the fathers to the children and the children's hearts to the fathers. Yet in Luke 1 He prophesies the coming Messianic age of deliverance and resurrection to full humanity in the midst of unprecedented signs and wonders. In that context He will turn the hearts of the fathers to the children regardless of the response. That is how seriously God takes parenting.

So what is the purpose of authentic parenting?

The ancient covenant accepted by Christian parents baptizing their children expects them to raise children so they strive for justice and peace, and serve all persons in a love that transcends love of self. They commit to raising children who speak openly of the source of their humanity in God, who see their humanity as a work in progress requiring periodic re-focus–and occasional course corrections–toward God in Christ, and continual submission to God through His Holy Spirit in terms of what He has revealed through Word, Tradition, and Encounter. They are expected to understand that keeping these commitments is their purpose as parents.

There is plenty of room for debate as to how best to implement these principles, and plenty of hot air expelled between the denominations on the subject. There are those who object to naming God as essential to the process, and they too are entitled to their perspective. (I would love to hear how it works out to divorce the Creator of humanity from the process of becoming human.) Others would wonder how food, shelter, and a loving family in which to grow into their full and unique potential got left out–but these things are pre-supposed in the covenant unless anyone thinks children reach their full humanity without them.

The bottom line is that we are called as parents to raise our children for their benefit, not ours, and that old covenant provides an awfully good blueprint. It provides an amazingly good blueprint for us parents to live out our humanity into the bargain.

Maybe Somebody planned it that way.

THANKSGIVING IS THE BEGINNING

Bart was a priest I knew thirty years ago, when I was still in seminary and needing a mentor. Shortly after he agreed to be in this mentoring relationship with me he revealed that he was being tested for a disease that robbed him of muscle control at the same time it seemed to be scrambling his brain and messing with various other bodily functions. One of the possible diagnoses was Alzheimer's Disease. I asked him how he was praying for himself and–by extension–how I could pray for him. He said his prayer was, "God grant me a eucharistic heart." The word is Greek for great thanksgiving. It is the name we Anglicans give the Lord's Supper–the Holy Communion.

Thanksgiving is not everything; it can be saccharine and sentimental if we just blandly and uncritically say thanks for everything, as though there were nothing we might beg a loving God to change in our circumstances. But if we understand–as I do–that communion with our Lord Jesus is the core and context of our acts of worship–the name begins to make sense. As I understand worship this context begins with praising God–and thanking Him for the opportunity. It continues with hearing and commenting on His Word in Scripture–and thanking Him for the enlightenment and the marching orders He brings. We acknowledge the shape of our faith in the words of the ancient creedal summary–and thank Him for giving a dependable shape to our belief. We pray for those in need of healing, shelter, peace, and deliverance from evil–and thank Him for loving them more than we can. And we thankfully celebrate the reality of His death and resurrection for the sake of our larger life; all this as we thankfully hail his sovereignty and protection over us while standing invisibly in our midst. From inside the whole process of worship, this Eucharistic heart broadens our awareness and expands our vision of opportunities in the context of this lifestyle of thanksgiving. It is not a different viewpoint so much as it is a larger, more wholistic, and eagle-eyed perspective.

I would love to say Bart was miraculously healed of his medical condition, but that did not happen. He was eventually diagnosed with Multiple Sclerosis and he gave thanks it was not Alzheimer's. That was miracle enough for him and the peace of God was quite visible all over him the last time I saw him.

When the Pilgrims celebrated their first Thanksgiving in the New World they were starving and riddled with disease. The Native Americans who befriended them and joined their celebration were doing only marginally better. But these Pilgrims and their indigenous friends chose to believe the message of Romans 8:28 that God works all things together–ultimately–for good in those who love Him and are called according to His purposes. They asked for and received a

Eucharistic heart. Such a heart enabled them to be more conscious of what gifts they were given than of what needs had not yet been answered. It gave them both joy and a reason for that joy.

A story is told of a country parson in the UK who ran out of petrol while out calling on members of his flock. He knocked on the door of a church member's home just up the road and the family offered him as much petrol as he could carry from the tank in their garden. They added – regretfully – that the only container they had was a chamber pot. The parson answered that he was thankful for whatever he got – being assured this was God's gift and God's gift is always precisely what he needs. As he lugged the pot back to his car and began pouring the contents into the petrol tank a motorist drove by on the other side of the road and exclaimed, "Oh, if I only had faith like that!" That faith was indeed what he needed, but not what he thought.

The faith displayed by the parson was not an unshakable conviction that God can transform human waste into motor fuel; of course He can and of course He wasn't. The faith was as the parson said – that whatever we receive from God is precisely what we need for God's good purposes to unfold in our lives, when we receive it. Developing a eucharistic heart is the work of a lifetime. It is the work that – from our end – enables a life to be lived well. May readers enjoy a Thanksgiving as memorable as it is blessed.

And may they – we – go public with it.

ABOUT THE AUTHOR

James Wilson's ministry spans four decades as pastor, teacher, and Kingdom ambassador. He holds Master of Arts degrees in Education and Divinity. He celebrates God's Holy Spirit in charismatic, evangelical and mainline bodies with equal awe and enthusiasm. Jim and his wife, Diana, launched PrayNorthState in February 2001.

Jim's focus is community transformation as he shares God's call for repentance leading to a Great Awakening in more than thirty states and twenty nations. He has authored Living As Ambassadors of Relationships and The Holy Spirit and the End Times. He hosts PrayNorthState Radio and appears as a periodic guest and guest host on syndicated radio and television programs across the nation. He hosted PrayNorthState Television from 2004 through 2011. His books are recommended by the Miracle Channel and the International Healing Rooms.

He coordinates the California Governor's Prayer Team, is a co-director of National Day of Repentance, and is a popular conference speaker. His blog enjoys a circulation of more than 400,000. But most of all he goes where God tells him to go and comes alongside people and ministries to whom God directs him–whatever their denomination or stream.

Jim has ministered and taught God's miracles for more than a quarter century. He watches limbs grow, cancers eliminated, and auto immune systems restored in more than thirty states and twenty nations. He has always said, "We don't have the gifts; the gifts have us because we have the Spirit of the Living God." The overarching purpose of **Jim's** teaching, broadcasting, and writing is to rouse and prepare the Body of Christ to "go forth in the spirit and power of Elijah, to turn the hearts of the fathers to the children, to prepare a people for righteousness" as God promises in Luke 1:17.

God Himself has now announced we need no longer wait for the Great Awakening; it is underway. He adds that His call to prepare for it through repentance – progressively re-focusing our attention on Him – is more urgent than ever if we would accept our role in what God is doing. Kingdom in Pursuit is Jim's way of saying, "It is time."

CPSIA information can be obtained at www.ICGtesting.com
Printed in the USA
LVOW07s0047250615

443723LV00001BA/1/P